Piracy and the Decline of Venice

Piracy and the Decline of Venice 1580–1615

ALBERTO TENENTI

translated from
Venezia e i corsari, 1580–1615 (*Bari, 1961*),
*with an introduction and glossary,
by Janet and Brian Pullan*

UNIVERSITY OF CALIFORNIA PRESS
BERKELEY AND LOS ANGELES
1967

First published in Italian, 1961
© *Gius Laterza e Figli, 1961*
English translation first published 1967
© *Longmans, Green & Co. Ltd, 1967*

UNIVERSITY OF CALIFORNIA PRESS
Berkeley and Los Angeles

Printed in Great Britain

It was indeed at this time that the Venetian Republic suffered the interruption of its maritime trade, which had hitherto proceeded so successfully: for not only did the Uskoks plunder in the Adriatic and almost on the shores of Venice itself . . . but it even seemed as though all who sailed the sea had joined together in a plot to plunder Venetian shipping.

Nicolò Contarini, Historie

Contents

Foreword	xi
Introduction	xv

PART I THE PIRATES

1 The Uskoks	3
2 The Barbary Corsairs	16
3 Maltese, Florentines and Spaniards	32
4 The English	56

PART II THE ORGANIZATION OF THE VENETIAN NAVY

5 The Merchant Fleet	89
6 The Light Galleys	110
7 Galleasses and Galleon	132
Conclusion	150
Glossary	152
Notes	157
Bibliography	193
Index	199

Illustrations

facing page

Uskoks attacking merchantmen (from G. Rosaccio, *Viaggio da Venetia a Costantinopoli*, Venice, 1606)   42

A Venetian galley in pursuit of Uskoks off the island of Pago (from G. Rosaccio, *op. cit.*)   43

Algiers (from G. Braun, *De praecipius totius universi urbibus liber secundus*, Colonia, 1575)   58

Malta (from P. Bertelli, *Theatrum urbium italicarum*, Venice, 1599)   59

Taranto (from P. Bertelli, *op. cit.*)   90

The northern ships called *bertoni* by the Venetians, which, especially in English hands, proved themselves to be formidable pirate craft (engraved by H. Cock, from a drawing by F. H. Brueghel, *circa* 1565)   91

Bertoni at sea (engraved by H. Cock from a drawing by F. H. Brueghel, *circa* 1565)   106

Typical renegade Christians, who formed the crews of Turkish pirate ships (from N. de Nicolay, *Les quatre premiers livres des navigations et pérégrinations orientales*, Lyon, G. Roville, 1568)   107

Foreword

In this study of piracy, Professor Alberto Tenenti has extended and deepened historical knowledge of the decline of Venice as a great seapower and an international entrepôt. He has enabled historians to know more about the decisive shift in the economic hegemony of Europe which occurred in the first half of the seventeenth century: more, too, about the methods used by the English and Dutch to extend their influence into the Mediterranean, at the expense of some of its former masters.

The years from the mid-fourteenth century to about 1620 linked two periods of crisis and depression which deeply affected, not only the advanced economies of northern Italy, but a large part of Europe as well. It may be that the crisis of the mid-fourteenth century brought relative decline to northern Italy, and that of the early seventeenth absolute decline. It would, however, be hard to prove this conclusively on the available evidence. In the course of the fifteenth and sixteenth centuries, Venice, like Florence and Genoa, had faced severe challenges. But she had succeeded in partially compensating for the losses suffered in traditional spheres of activity by exploring new ones. In the fifteenth century, Venice had expanded westwards on to the mainland of Italy and entered the Italian power-struggle. Later in the century, she lost to the advancing Ottoman Turks many valuable colonial possessions in the Eastern Mediterranean; but in 1489 she acquired

FOREWORD

direct dominion over the island of Cyprus, an invaluable stepping-stone to the Levant. This she held till it was torn from her by the Turks in 1571.

Early in the sixteenth century, after the Portuguese discovery of the oceanic route round the Cape of Good Hope to India and the East Indies, the Mediterranean ceased to be the only channel of intercontinental trade, the sole distributor of oriental goods to Europe. Lisbon and Antwerp, site of the Portuguese spice staple till 1549, became formidable rivals to Venice. Nevertheless, the Portuguese failed to secure an effective monopoly of eastern merchandise, and the oceanic and Mediterranean routes continued to compete on fairly even terms throughout the sixteenth century. Changes in the political situation, outbreaks of war or piracy on either route, tipped the balance temporarily one way or the other. The Mediterranean at any rate continued to supply France with a high proportion of its spices, through the Italian-dominated port and market of Marseilles and Lyons. Venice suffered to some extent from competition within the Mediterranean: from Marseilles, Ragusa and even Ancona. In spite of this, even as entrepôt trade in oriental goods shifted away from Venice, the textile industry migrated towards it. From 1520 onwards, Venetian woollen production expanded, reaching a first peak in 1569. This depended heavily on the Levantine market, and Venice in a sense battened economically on the Ottoman Empire even as her ancient rival, Genoa, exported goods and services to the Spaniards. This industrial advance greatly contributed to maintaining Levantine trade. Meanwhile, and especially between 1540 and 1570 (when population pressure was heaviest), Venetian capital was also devoted to the more intense exploitation of the mainland.

But towards the close of the sixteenth century, the final blows to Venetian prosperity were being prepared. These were dealt, not by the Portuguese, the Turks or the Spaniards, but by the aggressive northern enemies of Spain — the English and

FOREWORD

Dutch. They both by-passed and invaded the Mediterranean, ousting the Portuguese from their precarious supremacy in the Far East, and inserting themselves, with the enthusiastic approval of anti-Spanish Ottoman authorities, into the Levantine markets that supported Venice. Much of Professor Tenenti's book is concerned with analysing the decisive impact of northern piracy on the trade of the Venetian Republic and explaining the failure of Venice to resist this final threat. During the first third of the seventeenth century, Venetian prosperity was irreparably damaged, not only by the effects of ill-controlled piracy, and not only by competition from the north: but also by a severe shipbuilding crisis, a dearth of essential materials, that had begun in the mid-sixteenth century. In 1630–31 a disastrous plague created a labour shortage which increased wages; gild pressure maintained its high level and weakened the power of Venetian industry to compete with its northern and French rivals. The conservatism of powerful gilds strangled the adaptability and inventiveness that might have saved the textile trade. From the presence of vigorous aliens in the Mediterranean, only ports like Leghorn could hope to prosper. Leghorn was the artificial creation of the benevolent, commercially-minded absolutism of the Medici Grand Dukes of Tuscany. Geographically well placed, it offered the cheapest facilities to northerners to use it as a base for trade with the Levant. The Venetians' proud fear of deteriorating into a mere forwarding-station like Leghorn or Marseilles prevented them from lowering their own import and export duties, and anchorage and other taxes, and from permitting foreigners to trade with the Levant on the same terms as Venetians.

In early modern Europe, non-economic forces such as war, disease and weather often effected decisive economic change. Commercial rivals had often to be outfought before they could be out-traded or vital monopolies secured. Naval or military failure was often the prelude to commercial decline. The

FOREWORD

English and Dutch outfought the Venetians, though not in any one pitched battle. Perhaps, as Tenenti shows, Venice failed most dismally in the sphere where pride was strongest and tradition most enduring — the organization, equipment and discipline of her famous navy. This failure meant the decay of Venetian seapower: its absolute decline, without compensation or reprieve.

B.S.P.

Introduction

Every Mediterranean chronicle of the fourteenth or fifteenth century — Ragusan or Neapolitan, Venetian or Genoese — and every record or portrait of sea life at that time, is packed with accounts of pirates or corsairs. But almost nobody has thought of studying them systematically, of building up a synoptic view of their activities and of looking beyond those appearances of theirs which cannot be treated as other than sporadic. As far as the sixteenth century is concerned, the results of the historical researches hitherto carried out seem to be rather better. Everyone has heard of Barbarossa, and this is undoubtedly thanks to the studies which have focused on him. But in reality the attention devoted to the Turkish pirate-admiral has fully demonstrated the flaws and one-sidedness of this type of inquiry. The problem has not been examined in all its aspects, but considered almost exclusively in military terms; and, in their excessive delight at finding a worthy opponent for Andrea Doria or Charles V, historians have too easily abandoned themselves to a dramatic reconstruction of their duels. Again, the light directed upon the middle years of the sixteenth century makes its beginning and end seem unimportant or even unremarkable. But we ought rather to acknowledge that its problems have simply been ignored. Hence I have felt the need to prove certain contentions which are essential to historical understanding: that the beginning of

INTRODUCTION

the sixteenth century marks the opening of a new phase in Mediterranean history, and that Lepanto marks, not only the beginning of a *status quo*, but also the start of an original period very different from its predecessors.

This book sets out to deal with the second of these problems. Up to 1572, the underlying reality beneath all Mediterranean life can rightly be seen as the enmity between the Christian and the Islamic world. In spite of disputes and rivalry, both at Prevesa and at Lepanto, Genoese and Venetians, Papalists and Spaniards found themselves side-by-side and forming a united front against Ottoman power. A discordant element in this situation – which in a way anticipated later developments – was the Franco-Turkish entente. But this was never decisively important, and the naval collaboration which rose out of it created much alarm but achieved unimpressive results. Immediately after Lepanto the French navy was feeling the effects of the terrible crisis afflicting the whole of France, and for a long time it was no more formidable than the Maltese fleet. But the splendid triumph of Catholic Spain was very soon to be tarnished. The Calvinists of the Low Countries soon added themselves to the growing Protestant power of Elizabeth. The English and Dutch navies did not hesitate to force their way into the Mediterranean from the years 1575-80 onwards. Combining trade and piracy, they succeeded in installing themselves at certain vital points, such as Tunis and Leghorn, Constantinople and Venice. After Lepanto, then, peace was only apparent. The rivalry between Spaniards and Protestants was added to the old antagonism between Christians and Infidels. This was the start of a new political and commercial contest destined to continue at least until the opening of the Thirty Years' War.

I maintain that the problem can conveniently be studied by centring researches on Venice. The sea regions in which Venetian power was present more or less formed the theatre in which the chief antagonists fought their battles: the eastern

INTRODUCTION

Mediterranean especially, and then the Aegean, the Ionian sea, the Adriatic, and finally the route between Sicily and Gibraltar. The coasts of Spain, the Gulf of Leon and the Tyrrhenean Sea certainly did not escape entirely, but the Barbary pirates seldom penetrated as far as these shores, save for their attacks on Roman beaches, while northern penetration into those regions remained essentially peaceful. Indeed, Florentines and Papalists, Spaniards and Maltese carried the offensive into the Levant and the Archipelago, and along the coasts of Morea and Barbary. This, then, is the meaning of the title of this volume: the study of a prominent aspect of Mediterranean life — pirate warfare. On one side was Venice, which, in spite of its huge navy and a merchant fleet which was still a considerable size, observed the strictest neutrality and sought only to protect its own trade. On the other were potentially or openly hostile navies, which clashed with one another and frequently also skirmished with Venetian shipping.

Although in my opinion the subject could usefully be treated again with fuller documentation, I maintain that the fundamental argument mentioned above is fully valid. After Lepanto, the waters of the Mediterranean became, more than ever before, a theatre of European history, and the scenes enacted there directly involved apparently distant regions like the Low Countries, England and Northern Germany. Venice was well aware of this, for she sought support from the Protestant powers perhaps even more than the friendship of France. She favoured their anti-Spanish policy and their business activities in the Mediterranean. Certainly, the northern expansion and the victory of English and Flemish and to some extent French competitors in the Mediterranean dealt a last blow to Venetian trade. In the hard choice between political independence and commercial success, in her uncertainty about her own fate, the proud determination of Venice still shone forth above all her mistaken and her shabby actions. Instead of choosing, like her neighbour Ragusa, a life with no risks and no history, the old city-state refused to give way to the predominance of any power, be it Turkish or Papal, Spanish or Habsburg.*

* Some years ago, I had occasion to examine closely various documents on Venetian sea life at the turn of the sixteenth to the seventeenth century. I have now set out to take up a part of them which had not been sufficiently exploited and to combine them with the results of new researches subsequently undertaken. The present volume, therefore, has a character of its own, very different from the recent work which appeared under the title *Naufrages, corsaires et assurances maritimes à Venise (1592-1609)*. The reader can easily see this for himself.

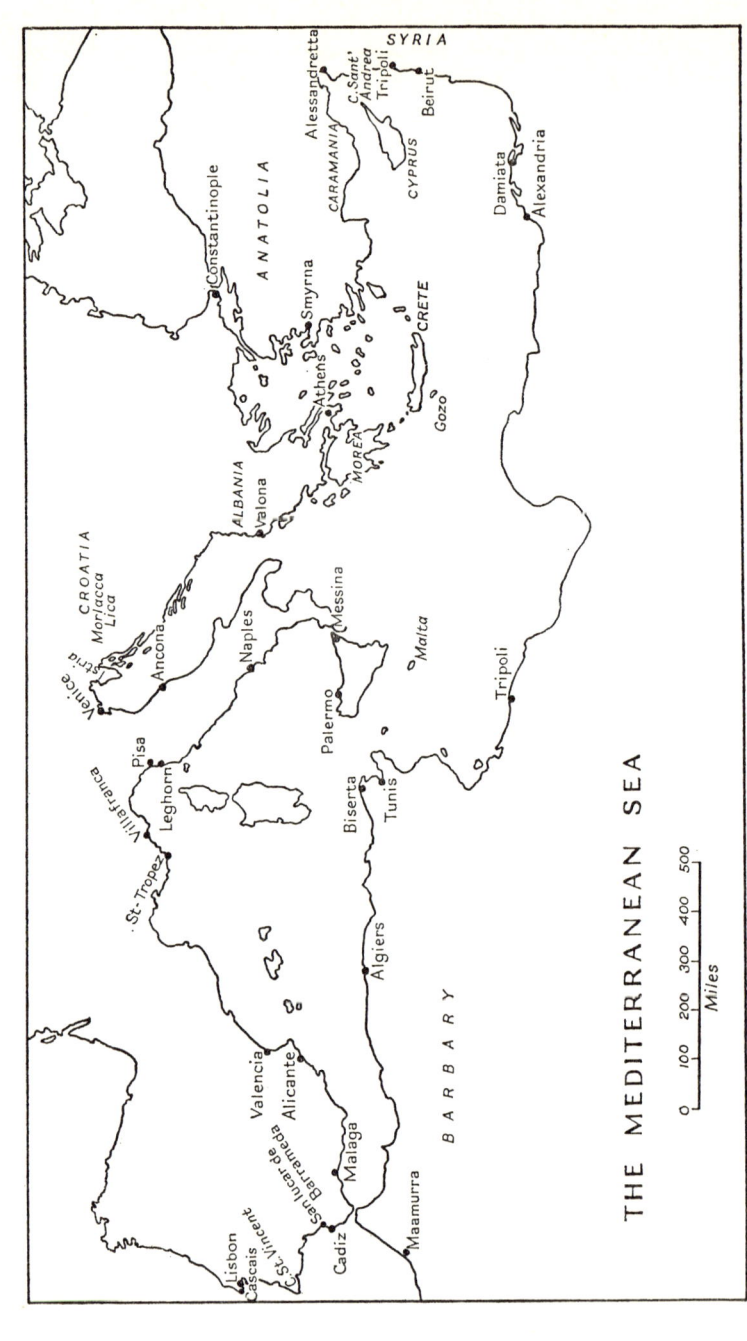

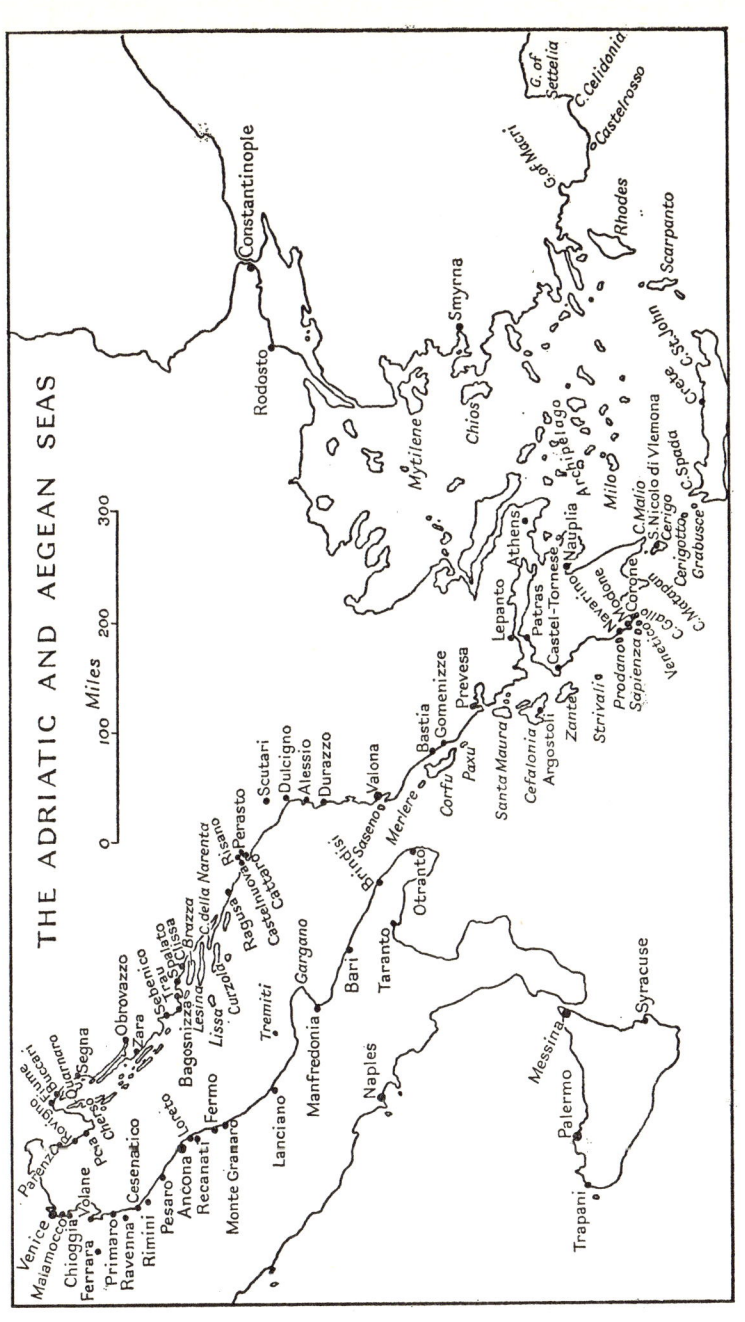

PART I

The Pirates

Chapter 1

The Uskoks

Situated in the region of Fiume at the foot of barren Mount Morlacca, waterless, without soil and almost treeless for a mile or two inland, Segna had not even a harbour or a safe bay in which to receive ships. The savage winds which frequently swept the waters before it prevented any ship from anchoring there. Impregnable from the sea (in spite of the opinion of certain Venetian admirals to the contrary), the town was also secure on the landward side: not so much because of the fortress which defended it, nor on account of its little Habsburg garrison, as because the Turks could not bring their artillery from the interior to attack it. It was in this 'infamous lair' that the Uskok pirates had their principal base.

Robbers, a tribe of ruffians, iniquitous rogues: such epithets were commonly applied to them. Sometimes the authority of Livy was directly invoked, for he had called them *'gentes Illyriorum latrociniis maritimis infames'* and eloquently portrayed them as 'an arrogant, haughty, gluttonous, rapacious people, drunken in the extreme, and so they consume their ill-gotten booty'.[1] Seldom has so small a group of men created such a persistent international problem. For more than a century after about 1540 the problem of the Uskoks recurred constantly in diplomatic despatches. It poisoned relations between Venice and the Austrian royal house, and also with the Pope and with the Turks. The Turks, having conquered most of the kingdom of Hungary — of which Segna, together with Croatia, formed part — had stopped at the threshold of the Quarnaro. The Habsburgs, who had inherited rights to the Hungarian crown, had welcomed into their service a certain number of families who had taken refuge on this strip of land. For many years the Ottoman Empire did not seriously resume its offensive, nor was Austria in a position to embark upon a counterattack. However, there were frequent and lively skirmishes between the two adversaries. In this little frontier war, these fugitives — for such is the meaning of the word *uskok* — felt completely at home. Sure of imperial protection, helped by the Pope, who saw them as crusaders,[2] they soon understood that venting their own resentment against the Turks could become a profitable trade. Indeed, not only did the important traffic which gave life to the port of Venice regularly follow the Dalmatian-Istrian route, but a multitude of smaller craft also sailed from one Adriatic island to another, or engaged in coastal trade along the Illyrian shores. What was more, the peoples of the hinterland, subject to the Turks, traded gladly with the Dalmatians and with the Venetians, especially across the estuary of the Narenta. Anybody, perhaps, might have become a pirate in the face of such propitious circumstances.

The problem rapidly became insoluble. Venice, in the peace treaty with the Porte which followed Lepanto, had procured a clause stating that Turkish warships should not penetrate into the Adriatic. By way of compensation Venice guaranteed the safety of Ottoman trade. Therefore, after every Uskok attack, in addition to protesting against the Venetian Republic, the Sultan would renew the threat to despatch his own fleet into the Adriatic. Venice then turned to the Emperor to obtain his intervention against these turbulent vassals: but it was time wasted. The Habsburgs were delighted to upset Turco-

Venetian relations, to damage Ottoman subjects, and to affirm indirectly their sovereignty over one part of the Adriatic at least. The Venetian requests appeared to find a warmer welcome at Rome, but the Pope limited himself to ineffective intervention at the Viennese Court, obtaining nothing more than promises. Soon the incidents began again.

Only a handful of men was involved, never more than a thousand, but they succeeded in building an organization for robbing the public so efficient that nothing could uproot it. Above all, they were protected by an almost perfect conspiracy of silence, encouraged by the gossip of interested parties. 'Moreover, there is the universal inclination of all Dalmatia to favour these brigands', said Almorò Tiepolo to the Senate, 'for these people entertain the heresy (so to speak) that the preservation and maintenance of the Province depends upon the ravages of Uskoks.'[3] Certainly it was not difficult to find informers amongst the Dalmatians, many of whom were discontented with Venetian government: there were also informers in Venice itself. In September 1586 the Council of Ten discovered that a clerical official from Lesina, Francesco da Bruzza, was a spy: he not only informed the Uskoks of the departure of every vessel, but pointed out where goods belonging to Turkish subjects might be found.[4] The inhabitants of Segna, thanks to the network of their accomplices, were thus nearly always well-informed of the movements of Venetian shipping; nor did the Uskoks fail to revenge themselves savagely on those who had betrayed them. The terror was such that Dalmatian subjects preferred to incur the rigours of Venetian law rather than expose themselves to the reprisals of these plunderers. The Uskoks therefore did their work with impunity, but if by chance they ran into the Venetian naval force, they repaired to land with their spoils, taking refuge for weeks and even months in safe hiding places prepared by their supporters.[5]

The tactics they followed helped to make them impossible

to catch. When pursuing a limited objective, they would not even use their own boats but would get possession of other people's. However, their own *brazzere* (so called after the island of Brazza) were excellently designed for pirate warfare in that region: very small, they normally had six to eight oars, whilst the biggest had twelve or at the most sixteen. Their crew was three or four times that number of men, who changed places every hour, thus enabling the boat to travel far faster than Venetian galleys and also to cover great distances — up to one hundred miles in a single night. Small and manœuvrable, these vessels could easily hide themselves in inlets or behind rocks; nor was it difficult to pull them ashore. When danger was imminent the crews, as a last resort, would fill them with water and sink them to save them from capture by means of a hole bored in the hull.[6]

Thanks to the people's connivance and to these devices, the Uskoks, particularly after their good luck in seizing the ship *Contarina* in 1574, constantly threatened a vast area of about 300 miles. The Quarnaro, the straits of Novigrade, the Obrovazzo river, the coasts of Sebenico and Trau were all under their control, which thrust still farther south, down to the islands of Lesina and Curzola and even to the gates of Ragusa. Two-thirds of Dalmatia, as well as the Istrian coasts, were therefore menaced by the Uskoks. In 1614 Filippo Pasqualigo confirmed in the Senate that, whilst it was difficult to prevent them putting to sea in the good season, it was impossible to do so in winter.[7] One intensely exploited base was the island of Brazza, whose inhabitants bought slaves captured on neighbouring Turkish territory. The Uskoks particularly appreciated it because, hiding there for weeks at a time, they could watch the near-by mouth of the Narenta, which was much frequented by merchants. The well-known practice of using galleys for the voyage to Spalato was mainly due to their constant menace, which threatened to divert irrevocably to Ragusa the trade coming from the Turkish hinterland. However, even this formidable vessel was not safe from attack. Venetian admirals always recommended an escort for it. In August 1588, for example, a galley on this route escaped being plundered merely because it had just unloaded its goods. The Uskoks, however, succeeded in boarding it, took the money they found, and left it only because two other galleys arrived on the scene.

The activity of these pirates, taken as a whole, was like a running sore which utterly exhausted the Venetians. But if they struck innumerable blows against the Dalmatian islands, and against the smaller craft — *fregate, saettie and marciliane* — which sailed the waters of the northern Adriatic, the attacks upon more important ships were also frequent enough. In January 1580 two big ships coming from Cyprus and Syria — the *Costantina* and the *Balbiana* — were put to flight in the waters of Zara by Uskok boats. But the Ragusan galleon commanded by Nicolò Rusco did not escape them in February 1586: forty-two bales of scarlet and purple cloth formed the bulk of the booty. Other galleons were later to be ransacked, like that commanded by Domenico Surbi in 1596, or else directly taken, like the galleon *Tegiachin*, master Filandro Penzo,[8] captured the following year. Certainly the best opportunity for such enterprises was a shipwreck, and Francesco Molin describes one in his *Compendio delle cose che reputerò degne di tenerne particolar memoria*: 'At the end of February 1592 occurred the wreck of the *saettia Vidala*, laden with many cloths of wool and silk and other very important merchandise, whose value approached the sum of 130,000 ducats: this ship left Venice and encountered a very violent storm at sea, went to take refuge in a cove (*sorzadore*) on the island of Cherso, and having dropped anchor, as the ship was not a good one, she split open and went to the bottom, although there was no loss of life. There, however, good fortune ended: fifteen Uskok boats appeared, with perhaps 350 to 400 men, drums beating and flags flying: and they took and bound the sailors who did not resist, and tortured them to make them reveal where the cash was, which they did. The Uskoks ransacked the *saettia* and removed from it all the silken and woollen cloth, which could all have been safely recovered because the ship had sunk in shallow water. And the Uskoks joyfully divided the booty.'[9]

These pirates were in reality plain and simple robbers. There was a religious pretext behind their activities: they had to fight the infidels — but they attacked their property rather than their persons. On the other hand, granted that they were usually in pursuit of merchandise owned by Turks and Jews, was it not Christians who were transporting or purchasing it? Subjects of the Pope, especially from Ancona, even more than Venetian subjects or Ragusans, engaged in and promoted trade of this kind, but very few ships traded in the Adriatic without some infidels having a stake in them. But, so long as there was a scrap of cloth or the least bit of merchandise belonging to infidels aboard, the Uskoks regarded themselves as crusaders. There is no doubt that in all this area the Christians suffered most. It would be possible to list a considerable number of ships which came from Ancona and were captured in the neighbourhood of Ragusa, like the ship which, in January 1592, in spite of using its guns, was taken and ransacked by sixteen Uskok boats, which carried off rich booty.[10] Nevertheless, as we shall see, the systematic plundering to which the struggle against the infidels in the Adriatic gave rise was common to all the Mediterranean. Everywhere religious fanaticism served as an excellent pretext for energetic pirate warfare.

Certainly the Uskoks were not the least pious of Christians. Sometimes we read, as in the report presented by Vittore Barbaro to Filippo Pasqualigo on 25 April 1601, that the inhabitants of Segna were seen going from the harbour to the churches on their bare knees to give thanks for their uninterrupted robberies. With much greater asperity, Nicolò Donà declared in the Senate 'they do not hold it a sin to rob, although in other things they apparently live piously, going to Communion and confession and often having recourse to God with public prayers and vows, and even handing over the tenth part of their booty to their bishops'.[11] At Segna there were two friaries, one of Franciscans and the other of Dominicans: in the division of the spoils, one-tenth was reserved to them. In exchange, these priests and friars personally took part in the raids, or directly contributed to them. In addition the friars preached in public places the necessity of intensifying the raids. Thus anyone who did not take part was reputed to be cowardly, and it was nearly impossible to find, among the banners which decorated the tombs in the churches, anyone buried there who had died in his own bed. A certain mystique of violence pervaded this extraordinary society. The families which could boast the greatest number of men hanged or cut in pieces were the most honoured and well thought of: young men were taught the use of arms rather than the alphabet, and infants scarcely able to walk threw stones at one another until they drew blood. No less did the women incite their husbands to robbery, despite the risks. When they heard of their deaths they flaunted their savage grief for a few hours, but before they had finished weeping they had already found a new companion. 'So that they would usually celebrate the burial of one husband and marriage with another in the same day.'[12] In this community, where everyone engaged in the pirate's trade, everyone shared the profits. Anyone who, because of age or sickness, could not take part in person paid a partner to do so, or else fitted out his own boat, or provided towards its stores a quota of thirty loaves and one ducat. It is certain that had Segna not received a continuous although limited supply of reinforcements, in the long run this centre of piracy would have died out. We do not know how many refugees continued to arrive from the Turkish zone; their number seems slight, but a word had been coined to distinguish them from the first arrivals — they were called *venturini*. This name, however, apparently referred especially to those who came from Venetian dominions, from the Italian coast of the Adriatic, or even from the Venetian fleet itself. A special phrase — *farsi uscocco* — was coined to describe this. When a Dalmatian subject had incurred some penalty, or when a galleot had been banished, and there were many instances of this, he would quite often choose to take refuge at Segna. But he would not on that account consider himself condemned to stay there: on the contrary, if he escaped death, he would need little time to make a tidy fortune through robbery; nor was it difficult to obtain a pardon from the Venetian authorities. Indeed, the commanders of naval squadrons were empowered to grant such pardons, and such was their need of crews that they would content themselves with imposing a year or two of service at the oars of the galleys as punishment, sometimes without pay, sometimes at half-pay. They would even agree to take on another man in the place of the culprit. These abuses in their turn acted as an incentive to many people who are 'by their example induced to do the same, seeing that these men taken from the hoe and the plough, barefoot and in rags, have in a brief space of time become prosperous and well-favoured'.[13] It was therefore not surprising if after years of open warfare and of struggles to the death these pirates seemed like so many hydras: for however many heads were cut off, there always remained about 600 of them.

The heads of the Uskoks were quite literally cut off by the Venetians when they succeeded in capturing them; cut off from the shoulders, and publicly displayed on the proclamation stone, they were the pride of commanders returning from the Uskok region. This form of revenge and of expressing their feelings served in its way to placate the Venetian government, and perhaps even public opinion as well, but the attacks were renewed, and there were more ships plundered than pirates beheaded. Against a few hundred men provided with a single base and armed with nothing better than arquebuses, the Republic employed almost every means at its disposal. But the leading senators showed little skill in selecting them, and even the best admirals little aptitude in applying them. Up to 1582 the fleet had despatched a few armed boats against the Uskoks; then they took to using *fuste*; but soon (in 1586) they resorted to light galleys. Almorò Tiepolo had as many as seventeen galleys at his command in order to besiege the pirates in their few lairs, but at the end of his tour of duty he pleaded again the need to employ small armed craft in addition to the bigger ships. For the rest he frankly admitted that in a year and a half he had never succeeded in inflicting a real defeat on the inhabitants of Segna, and added: 'Although during my period of office I met and molested them many times, the victory was so costly that in truth I have gained little by this means.'[14]

It was true that the guns could do little against such minute targets as the enemy boats, which were mostly piloted by men who knew the ins-and-outs of the Dalmatian coasts perfectly. The Uskoks often showed no fear of the galleys, even when they did not actually succeed in deliberately luring them into an ambush. In May 1587, near the mouth of the Narenta, they purposely caused a trireme to follow two or three of their boats. The captain, in pursuing these boats, allowed himself to be lured into a narrow stretch of river which the galley could scarcely enter, whereupon from both sides of this narrow place they were ambushed by 300 Uskoks who suddenly let loose a volley of arquebus fire, wounding many but killing only one. With other small craft they struck fear into the hearts of the crew, and from a number of boats boarded and captured the galley. They removed from it its provisions, the powder and shot, silver, and other possessions of the commander, and took one of his brothers prisoner.[15]

So the pirates were again revealed for what they were: plunderers, not real enemies of the Venetians. But even the Venetians hesitated to launch a full-scale attack. The previous year, when with two galleys they could have trapped 150 Uskoks who were struggling with the Turkish Bey of Lica, they not only withdrew, but on hearing the Uskoks' war cry of 'Iesu, Iesu', they too replied 'Iesu, Iesu'. It is not surprising that these pirates should refuse to tolerate the attempts of Venetian magistrates to prevent them from attacking non-Venetian ships, or that they should threaten reprisals when, for example, the guns of Curzola protected by their fire Turkish ships passing between Ancona and Narenta. At the beginning of the seventeenth century, Vittore Barbaro wrote again: 'They think the damage which they inflict on possessions and subjects of Your Serenity to be fully justified, because Venice prevents them from going to plunder the Turks, and they hold this belief because it is taught and preached to them by their friars and priests, who are ignorant and iniquitous knaves.'[16]

Faced by this worsening situation, the Republic gradually decided to take steps against it. In the summer of 1590, despite the blockade of Segna by four galleys, sixteen Uskok boats managed to take to sea and to reach the fruitful waters between Curzola and Ragusa. But, after the plunder of the *saettia Vidala* in February 1592, the advocates of a benevolent neutrality no longer obtained a hearing. Nor did the defeatists who would have agreed to invite the Turkish fleet right into the Adriatic. Venice understood that she was the only one who could act, and that no one else would bestir himself merely in order to defend her trade. The expense at once turned out to be considerable: at least 120,000 ducats a year up to the end of the sixteenth century, increasing to 200,000 in the first fifteen years of the following century. The results, moreover, were far from being decisive, especially at the beginning; and expedition followed expedition. There was already a small squadron, reserved for the surveillance of this area, under the command of a *Capitano contra Uscocchi*. In 1592, fittingly, an admiral was appointed to fight them: the *Provveditore generale in Golfo*.[17]

After some years, the operations began to produce results: in the spring of 1598 the *Provveditore* Giovanni Bembo attacked a fortified position between Buccari and Segna and cut to pieces a hundred Uskoks. At the beginning of winter the galley of Antonio Giustinian, *Capitano del Golfo*, snatched away a French *saettia* singlehanded from sixteen boats which had captured it off Pola. However, Venice brought about the real change in the situation only indirectly: in 1600 the Habsburgs decided to intervene at Segna. One energetic agent of theirs sufficed to halve the number of pirates who lived there. In 1599 the report sent to the Senate by Nicolò Donà, the fourth in the succession of *Provveditori* in this area, again showed up all the uncertainties of Venetian tactics. He proposed, on the one hand, the erection of watch-towers, as he was convinced that it was impossible either to occupy Segna or to destroy the fortress; and, on the other, the substitution for the galleys of a dozen armed boats, and even of genuine *brazzere*. On the diplomatic level, Vittore Barbaro in 1601 did not appear entirely convinced of the necessity of eliminating the Uskoks: whilst he recognized that their presence in the Quarnaro was useful to Austria, it also seemed to him that it was fairly advantageous to Venice.

At the beginning of the seventeenth century the situation had become considerably worse, and the Republic was gratified by the imperial intervention at Segna. But the Habsburg agents in the preceding century had been the principal accomplices of the Uskoks, who reserved for them the best part of their booty. After a few years of relative calm the pirates soon found the atmosphere propitious for further attacks and robbery. 'The Uskoks', wrote the Senate on 31 July 1607, 'have passed with six boats above Parenzo and Rovigno, where they plundered and sacked the vessel of Nicolò Lupo and Zuane Mathcovich, which was destined for Scutari and other places in Albania and laden with Turkish and Jewish goods. As well as several other of our vessels and boats, they have plundered one of our *fregate* from Cattaro, and taken the letters addressed by us to our Ambassador in Constantinople. These acts are the more disturbing to us because there is little doubt that after the interval of peace and inactivity on their part, they are bound suddenly to return afresh to insolence of this sort.'[18] However, already in the previous year the inhabitants of Segna had taken the initiative again, and the Venetian *Provveditore* had captured one of their boats and hanged sixteen of their men. In 1607 three hundred of them came out in seven boats, and their booty, which was more substantial (about 150,000 crowns), was won at the cost of bloody losses. The seventy Turks of the boarded ship were carrying 150 arquebuses by way of contraband, and defended themselves until they were cut to pieces. Later the pirates actually succeeded in capturing a Venetian galley and killing the commanding officer, a Venier.

Thus the eclipse of Segna did not last for long. On the other hand, the tension between Spain and Venice soon gave new vigour and unexpected scope to the Uskok revival. During the sixteenth century the Uskoks had in fact been merely on the fringe of the Crusade. They had been the gangsters of the Illyrian seas, never attaining the dignity of genuine corsairs. Up to the beginning of the seventeenth century, banished criminals from neighbouring states took refuge in their harbour and leagued themselves with these plunderers in a robbers' gang of limited range. After 1615, however, their forays extended almost throughout the whole Adriatic. In 1617 they captured several Chioggian boats on the beaches of the Marches, and they reached Caorle and even Malamocco; a little later, others installed themselves at Brindisi.[19] One Ferletich went straight to Naples to obtain from the Viceroy a corsair's licence, and, having obtained it, did not hesitate to venture into the Adriatic, setting his course for Venice. It was unfortunate for him that in August 1619 the Admiral Giust'Antonio Belegno surprised him off the Lido, forcing him to stop his embarkation and flee. But the Duke of Ossuna later provided him with new vessels.[20]

The Spanish–Uskok alliance raised new problems. About 1615 the Republic seemed to have agreed upon the tactics to follow, accepting Donà's advice and arming dozens of small craft: unwillingly it had consented at first to spend 20–25,000 ducats a month, and later 30,000. But in April 1620, when the galleys had compelled Ferletich's two ships, laden with Uskok pirates, to take refuge in the port of Manfredonia, no one dared to order an attack: instead they must be held 'as in a siege'. The following year Marino da Molin and Benedetto da Canal were chosen as captains of two large armed ships 'to be kept continuously at sea near Segna, together with several *fuste*, for use against the Uskoks, for we hear that they have many vessels at sea'.[21] Perhaps the Venetians had forgotten that these pirates were also sorcerers. Lighting certain fires in the grottoes of the neighbourhood, the women of Segna succeeded in causing 'the lucky *buora* wind to blow whenever they pleased'. Vittore Barbaro assures us that in this way they had many times snatched their husbands from the hands of the Venetian navy, and even a man like Nicolò Donà had said in the Senate: 'Certainly I have seen clouds piling up against one another over those mountains so violently that this seemed the result of sorcery rather than of nature.'[22]

Corsairs, hydras and wizards, the Uskoks seemed to have been created expressly to escape capture. The Venetians, opulent and noble lords, though face to face with them and having them within easy reach, all too rarely overcame their feelings of anger and disdain towards them: just as they did not really perceive that Istria, 'a dying body almost deprived of spirit', was 'languishing, so to speak, beneath the very eyes of its prince'.[23]

Chapter 2

The Barbary Corsairs

It is much harder to define the activities and composition of the Barbary corsairs than to describe those of the Uskoks. Before trying to do so, it is necessary to make it clear that the corsairs from North Africa were not the only ones infesting the Mediterranean waters. More active, more famous and more powerful than the others, they had friends and comrades along all the coasts dependent on the Porte. After Lepanto, Ottoman aggression no longer took the form of naval operations of great scope or vast range: but aggressiveness towards the Christian world did not diminish. In spite of the peace, the Turkish fleet and the Catholic (except the Venetians) still considered themselves enemies — if they did not always seek one another out, when they did meet they aimed at destroying one another. Islam and Christendom, in short, considered that their duel was anything but finished; but the two empires, Turkish and Spanish, no longer assembled great navies, and generally kept their squadrons within their respective territorial waters or zones of influence.

In these circumstances it is more than justifiable to describe as a 'war of corsairs' (*guerra di corsa*) the vast complex of naval operations, of attacks and raids, which disturbed the Mediterranean seas and coasts and made the years after the battle of Lepanto the ones in which navigation was at its most insecure. On the Turkish side, without a doubt, those who proved themselves boldest and most dangerous were the Barbary corsairs: one can say that around the years 1580–90 there was no harbour and no coastline belonging to Catholic states which escaped their attacks. The coast around Rome, which was particularly badly defended by the Papal forces, formed one of the areas most favoured by these corsairs: but they also continually threatened Tuscan and Ligurian waters, as well as the coasts of Sicily and Calabria — nor, as we shall see, did they neglect the Adriatic. All the Catholic navies were devoted to the struggle against these infidels. The advance guard and assault troops were provided by the Orders of St John and St Stephen, the first based at Malta, the second at Leghorn and Pisa. These 'Knights', who considered themselves true crusaders, did not confine their activities to patrolling Christian coasts — on the contrary, they invariably left them to betake themselves to the waters off the Barbary coast, the Ionian sea or the Levant. It was not long before the English joined in this game.

As for Venice, she was the only Mediterranean power which was truly neutral, the only one which respected the treaty made with the Porte. Her ships, men-of-war or merchant vessels, refused to be involved in the hundreds of engagements which took place at sea: the Venetian authorities in the Adriatic, Ionia and the Levant avoided as far as possible acts of favouritism towards any of the contestants. Venice, as she had done before Lepanto, continued thereafter to believe that the best policy was to make no alliance, either with Islamic East or with Christian West: she tenaciously pursued this line of conduct as if her good fortune and her very life depended on safeguarding the trade which was the source of her wealth. And because, as has already been pointed out, the Mediterranean and European situation, which had already changed during the sixteenth century, was after 1580 entering a radically different phase, we shall see that this programme not only failed, but played itself out and came to nothing in the years we are about to examine. Venice was to remain a centre of European importance, thanks above all to her financial activities, and she would owe her continuing prosperity largely to the increasing value of her mainland possessions. But the merchant fleet and even the navy were to lose so much of their power and strength that they had to fall back into positions of secondary importance.

Up to the beginning of the sixteenth century Venetian shipping did not blame its misfortunes outright on the competition from other fleets or on the insecurity of the Mediterranean routes. While we await a fuller study of the period between 1525 and 1570, we can still establish that immediately after Lepanto the old trading system of the Republic did not decline: Venetian ships were still travelling the western routes as far as distant England, even if they did so rarely. After 1610, however, it was English and Dutch ships which mainly guaranteed Venice's trade with the Levant. One might assert, nevertheless, that neutrality was the best policy the Republic could follow. The fact remains that the Venetians found themselves — as in the past, and indeed even more so — literally caught in the mesh of remorseless pirate warfare. Although at peace with the Porte, her ships were scarcely ever respected by the Turkish corsairs: and Spaniards and Maltese and later the English very seldom allowed themselves to be restrained by promises or scruples. Precisely because of their function as commercial intermediaries, the ships of the Republic were destined to be the target for both sides: they became the principal victims of this situation.

The chief hotbeds of Muslim piracy, apart from the African ports, were those of Albania and the Morea. Later, towards 1615, some such pirates appeared actually within the Adriatic. Under the pretext of fighting the Uskoks, the Turks armed small *fregate* at the mouth of the Narenta, at Castelnuovo and at Risano. But in the preceding decades the most tangible threat to shipping came from Valona and Durazzo, as well as from Algiers and Tripoli. From the beginning of the sixteenth century there flourished in the Albanian ports piracy of a more limited scope; this was conducted by small fast-moving ships called *fuste*. The Venetians did not always succeed in overtaking them with their triremes: sometimes they did so only after a very long chase. In May 1581, for example, three galleys had to sail ninety-five miles before capturing one of these ships which they had sighted near Tremiti, but the other two which had accompanied it were lost from sight and nightfall secured them from danger.[1] The *fuste* had on average about fifteen ranks of rowers, with two galleots (generally slaves and very often Christians) to an oar. They did not possess any genuine artillery, but relied especially on arquebuses, carbines and bows. It was not always easy, however, to distinguish *fuste* from *galeotte*. The first of these terms must have had a wider meaning and was applied even to larger ships. Moreover, if a pirate had the means, he would have his *fusta* cut in half to insert a supplementary section of hull and transform it into a *galeotta*. Certainly at Valona, in addition to the *galeotte* from Barbary which passed through rapidly, a number of ships which were more powerful than *fuste* made a longer stay. Between October and November 1586, in the space of a single week, the same vessel was described, first as *fusta*, then as *galeotta*, in two different despatches sent from Venice to Florence: it had twenty-two benches and there were at least 150 Turks on board. The story of this ship, which the *Provveditore dell'Armata*, Tiepolo, captured at Cape Lachi, near Corfù, is a typical one, also because her captain was found to be a certain Angelo da Mola, a renegade Christian and an outlaw. Another such captain was one Francesco da Chioggia.[2]

Even when, as almost invariably happened, the pirates really were Turks, they were never persons authorized by the Porte to engage in pirate warfare with the Venetians. Nor can we say that the local Ottoman authorities systematically disobeyed the orders from Constantinople. In practice they made themselves accomplices of the corsairs and received some reward from them. Directly opposite the Albanian coast lay Apulia, a Catholic country subject to the King of Spain. For the Turk it was wholly legitimate to attack its coast and its towns, and to damage its trade. Now, on these very coasts a great number of Venetian ships went to sell, but above all to carry, various products and especially oil, so necessary for the textile industries of the time. The corsairs always claimed that Venetian merchandise was not at stake. How could a Turkish official confiscate booty from one who had seized it from the infidels, even at the cost of his life?

There was no lack of legal and especially of diplomatic controversy between Venice and the Porte throughout this whole period. Indeed, after Lepanto it did not seem that the authorities of the Republic insisted on recovering the stolen goods, which were immediately sold by the corsairs. On the other hand, Constantinople allowed the galleys to give chase to the *fuste*, never protesting too much and tacitly admitting that all of them deserved punishment. It must be said immediately that, if the Venetian admirals were more fortunate in this respect, they never showed themselves merciful towards their daring adversaries.[3] It was in fact their custom to cut both Turks and renegade Christians to pieces. The captains of the galleys followed up their pitiless extermination of the Turks by freeing the Christian slaves, but their triumph was complete only when they could tow the pirate ship into port. 'As he had not yet left Venice', we read in a despatch from Venice of May 1587, 'Signor Carlo Contarini, designated Commander of the Cretan fleet, was sent out on the orders of this most illustrious government because there were four *fuste* doing damage. This month, on Easter Day, he captured one of them which had on board fifty-seven or fifty-eight men, who fought valiantly and wounded about fifty of the galley's crew; only one of them died, however. He fell in the sea and was drowned. And finally the *fusta* was taken, the Turks were cut in pieces and nine Christian slaves were rescued. This galley commander returned victoriously the following Monday towing the said *fusta* astern of the galley, which had many arrow holes in its lantern and in many other places.'[4]

In spite of the marked superiority of the galleys and the risks they ran, the *fuste* — as appears from this document — did not hesitate to venture as far up as Venice. Such feats of daring were quite common, especially before 1600. Venice, it is true, did not possess a single base along the Italian coast of the Adriatic; furthermore, there were not many ports capable of accommodating galleys, and their commanders seldom left the Dalmatian bases to patrol waters where their ships could not easily find shelter. The pirates, for their part, were sure that they would not meet flotillas of local origin: neither Spain nor the Pope, much less the Duke of Ferrara, disposed of ships in the Adriatic to protect their own merchantmen. But, which was most important, the coasts of Emilia, the Marches, Abruzzo and Apulia, were alive with busy coastal trade, conducted by ships of small tonnage which could never defend themselves against the *fuste*. Hence the *fuste* were the masters here, especially between the Po delta and the promontory of Gargano. The best opportunities were afforded them by the fairs of Lanciano and Recanati. There were numerous Venetian merchants who, in order to transport their goods to the region of Naples, preferred to send them by sea as far as the little ports of the Abruzzo and thence send them on by land. Pilgrims all too frequently sailed for Loreto. If, therefore, the *fuste* had to beware of the thrusts which the galleys could make from their base of Corfù towards the shores of Apulia, and if it was inadvisable to raise the alarm as far as Venice itself, in the central part of the Adriatic they could operate almost with impunity.

Nothing escaped their attacks. Not even the boat load of Franciscans who, in the spring of 1587, were travelling to Fermo for the Chapter-General; nor yet the other boat which in the summer of 1580 was carrying only water melons. The Franciscans were enslaved whilst the water melons served at least 'to refresh the crew'. The Franciscans' fate frequently overtook pilgrims like, for example, the ones who were going on two boats to Loreto in April 1582. They were seized no less eagerly than the goods destined for Pesaro and Ancona, which were stolen from other cargoes.[5] It is impossible to enumerate here all the *marciliane*, *grippi* and other smaller craft which were regular victims of the *fuste*. The *fuste*, indeed, were sometimes actually lost because of the abundance of the booty and the ease of obtaining it. In Autumn 1584 a *fusta* was wrecked between Rimini and Cesenatico: the thirty-seven Turks were taken prisoner by the peasants and two slaves were freed. In August, two other *fuste* already well laden with 'souls' and merchandise had wanted to plunder another well-laden boat two miles from Ravenna, but the ships could absorb no more and ran aground. 'They were aground until three o'clock in the afternoon, but nevertheless people from Ravenna did not come out to them as they had done on other occasions.'[6]

The *fuste* took to sea in the most varied formations. Often they joined forces with *galeotte*, forming genuine squadrons, but just as frequently they went out in small groups or even alone. In April 1582 there were three of them engaged, unmolested, in piracy in the region of Chioggia. In March 1583 two were sighted in the waters of Primaro, where others also appeared at the beginning of May. The following year a flotilla ventured as far as Parenzo and captured a boat there, having already taken three boats destined for Loreto. A more sizeable squadron, consisting of eleven *fuste*, left Valona in the spring of 1585 and penetrated deeply into the Adriatic. The Venetian fleet was alerted: this time a vessel with seventeen benches of rowers arrived within sight of Chioggia, but

Girolamo Capello's galley overtook it near Valona and towed it to the Basin of St Mark.[7] These profitable sorties of Venetian commanders were not rare in these years, especially in the spring, when there was always some vessel on the point of leaving the lagoon to join the fleet. Thus, towards the middle of May 1586, Donato Marcello, commander of the convict galleys, could easily go out to pursue several *fuste* from Valona which had robbed at least half a dozen small craft before the Po delta. He was to capture one of them near Fano and tow it to Chioggia.[8]

Up to the end of the sixteenth century, these pirate vessels were such frequent visitors that they seemed almost at home — there existed between the inhabitants of the coastal regions and the pirates feelings compounded of fear, familiarity and understanding. Often, indeed, the booty was too conspicuous and opportunities for reselling it were created. Certain established procedures had only to be followed for everyone to understand. At the beginning of May 1587 the news went round in Venice that the *fuste* had captured fifty Observantine Franciscans in the region of Tremiti. Isidoro Manfredi, who passed the news on to Florence, at once added: 'Nobody knows whether they will hold them to ransom, as they usually do on the coasts, by showing a white flag, or whether they will take them away.'[9] A description of these transactions which is almost a literary work but is still true to life is offered by Ludovico Agostini of Pesaro, writing about 1573, in his *Giornate Soriane*. He witnessed from near by the approach of the pirates, who raised the ransom flag, and at once he saw a small crowd run out from the city. 'It greatly amused us to see many of our citizens trading with these scoundrels, who, for the sake of money (as we afterwards heard) gave valuable things at a very low price, so that they could the more freely apply themselves to the misdeeds they had embarked upon; and it was believed that they had plundered to the value of 10,000 crowns and more. Some subjects of this State found themselves prisoners in their hands, and they, with the aid of their friends and relations, furnished themselves with the price of 3,000 crowns which had been set upon their heads.'[10] These practices persisted — not without giving rise to some incidents[11] — and the Jews willingly acted as intermediaries between Christians and Turks.

Raids and attacks also persisted — though the *fuste* seemed to approach Venice less often after 1600. If they did not always get as far as the Quarnaro, as they were still doing in 1591, dozens of ships continued to fall into their clutches every year. Naturally the pirates of Valona did not neglect the Dalmatian coasts, and especially those of Albania and Greece. The sea routes ending at Cattaro, Dulcigno, Alessio, Perasto, Durazzo and the Ionian islands, which were mainly Venetian, were not adequately protected by Venetian squadrons. But, without a doubt, the most severe damage was done by the *galeotte*, often assisted by smaller ships. The ships concerned had on average twenty-four benches of rowers, so that they were scarcely less powerful than ordinary galleys and always strong enough to attack even merchant ships of greater tonnage. They were as numerous as the *fuste*, and inspired fear in the Venetian squadrons. They generally came from the Barbary coast, but the waters of the Ionian and Adriatic Seas held a particular attraction for them. There indeed they could exploit the very convenient Turkish bases of the Archipelago, the Morea and Albania. Genuine squadrons of fifteen, twenty and even forty vessels are found causing alarm in these seas. Not even the *galeotte*, even if they came from Constantinople or were headed there to pay homage to the Sultan, were authorized to attack and plunder Venetian ships, but they would deliberately make calls at Modone, Santa Maura or Valona to indulge in profitable diversions at the expense of anyone they met.

They did not always get the better of the Venetian ships. The *Mosta e Moceniga*, for example, attacked by the Barbary pirates forty miles from Palermo in spring 1580, not only fought them valiantly but actually fended them off, and even saved a smaller, richly laden vessel which had taken refuge under its wing. The galleon *Garzoni*, coming from Crete in May 1586, put up an effective resistance to two *galeotte* which had attacked it in the Adriatic. When Hassan Aga, the Viceroy of Algiers, attacked the ship *Nana* and the *saettia Vidala* near Cape Matapan, gunfire and a favourable wind enabled the *Nana* to get away, and only the *Vidala* was captured, with a cargo of kerseys. The pirates again got the worst of it in the autumn of 1608 against the *bertone Veniero*, which was attacked between Modone and Corone, whilst bringing new Cretan wine to Venice.[12] Despite these and other episodes the damage inflicted by the *galeotte* was at all times considerable. If, in the autumn of 1580, it was calculated at Venice that in the region of Cattaro alone at least twenty-five vessels had been captured by the Barbary corsairs in about a month, we must remember that at this time their sphere of action extended from the Aegean to Sicily and to Spain.

Certainly the progressive withdrawal of Venetian shipping from the western Mediterranean helps to account for the fact that the traps for the Venetian merchant fleet were very soon laid along the Ionic–Adriatic route. Thus, in August 1586, two famous corsairs appeared simultaneously in these waters. Memi Arnaut, nephew of the Queen of Fez, commanded at least five *galeotte* (though another account speaks of twelve or fourteen) and Hassan Aga had fifteen or twenty with him. Soon afterwards Hassan Aga rounded the Cape of Otranto, headed towards Africa, with a galleon and a ship in tow. As for Arnaut, he took two *marciliane*, one belonging to the Coletti, the other to the Airoldi.[13] Galleons like the *Diedo*, which in 1588 was bringing an important cargo of silk from Smyrna, and ships like the *Canevala* which was returning with a valuable cargo from Tripoli in Syria, continued thereafter to join the ranks of the smaller vessels which were the normal victims of the pirates. If the pirates needed slaves they seized them even from the Dalmatian islands, as did the fourteen *galeotte* which, in 1591, took about 200.[14] After 1600, the ventures of the Barbary corsairs, though necessarily varying in scale from year to year, did not tend to diminish. Even before the summer of 1605 was over the losses amounted to about fifteen ships: a good half of them actually belonged to Venetian merchants, but the others too were trading on their account. Nor were they only *marciliane*, like the *Fanzaga, Bona, Gottarda, Tosa* and *Vidala*: two of Francesco Morosini's *bertoni* were also lost, and likewise a roundship, the *Cigala e Mozzocca*, which was bringing a vast quantity of cotton from Smyrna.[15]

The Republic's fleet, despite its deficiencies and the real difficulties of controlling such a situation, hastened to come to the rescue. It was against the Barbary corsairs, as against the Turks of Valona and Durazzo, that it achieved the best results. In this whole period, although an impressive number of *galeotte* was captured, only one galley fell into the corsairs' hands, between Sebenico and Spalato. On the evening of 5 May 1594 the Venetian galley had stopped at Bagosnizza to spend the night there: the commander, Marino Gradenigo, and several other gentlemen went on shore and stayed there until a late hour. 'When all had settled down to sleep', continues the despatch, 'the said galley was overtaken and seized by two *galeotte*, being unable to defend itself, because the gangplank was not in place and because they were unable to manœuvre the galley into a direct firing position. The Turks immediately towed this trireme out of the harbour and, favoured by the northerly wind, were soon far away.'[16] If, as seems likely, the victorious corsair was Arnaut Memi, he had to some extent avenged the Venetians' successful action ten years previously at the expense of a huge Turkish galley of twenty-six benches which was bearing the son of Ramadan Pasha and his mother to Tripoli. On 17 October 1584, Gabriele Emo, commander of the convict galleys, had attacked the

Barbary ship opposite Porto Ferro in Cefalonia, and, with the help of two other galleys, after an engagement lasting at least six hours, had taken possession of it. All the crew — fifty Moors, seventy-five Turks and 174 renegade Christians — were cut to pieces, together with forty-five women from the princess's retinue: the 200 Christian slaves were set free.[17]

We do not always possess the information necessary to appreciate the struggle in which the galleys engaged. Sometimes (as with Hassan Aga in the summer of 1587) we learn that the *galeotte*, as well as being equipped with a considerable number of soldiers (200 for each *galeotta*) were 'reinforced', so that instead of having three or four men per oar they had as many as six. Sometimes, as with Arnaut's seven warships in 1581, we only know that they were excellently armed: but the flagship had at least 100 extra men. Sometimes the capture of a Barbary ship is merely registered. The galley *Quirina* captured one in March 1588 (two years later, again in Apulian waters, the same trireme sank a *fusta* from Valona and carried another off to Venice). The following year the *Provveditore dell'Armata* took possession of another *galeotta* of twenty-four benches after a fierce engagement lasting four hours.[18] The encounters followed one another at unpredictable intervals. There was, for example, the collision in July 1596 between Filippo Pasqualigo and Mehemet Remer, whom he had sighted off Saseno, when Venetian success was, one could say, complete. Seven 'reinforced' galleys captured four of the five *galeotte* and cut to pieces all the pirates including their chief. In August 1605 the *Provveditore dell'Armata* sank three Berber ships, two *fuste* and a *galeotta*, in the Archipelago, after first removing from them their very rich booty. Another three *galeotte* were taken by his successor in the summer of 1613 with two *marciliane* which had previously been seized by the corsair Musli Rais.[19]

All in all genuine encounters bringing victory or extermination were rare occurrences, partly because the Republic's admirals never exposed their warships to danger unless they were certain of being superior to the enemy. Barbary vessels were nearly always well equipped for battle, and there could be surprises in store for those who attacked them.[20] So it happened that the fleet commander withdrew from Corfù to Zara to re-form his own squadron. It even happened that he refused to counterattack until he had received the instructions requested of the Senate. And not even when the Venetians seemed to be ready to reply, and when the pirates were almost within their grasp, was it certain that they would reach them. In a long despatch of 19 June 1610, the *Capitano del Golfo* described the unsuccessful pursuit of four *galeotte* off the Ionian islands. His own three galleys had just left the port of Corfù on the morning of 18 June to try to intercept two *fuste* from Prevesa, when a number of cannon shots recalled them. These shots had been fired by a fourth trireme which ought already to have joined the other three, and which was now to advise the *Capitano del Golfo* to aim for the Gomenizze, where the Barbary *galeotte* were attacking two ships. But the commander of this galley, Camillo Morosini, not having wished to leave Corfù and join his own ship on time, delayed the whole operation for several hours. 'I did all I could', wrote Francesco Molin, 'by hoisting more sail to make up the time which had been lost through another man's fault, and, followed only by the Signori Loredano and Balbi, contrived to reach Leftimo in the nick of time. The patrols there told me that the *galeotte* were making off towards the rock of Paxu with the booty. When I myself reached Paxu I was informed that they were sailing way ahead in the direction of Santa Maura. However, I continued the voyage at the same speed and at eleven o'clock at night I finally found them, but they were over fifteen miles away from me, and, having a very favourable wind behind them and being already very near to the aforesaid Santa Maura, they managed to save themselves.' The *Capitano del Golfo*, though now abandoning hope of overtaking them, still urged on his men and followed them until two o'clock in the morning. But after daybreak he had to admit that they were certainly at Santa Maura with one of the plundered vessels: the other, which had run aground a short distance from the entrance to the harbour, could not be pulled off in spite of all the efforts of the Venetians.[21]

Much more frequent than direct encounters were alarms communicated to Venice either by a whole network of informers from both coasts of the Adriatic or else directly from Rome, concentrations of naval forces which were often fruitless, and pursuits seldom crowned with success. Everyday life was composed of ambushes and surprise attacks, of which the very numerous merchant vessels were usually the victims. Navigation was full of unexpected encounters and adventures. The Venetians knew that when they met a Turkish squadron they had to offer its commander a gift — a present which was in fact a tribute. In spite of this burden, they were delighted to avoid anything worse. Dandolo da Milo, master of the ship *Barella*, which had returned from Syria, described for example how the eight Turkish galleys of the Bey of Rhodes and the Bey of Mytilene had on 29 May 1599 begun to tow his ship away because the 'present' was slow to appear.[22] Hassan Aga created genuine astonishment when he not only renounced this acquired right but even offered 'refreshments' to the sailors and their passengers whom he encountered off Zante. It was the Christians who hesitantly insisted that he should allow some of the commanders of his *fuste* to accept some cloths as a gift, 'and he would scarcely consent'.[23] It seemed like a happy dream, but nightmares were much more frequent. Some — not always the most desirable ones — were short. In the summer of 1607 two *galeotte* met a vessel coming from Durazzo, manned for the most part by Turks: they cut them to pieces just the same. The same fate overtook a Greek ship driven by storms into the canal of Cattaro, below Castelnuovo, towards the end of 1586.[24]

Fortune sometimes both smiled and frowned in a brief space of time. This happened to the French vessel which the *Provveditore dell'Armata* seized from the hands of the pirates in 1602, and to the *bertone Beltrame*, which was recovered and taken to Corfù by galleys, which even succeeded between June and July 1607 in capturing two of the *galeotte* which had attacked her. It happened also to the ship *Pasqualiga*, rescued from the Barbary pirates by the Knights of Santo Stefano and taken to Leghorn, between 1609 and 1610.[25] One could escape from *fuste* and *galeotte*, but they were everywhere and always ready to attack. In February 1586 two vessels from Valona saw a low-lying ship without oars and mistook it for one of those galley hulls which the Republic often sent to the Levant. The bigger *fusta* did not hesitate to close with it, but it turned out to be a galley which, though it had lost nearly all its oars in a storm, was still strong enough to win the engagement and cut all the pirates to pieces. Only too simple was the capture of another *fusta* in the spring of 1593. 'The merchant galleasses', we read in a report of 22 May, 'have taken a Turkish *fusta* above Corfù, which fell into their hands like a hare caught in a trap. The wretches had lost their compass and sailed for a good part of the night keeping the lantern of the galleasses always in sight, thinking this was the North Star, so that at daybreak, they found themselves beside these galleasses within firing range, and so became the victims of this supposed "star".'[26]

We have certainly not been able to list in these pages all the *fuste* and *galeotte* which fell into the hands of the Venetian squadrons, not even those for which trustworthy evidence has been found. There were far more of them than in the years before Lepanto, but it does not seem paradoxical to treat this as an additional proof that they had strikingly increased in number. The Venetian fleet in these years — as we shall see later — would have been unable to appear so much more efficient than its predecessor in the mid-sixteenth century had not occasion for action become more frequent and indeed so common as to enable every well-disposed admiral and almost every captain to distinguish himself often and brilliantly. There is one other decisive explanation for both these things: the absence of large Ottoman naval concentrations. As a result, the Turkish corsairs of Albania and the Morea, of Anatolia and the Barbary coasts enjoyed greater freedom of action, whilst on the other side Venetian squadrons were no longer obliged to shut themselves up in the Adriatic almost every year (as in the mid-sixteenth century) in order to avoid, in just those months most favourable to piracy, dramatic incidents or dangerous skirmishes with the Muslim navy.[27]

Chapter 3

Maltese, Florentines and Spaniards

Nicolò Surian, who had served as commander of the Venetian fleet for several years, read an important report in the Senate at the beginning of 1584. The words of the *Provveditore* again presented to the patricians' views which were soon to appear unsatisfactory to them. He recommended the greatest caution in encounters, not only with future Turkish navies, but even with Barbary corsairs. According to the admiral it was inadvisable that galleys should go out to pursue them into the Gulf of Taranto or along the Calabrian coasts. There were now few Venetian merchantmen regularly sailing this route. Nor should Venice concern herself with defending the coasts of the Viceroyalty of Naples. Surian, moreover, did not wish Venetian squadrons to interfere with the movements or the landing-places of the *galeotte* along the shores and within the ports of the Morea. 'There is no need to seek out Levantine *fuste* between Cape Malio and Zante, because they do not stop to plunder in those places. For there are few ships carrying goods of any value in that sea. If there are any, they are so large that they little fear pirate *fuste* of the calibre of the present ones.' In fact he exhorted the Senators to concentrate the galleys in the Adriatic for a merciless struggle against the pirates which infested it. At the same time he tried to persuade them to allow the Barbary corsairs to circulate freely in the Ionian Sea to avoid encounters with unforeseeable consequences.

The admiral's outlook was evidently that of a man whose ideas were formed before Lepanto, and whose past experience counselled prudence and circumspection in the face of the Turkish Empire. Even after the Christian victory he saw in the Ottoman colossus the greatest danger to the future of his country. Besides, it is significant that by 1580 Surian had still not realized that Barbary piracy was spreading eastwards — which is one more proof that the beginning of the new and systematic Berber offensive must be dated at about this time. If the threat of a Turkish advance and of its possible renewal still prevailed throughout the Mediterranean in these years, the voice of the *Provveditore* still obtained a hearing. As we have seen, even in the following years, Venetians continued to attack *fuste* and *galeotte*, especially in the Adriatic and around the Straits of Otranto. No less characteristic is the attitude towards Westerners which this report reveals. The admiral maintained that there must be stern vigilance against them. After mentioning that many sailors and oarsmen on Christian ships came from the galleys of Venice, he stressed the fact that this made them certain of unwavering support and sure co-operation in Venetian territories in the Levant. 'When they arrive at these places, they disembark in the utmost security and receive as much reliable information about the ships of Your Serenity as they can possibly want. If, on the other hand, Your Serenity's galleys put in to a place where such Western ships have been, these ships are protected by your subjects with false information so that they can sail your seas in safety. Nor is it possible to cure your subjects of this great love for Westerners, even though Your Serenity has forbidden under the severest penalties that they should harbour such people.'

Another reflection of an earlier situation is the fact that

Surian identified these pirates chiefly as Florentines and Maltese, whilst (he added) others came from Messina but with 'smaller vessels such as *fuste* and *fregate*'. His principal concern, in dealing with ships entirely devoted to piracy, was that the galleys should be sufficiently numerous and well-armed to dissuade pirates from approaching Venetian waters, and should ultimately be capable of disarming them. Hence he proposed to increase to seven warships the strength of the squadron employed in guarding the island of Crete, and to keep them at sea in winter — the season preferred by these pirates — between Crete, Cerigo and Cape Matapan. It would then be sufficient that some other warship based on Corfù should complete the security force patrolling between Zante, Cefalonia and Paxu.[1]

The Senate had already accepted the first proposition of this retiring *Provveditore dell'Armata*, and from 1581 Filippo Pasqualigo, the new Commander of the fleet guarding Crete, had at his disposal a squadron of seven galleys. A capable admiral, he did not wait long to make use of it. The Knights of St Stephen, though they conducted regular crusading expeditions to the Levant, from now on respected their instructions to beware 'of enemies and likewise of Venetian galleys of superior strength, avoiding all entanglements with them'.[2] It goes without saying that not even these newest crusaders cared much about fighting the infidels as such. Nevertheless, we have a particularly clear illustration from these years. Half-way through 1583, it was learnt in Venice that the ship *Ragazzona*, returning from Syria and Cyprus, had in these regions encountered first, six Turkish galleys guarding Rhodes, which were 'ill-equipped and poorly armed', and the following day the four galleys of Tuscany, 'as well-equipped as any that sail the sea'. The Venetian ship had informed the Knights of this excellent opportunity, but 'they chose not to go and fight them, saying that they wanted to continue their voyage to Cyprus and Syria in order to plunder'.[3]

The Order of the Knights of Malta was much more a company of international adventurers than was the Pisan Order of St Stephen — which, moreover, the Grand Duke held firmly under control. Pasqualigo had to act against the Knights of Malta when he received the order to disarm the galleys of St Stephen, together with every other armed vessel from the West which entered Venetian waters. On the night of 18 February 1583 the Commander of the Cretan fleet surprised a Maltese vessel with two Turkish caramussals at anchor in the port of San Nicolò della Vlemona (Cerigo), and captured them without a blow being struck. In fact the ship had little that was Maltese about it. The Captain was Don Diego Brocchiero de Anaya, a native of Salamanca; together with various other knights and about 200 soldiers he had scoured the seas of the Levant, and the booty, worth 80–100,000 golden ducats, attested the success of his venture. The ship, too, had its history: it was an English galley, which the previous year had carried out a raid in the Mediterranean and was then driven by a storm on to the island of Malta. The crew were despatched to Rome as heretics: we know that the Inquisition, having failed to force these Protestants to abjure their faith, then had them tortured and roasted alive in a public square before the eyes of the Romans. Brocchiero had bought the ship, which was equipped with very powerful artillery (at least sixty guns), and had it refitted at Messina. This was a foretaste of the contribution which the northerners were shortly to make to navigation and pirate warfare in the Mediterranean.[4]

Meanwhile the Maltese fleet had set out to sea, and in the spring had captured the ship despatched by Hassan Aga to Constantinople with 150 janissaries, 40,000 sultanins in cash, and goods to the value of 60,000 ducats. Four galleys of the Order of St John were then sent towards the Levant. While Pasqualigo was forced by the passing Turkish navy to remain in the port of Candia, the Grand Master's galley and that of the Knight Bandino skirted the island and preyed on the coasts near Cape Salamon. Having encountered the vessel belonging to Giorgio and Bernardino Pizzamano, the pirates put some of their men on board, to take it to Malta. But the winds drove it almost on to the Barbary coast, and then flung it back upon Crete: 'being then becalmed, it could not depart from those coasts. Hence the Westerners who were on board ... struck a bargain with the ship's master that half the Jewish goods on board should be freely granted to him; and so the ship was recovered, and taken to the Canea by the very persons who were in charge of her'.[5] In the end the Commander of the Cretan fleet was able to emerge with his seven galleys, and on 24 July he found himself face to face with the four warships of the Knights between Cerigotto and Grabusce. While one of them rapidly headed for the Archipelago, the other three, seeing themselves cut off from the west, hoisted their red flag with the white crosses, preparing themselves for battle. Pasqualigo, too, hoisted the standard of St Mark, but did everything he could to make it clear that he was only asking for sails to be reefed and for the right to inspect the ships. He fired powder without ball from his light guns, but his warning fire and smoke produced no effect. In the end — as he later told the Senate — 'it seemed to me that the reputation of this Most Serene Republic would have suffered, had I allowed them to test me by escaping, and not attempted to lay hands on them by any means at all'. However, when some shots had been fired and he was on the point of ramming the Grand Master's galley, this vessel — manœuvring its sails in a manner which was as masterly as it was unexpected — changed tack, and with 'marvellous speed' passed across the bows of the Venetian warships. The admiral then abandoned the pursuit to avoid losing the other two as well. These, the *San Giacomo* and *San Giovanni*, seeing their escape route barred, let themselves be taken without either fighting or pillaging, while the slaves, crying 'Freedom!', broke their chains with sheer strength and threw them into the sea. The Knights and soldiers of the *San Giacomo*, 'with the vilest cowardice', wrote Pasqualigo, 'threw themselves into the water, and as they were rescued were brought before me, all wet and naked'.[6] The commander of the patrol, after first pausing at Crete, hastened to leave for Corfù, and by this perspicacious move avoided being surprised by the Turkish admiral, who had flung himself into the pursuit in order to recover the two pirate vessels. By an astute move, after some delay, he sent to Constantinople only the thirty Turkish prisoners whom he had found on board, instead of freeing the 223 slaves at the oars.

The operations of the Venetian squadron did produce some results. The most immediate effect was, undoubtedly, the arrival from the Turkish islands of the Archipelago of the grain which Crete urgently needed, for it was capable of living off its own harvests for only four months of the year. Certainly, as well as winning satisfying prestige, Pasqualigo did for a short time drive the Westerners away from these seas. The events of 1583 were nevertheless the prelude to the worsening of relations between Venice and Malta. The Republic, perhaps fearing a counterattack in the spring of the following year, was already sending another three galleys to the fleet commander. Soon afterwards a Venetian ship was seized at Malta on its voyage from Crete to Spain: at the news of the first reprisals, the Knights clapped the crew in irons, removed the rest of the cargo, holed the ship and sank it.[7]

In the following years there is evidence of further incidents. One cannot say for certain that the Maltese, much less the Florentines, concentrated chiefly on Venetian shipping. The Knights of both the Orders, whose galleys often joined forces in order to carry out the most varied enterprises, went in pursuit especially of Turkish and Barbary ships. Sometimes they engaged in real battles. The exchange of blows with Muslim forces was continuous. Now the Tuscans captured booty worth 100,000 crowns in the region of Tunis; now the

Maltese got possession of a *germa* with 400 Moors and seventy Turks on board. If the galley of the Prince Aumale had to fight for a whole day before capturing and taking to Malta a Barbary vessel whose cargo was worth 50,000 crowns, Algerian *galeotte* captured the armed *galeotta* of the Knight Bandini, likewise in the waters of Gozo.[8]

Reports of all these operations reached Venice and there were rumours which no one hastened to check — for example, that five Algerian *galeotte* had surprised two Tuscan galleys on a Sicilian beach, or that the Tuscans and Genoese had captured a Turkish warship with 300 men in the Archipelago. There was more concern, perhaps, when a Ragusan ship was involved, merely because it had transported 'goods belonging to Levantine Jews'.[9] It was a fine thing to be neutral. In September 1586 two well-armed Maltese *fregate* attacked the *saettia Segura* in the waters of Cefalonia. It was carrying silken cloths and other goods worth 25,000 crowns: amongst the passengers there was a Saracen personage who was later to offer forty slaves and a large sum of money for his ransom. 'When he was taken by the crew of the *fregate*', the despatch continues, 'the ship's purser was killed, his nephew was tortured to make him say that the ship and its cargo belonged to Turks: and so, out of fear, the said nephew confessed and signed the statement which they wanted. Under this pretext they conducted the ship to Malta with eight prisoners on board, having disembarked the others.'[10]

When these methods were used, it was evident that no merchantman was safe from pillage. The Venetians therefore addressed themselves to the Pope, who delegated the examination of their suit to a commission of cardinals. The Pope could be a good ally: his subjects traded very actively with Turks and Jews, and his treasury drew a steady income from such trade. In July 1587 the Roman Congregation decided that Levantine Jews or Jews domiciled in Italy could ship goods without interference, as could Christians trading with Turks, so long as they did not carry certain goods which had for some time been forbidden. But the Knights of Jerusalem from Malta, at whom this decision was particularly aimed, paid no attention. In these very months the Knight Brocchiero and his galleon, equipped with fifty guns and 500 soldiers, began to attack Venetian shipping. On the Smyrna route, the *Balbiana* was plundered; the *marciliana Croce* was seized and taken to Malta; and the galleon *Baietto* may have suffered the same fate.[11] The Senate animatedly discussed whether it was better to apply to the Pope again or to give secret orders to the *Provveditore dell'Armata* to seize the pirates and put them all to the sword. The idea of refitting galleasses and equipping them with heavy guns made some progress: but the expense was great, and the delay in reaching a decision even greater. Meanwhile the Senate relieved its feelings by dubbing the Knights 'corsairs parading crosses'. More efficient than the Venetians, the Turks at the beginning of 1588 captured the *galeoncino* of a French *commandeur*, a 'serviceable vessel with twenty oars, equipped with ingenious devices which brought great advantages in combat'. The Scio patrol had been forced to struggle with it for three days.[12]

The situation undoubtedly created concern, and was no less delicate than the affair of the Uskoks; behind the Maltese galleys was Spain, which would not have tolerated Venetian reprisals without taking action. It seems indeed that after Pasqualigo's success the Venetian squadrons ceased to pursue these pirates to the death. And yet the Knights regularly went out to raid the seas, showing a preference for the Levant. And although one year, as in 1588, the Turkish fleet might succeed in intercepting and repelling them, the following year they made two expeditions to the eastern Mediterranean. From the first they returned with 300,000 crowns in cash; from the second with a huge quantity of booty and at least ten ships, one of them laden with a cargo of spices.[13] In September 1591 two Maltese warships dared to force the mouth of the Adriatic to try to surprise the merchant galleasses employed on the Corfù line: several shots were exchanged above Saseno, and sub-acid conversations took place in Venice between the Receiver of Malta and the Senators.

A document from the end of the sixteenth century, sent in the form of a report to the Grand Duke of Tuscany, provides the most typical description of a pirate cruise in these years. Leaving Messina on 25 April 1597, the Knights of St Stephen 'on the 28th sighted the mountains of Navarrino. At night they entered the straits between Speranza and Modone to see if there were any ships there, but found none. On the 29th of the same month they passed through the channel of Cerigo and Cerigotto in the still, calm water and during the night met seven galleys which they judged to be Venetian. And as the Tuscan vessels were in the moonlight, it is thought that they were first sighted by the Venetian galleys, which gave chase to them, sending up smoke and flares. Our galleys turned towards Cape St Angelo and were pursued for two hours and a half, although they would have disappeared from sight immediately had they not stopped on two occasions to wait for the flagship. In the morning they were out of sight and it was thought that the Venetians would retreat to the fortress of Cerigo. The Tuscans had then heard that the Venetians had taken three Turkish *galeotte* which had seized a Venetian ship with 60,000 ducats' worth of goods; this was restored to its owners and the Turks cut in pieces.[14]

'The Tuscans entered the Archipelago and on the first of May arrived at the island of San Giovanni di Sconia, where they gave chase to two brigantines of fifteen and eleven benches respectively, with sixty-four Turks on board. They drove them ashore and spent three days in pursuit of them. They captured fifty-one, whilst the others escaped into the caves. On the 6th of May they went out by night through the channel between Rhodes and Scarpanto. On the 8th they found a little boat on Castel Rosso with ten Christians, fugitives from

Famagusta in Cyprus, who said that in that city the Christian slaves had rebelled against the Turks and killed many of them, but then they did not know how to act because they had no leader: most of them were given up and cut to pieces by the Turks, whilst the remainder were savagely executed.[15]

'On the 9th of May, a high wind and a heavy sea forced them to take shelter on land and they anchored at Calamici, near the Gulf of Macri, where they took on water. On the 10th, in the said Gulf of Macri, they captured two vessels – the first a caramoussal laded with corn, manned by forty Turks, who dragged the boat on to land and fled, and the Tuscans found on it fifteen Jews, seven female, the rest male; whilst the other was a small vessel with a cargo of timber, manned by seven Greeks. The Tuscans found four Turks aboard, took the Greeks on board the galley, and sank both the said ships. On the 14th they seized a caramoussal with a capacity of about 400 *salme* and a cargo of timber, sixty miles from Cape Edidonza. This had sixty-four well-armed Turks on board and fought bravely. Three Knights were killed, as were six other officers, and some ninety persons wounded by arrows: the caramoussal was taken, with the loss of fourteen of their crew. It was coming from Constantinople and was headed for Cyprus and then Alexandria. It was sunk. The Tuscans took fifty slaves.

'On the 15th, they seized a *germa* with a capacity of 800 *salme*, carrying 300 baskets of rice: this came from Damiata. They cut it loose with thirty-four Christians aboard and left it ninety miles above Cape Celidonia. They had taken twenty-seven Moors off it. On the 17th, thirty miles from Cyprus, they seized a little vessel carrying 170 baskets of rice, coming from Damiata with fifteen Moors aboard: they towed it by the stern for three days. On the 20th they cut it loose eighty miles from the Seven Capes, where they took another small vessel. This had four Turks aboard, whilst the rest of the crew were Greeks, and carried eighty-four baskets of rice: it came from Damiata. They towed it for two days and then released it with twelve Christians aboard, in addition to the slaves. On the 20th, seventy miles from the Seven Capes, they seized a vessel with a cargo of timber, and ten bales of carpeting and another ten of leather. And even though the twenty-four Turks who were aboard attempted to escape on to land with the boat, the carpets and leather at any rate were taken and brought to the galley. The ship was handed over to all the Greeks who had been kept back from other vessels during the voyage, and they let them go as they pleased. There remained twenty-four slaves. Of the Greeks, a certain Father Penino and three others came to Malta and claimed compensation for one of the vessels loaded with timber, which had been sunk, saying that it and all its cargo belonged to him.

'On the 21st of May, ninety miles from the Seven Capes, where they were driven by thirst and great need of water, they sighted four vessels. A galleon of 3,500 *salme*, and a caramoussal of 800, well-equipped with crew and slaves, were sailing with a steady wind behind them and half a mile apart. On wise reflection (especially because of the steady wind, and because they anticipated the approach of a convoy of galleys of which they had news), they left them and went to find the other two caramoussals, and with their guns they made them take in sail by severing their yards from top to bottom, and because of the steady wind they kept bearing down on them astern. On the first, with a capacity of 600 *salme*, and a cargo of flax, rice and spices, they found twenty-four Turks. And the second was rammed during the fighting and the Tuscans killed fifteen of the enemy; two from the galleys died, but they wounded up to twenty men and took the ship by force. They found on it fifty-five Turks, Moors and negroes, both wounded and fit. Its capacity was 800 *salme*, and its cargo, flax, rice and spices. They were coming from Alexandria with the other two vessels, and gave more reliable news of the convoy which was approaching. The caramoussals were patched up and cut loose, and seventy-four Christians were put on both of them.

Uskoks attacking merchantmen (from G. Rosaccio, *Viaggio da Venetia a Costantinopoli*, Venice, 1606)

A Venetian galley in pursuit of Uskoks off the island of Pago (from G. Rosaccio, *op. cit.*)

They left them on the 22nd, 140 miles south-east of Crete. And of all the vessels cut loose — which were five in number, with 104 Christians on board, and rice, flax and spices to an estimated value of 50,000 crowns — not one has yet appeared, although they are very optimistic about them and confident of their arrival. God grant that it may be so! Including the ransom of the slaves (i.e., one *cadi chiaus*, three *rais* and fifteen Jews), and the sale of twenty-five negroes (six females and the rest males), there should be a prize of 100,000 crowns, including also the slaves at the oar at 100 crowns each.

'On the 25th, spurred on by thirst, they arrived in Crete, at the river Ciciri, and stayed near the coast for six days. They tarred three planks at Cape St John, and they left there on the 1st of June in bad weather. On the 6th, in the moonlight, they sighted Mongibello. On the 7th they drew into port with a fine volley from their guns and many flags flying from prow to stern, in good order and high spirits. On the 8th they took steps to ensure that there was no kind of sickness on board. They had brought all the bills that the ships were sound and clean and came from healthy countries. They had been absent forty-two days in all. They left on a Friday and returned on a Friday. The prize amounted to some 120,000 crowns.'[16]

Barbary pirates and Westerners had flung their nets across the Levantine seas where the most important trade of Venice took place. With the passing of the years both Barbary pirates and Westerners, now summoned less and less often to join the fleets of the Sultan and the King of Spain, observed that the most propitious moment for pirate warfare had now arrived. But very soon even the Spanish Viceroys of Naples and Sicily thought of using the squadrons at their disposal, and even of fitting out pirate ships on their own account. When this happened, the Venetians really found themselves badly situated. 'Since on account of the Uskoks nearly all the galleys had to remain in the Adriatic', wrote Vittore Barbaro in 1601, 'and since the Levantine fleet of the *Provveditore dell'Armata*, which used to have eighteen or twenty, had been left with only four to six, the many gains made by the corsairs began to be felt. And what was worse, squadrons of galleys, even very small ones, not from Spain but from Tuscany and elsewhere, have permitted themselves with excessive licence and insolence to enter the ports of Zante and Argostoli and the Corfù channel, and even to approach the fortresses there.'[17] Venice's richest vessels were captured or plundered, the northern vessels which transported precious goods on behalf of Venetians were seized all along this route: mere resentment against Spain heightened into hatred, and the Republic did everything of which it was capable to defend its shipping.

As Nicolò Contarini was later to relate in his *Historie*, the two Viceroys of Naples and Sicily were not slow to find reasons, which seemed excellent to them, to expand their own pirate industry. An ancient custom decreed that the booty should be regarded as tribute to the Viceroys' wives; if the ships concerned had been fitted out at their instigation half the booty fell to them, and even when the ship had been privately equipped a quarter of the profits had to be handed over. 'The Viceroy's wife', wrote Contarini of one of them, 'who, like a true Spanish lady, professed to have no stain on her conscience, declared that she had set theologians to work and been assured that there was no reason to feel any scruples, since her King had piously declared relentless war both upon heretics and upon infidels. Moreover, these contributions were the rightful portion of the King, who by paying for these vessels kept the seas free of pirates and blunted the pride of the Turks.'[18] The European situation, again, provided a new pretext and an additional motive for Spanish piracy. It was around 1580 that the new enemies of the Catholic King, the English and the Dutch, were entering the Mediterranean with their ships and were quick to establish profitable links with Venice. It therefore seemed that there could be no objection to fighting them in defiance of the Venetian Republic.[19]

The first series of important Spanish attacks took place around 1585–87. In these three years, at least four important Venetian ships were captured — the work mainly of galleys from Sicily. The *Rota*, master Nicolò Condocolo, was seized off Syracuse, the *Setta e Vidala* at Trapani; a similar fate overtook Master Giacomo Basso's ship returning from Palermo. But in 1586 the Spaniards ventured as far as Cefalonia to capture the ship *Patinota*, master Manoli da Cerigo, which was ambushed during the return voyage from Smyrna.[20] To the two sorts of Westerners mentioned by Surian, Florentines and Maltese, a third species, more dangerous than the others, was soon added. The Ragusans, too, had good reason to know this, for in 1587 they lost three ships, which were attacked by fourteen *galeotte* and captured after a savage battle lasting two days. The Venetians, for their part, sought to counterattack. The Commander of the Cretan fleet, with two galleys, captured a Sicilian *galeotta* in May 1588 between Zante and Cefalonia. He himself and many of his men were wounded in the encounter. As for the pirates, a relation of the Viceroy's butler was beheaded and all his men were hanged, while forty Turkish slaves recovered their freedom.[21]

While the Republic did not hesitate to brave Spanish wrath and face Spanish reprisals by pursuing these Westerners in its own seas, it could do practically nothing to defend the numerous northern vessels which were soon frequenting Venice, and they could not avoid, at least on leaving the Mediterranean, the risks involved in crossing Spanish waters. Thus, for example, the ship *Black Lion*, master Wilhelm Classen, which had left Venice on 20 March 1592 and in less than a month reached the Straits of Gibraltar, was there seized and taken to Cadiz: its cargo was sold, and the Adelantado put all the crew in chains to row in the galleys. A similar fate befell four other northern vessels in 1596. A German *orca*, master Mark Beckmann, was detained at Malaga, with its cargo of sulphur and silks. Two Flemish ships—the *Paradise*, master Dirk Wilemens, and the ship whose master was Tirvirch Naazar, carrying grapes and cotton, soap and mirrors — were captured in the waters off Corfù during the summer by the Spanish fleet, which in the same season and in the same place plundered the English ship whose master was Nicholas Nelson.[22] Next year it was the turn of three ships coming from Hamburg — the *Flying Fortune*, *Holy Trinity* and *Half Moon* — which were all detained at Lisbon with vast cargoes of grain. More typical was the adventure of the *St Peter*, master Luke Nerins, which was carrying malmsey and currants, carpets and glass ware to Danzig: between the end of 1597 and the beginning of 1598 the vessel was detained at Messina, and 'the said master and all the sailors were imprisoned, accused of being Lutherans in having eaten meat on Friday and Saturday, and of having said that they knew no Pope but bread and wine. They were also imprisoned because they were English, and were accused of committing acts of piracy in the aforesaid waters of Messina'.[23] Some further examples: Pieter Mayner's ship from Amsterdam was captured in Spanish waters with its cargo of lead and iron, as were the *St Peter* (master Hans Luber), the *Fortune* (master Fiche Zoistes), the *Red Lion*, *Bull*, *St Andrew*, *New Lily*, *Crescent Moon*, *Orange Tree* and *Fortune* (master Flores Heres). All but the last three were Dutch ships on their way to or from the Low Countries.[24]

Venetian merchants fared no better. They, however, were usually victims, not of the regular warships, but of private vessels equipped for the voyage with the approval of the Spanish authorities or with their active collaboration. The most violent outburst of this kind of piracy can probably be dated about the years 1595–1604. Various types of ship — *feluche*, *galeotte* and galleons — joined the Maltese and Florentines and dealt very severe blows to Venetian commerce. This series of attacks and this wave of Western piracy were probably unleashed by the attack on Patras launched in 1595 by the galleys of Naples and Sicily under the command of Don Pedro de Toledo and Don Pedro de Leyva. This action was the prelude to Spanish squadrons being frequently thrust into Levantine waters, not to a renewal of large-scale naval operations between the Turkish and Christian navies.

In the wake of these squadrons and in the atmosphere created by their expeditions many people organized private piracy of their own. The two Viceroys were among the first to do so. In the memoirs of Alonso de Contreras, the discovery of this lucrative pursuit by Bernardino de Cardenas, Duke of Maqueda and Viceroy of Sicily, comes almost as a surprise. Shortly after the Patras expedition he fitted out a *galeotta* which soon brought considerable spoils to Palermo: and then, in his enthusiasm, the Viceroy decided to equip two pirate galleons, the *Leone d'Oro* and *Leone d'Argento*. From their first voyage to the East, the plunder was very rich: Contreras, then a mere private soldier, recalls that for his share he got three hundred crowns and a hat filled to the brim with Spanish doubloons. 'The two galleons', he says, 'were sent again to the Levant, where we took unbelievably rich prizes on the sea and on the coasts, so fortunate was this Viceroy.'[25]

At this time the Neapolitans were no mere spectators. 'The Spanish Ambassador', we read in a despatch of November 1596, 'is in great difficulties because the Viceroy of Naples persists in detaining Venetian shipping and imprisoning the sailors: and every day he goes a step further.'[26] Western vessels slipped round the Ionian islands and penetrated into the Adriatic without the slightest scruple. The *Pisana e Mazza*, master Giovan Maria Furegon, was thoroughly plundered at Merlere, near Corfù, while the *Santa Maria di Loreto*, master Giovanni Morgante, coming from Rodosto on the sea of Marmara, was ambushed on the voyage by these new marauders and taken to Messina.[27] The Spanish Italians did not fail to employ the ruses proper to pirates, even when they were not actually making use of their own flag to enter

Venetian ports as friends and then plunder therein. 'Just as if war had been declared on the Republic', wrote Contarini, 'an armed frigate of the King's went like a friend to the pesthouse at Corfù, and thence, without respect for a friendly Prince or for the health regulations, like those voracious robbers that snatch their booty from the flames, they removed a Turk and a Jew who were in quarantine there with their merchandise; and on their return to Naples they were received with acclamations and cries of rejoicing by those who had a stake in the voyage.' The same author relates that two richly laden vessels, the *Soderina e Memma* and the *saettia Vidala e Cordes*, both on their way from the Levant, were captured by a trick that was manifestly piratical.[28]

The most important attacks by these Westerners on Venetian trade took place in the opening years of the seventeenth century. At the beginning of 1600, the *bertone* equipped by the Viceroy of Sicily captured the *San Giuseppe e Bonaventura*, commanded by Pietro d'Alvise, on its way to Constantinople. The following year, it was again Maqueda's ships that plundered the *Giustiniana* on its return from Syria. In these same months the *Memma e Constantina*, sailing from Corfù and compelled by foul weather to take refuge at Otranto, was forced to discharge its cargo by order of the Viceroy, on the pretext that the goods belonged to Jews.[29] Meanwhile, private adventurers and shipowners took advantage of the favourable situation. A Sevillan and a Frenchman, 'both outlaws and desperadoes on account of their wicked acts in the past', had equipped two galleons at Messina. Entering the waters of Cyprus, they lay in wait near Cape Sant' Andrea, and in those seas preyed on the *Pigna* and then on the *Leone*, stripping them even of their guns and provisions. Continuing their raid, they then headed north and on the coasts of Anatolia surprised and sacked the *Giustiniana*, returning from Syria, 'saying that all entries in the name of Christians were false and that the whole cargo really belonged to Turks and Jews. To prove this, they tortured the sailors and got them to say everything they wanted. At Prodano on the Morea', wrote Contarini, 'the *bertone Morosini* was treated worse than any other.'

Even the wife of the Viceroy of Naples had her champions and her plunder. Ferdinando d'Aragona and Giacomo Vinciguerra fitted out two large *bertoni* for her, and in the winter of 1600–01 they had the good fortune to hit upon two ships with valuable cargoes, the *Gagliana* and the *Martinella*. On the first, destined for Constantinople, the pirates left nothing but the Christian crew. The second, as it was a very fine ship and 'because its wealth could not be contained in their vessels', was actually taken to Naples. The pirates were welcomed 'like conquerors, with bonfires and celebrations, just as if they had returned after winning a decisive victory over a mighty and terrible foe. The Viceroy, too, received them as victors and as such invited them to sup with him; and though it was Lent and a Friday in March, nevertheless, using the Spaniard's privilege, they ate meat in public. One hundred and fifteen Turks and Jews had been seized from the plundered ships; and these were made to walk in front of the pirates as if they were trophies of the victory; and the pirates, though detested by all peoples, were honoured here like excellent and noble captains who had conquered by true skill and courage.'[30]

The vigorous diplomatic protests of the Venetian representatives at Madrid after the pillaging of the *Rossi*, and the almost simultaneous deaths of the two Viceroys, seem to mark a pause in this Western piracy. Maqueda died at the beginning of 1602; the Count of Lemos, Viceroy of Naples, had preceded him in October 1601. But their successors were no less deeply involved, and took advantage of the slowness of the interventions and negotiations at the Court of the Catholic King. When they realized that their Sovereign was about to forbid these lucrative enterprises, they hastened to equip the greatest possible number of pirate vessels in order to send them out before the King's orders arrived. Then, according to Contarini, once the letters from Madrid reached Palermo, they were kept secret by the new Viceroy of Sicily: Lorenzo Suarez de Figueroa y Cordoba, Duke of Ferra, published them only after sending his two pirate galleons to sea. In 1603 and 1604 other large Venetian ships fell into the hands of the Westerners. Thus, the *Silvestra*, master Leo Psoro, was savagely plundered in the Archipelago on her way to Constantinople. The *Martinenga* suffered the same fate near Alexandria, and so did the *Reniera*, master Giorgio Lefteri, which was returning from Syria.[31] On the other hand, it was easy for the two Viceroys to continue their irregular war by pretending to hand over their ships to private persons. Besides Vinciguerra, there appeared in Naples a certain Pietro d'Orange: together with Michele Vais, they took over, so to speak, the contract for this semi-official piracy. Further considerable prizes were acquired in this way: in addition to the *Pigna*, plundered by the galleon *Leone d'Oro*, at least two others, the *Vidala* and the *Nettuna*, were also captured.[32] Probably referring to 1603, Nicolò Contarini asserts that in one single year twelve big ships and a still greater number of *marciliane* were plundered or actually captured and taken to the ports of the two Viceroyalties of Southern Italy. Besides the losses to the public revenues and those suffered by Venetian artisans, Contarini calculated that the pirate warfare organized or instigated by the Spaniards had caused a loss of about eight million gold ducats that year.

Even if we have to discount a part of this figure, and even if we admit that it represents a peak never previously reached or subsequently overcome, we cannot fail to take account of it. And while the fury of the Spaniards increased, the Barbary pirates and the Turks did not cease their raids, and the Maltese and Florentines continued to inflict damage. In these years, moreover, Flemish and above all English piracy raged against the Venetians. As we shall see, the Venetian Republic was unable to defend herself simultaneously against all these; and it was not surprising that even her most vigorous counter-measures should prove inadequate. Again, her position as a neutral power, and, as it were, friend of the states which were fomenting the pirate warfare, blunted her weapons and forced her into concessions which were clearly contrary to her own interests. One might, for example, not agree with Francesco Molin, *Capitano del Golfo*, in describing all Western prisoners taken by the galleys as robbers 'by nature, birth and habit'. But it was difficult not to applaud this admiral's protests against systematically setting them free and so restoring them to piracy.

Certainly it was not easy for Venice to resist pressure from the representatives of Spain and the Papacy or even from the Receiver of Malta: but, argued Molin, addressing himself to the Doge and Senators, 'when they see that they have not received the punishment they deserve, but have even been set at liberty, they will return with fewer misgivings and greater confidence to committing other graver offences and acts of robbery, especially as they have learnt much about the navigation and become excellently informed about all the movements of Your Serenity's navy during the time they have been kept with it — informed, too, about the geography and topography and even the ports and markets of all the seaward possessions of the Venetian Republic. ... And let me say this', he continued, 'that perhaps all who have served Your Serenity in this seaman's trade and had occasion to seize some Western pirate vessel (as I know from my own experience) have found upon it, almost as a matter of course, some men who had previously been captured but then, by the mercy of Your Most Excellent Lordships, set at liberty at the instance of some agent of a Prince — men who, having become experienced pilots, are eager to take with them others whom they have led astray and seduced by the sweet hope of booty.'[33]

The evil of pirate warfare, difficult enough to extirpate by tearing up its roots, was one to which no mercy could be shown.

But the Venetians reserved their summary justice for Turks and Uskoks. Westerners, as subjects of Catholic powers, were merely put to the oars; and sooner or later they succeeded in returning to piracy, steadily increasing the scale of it.[34] A rapid glance at the first two decades of the seventeenth century shows how this pirate warfare proliferated. It was then that the *bertone* was definitely introduced and asserted itself increasingly in Mediterranean waters — this was a type of Atlantic ship with high sides, which was adopted by all navies and was used to impart a new vigour to piracy. Well before the beginning of the seventeenth century there was talk of Sicilian or Maltese *bertoni*; the Florentines and even the Barbary corsairs would not be slow to avail themselves of ships of this build. In the autumn of 1605 the news reached Venice that the *Giustiniana e Benvenuta*, returning from Syria, had first been attacked by a pirate *bertone*. She had succeeded in freeing herself after a bloody skirmish, but had then encountered the much more formidable *bertone* commanded by Spinola, which had forced her to surrender and had taken 50,000 thalers from her. Shortly before, the pirate Spinola had attacked the *Zena*, coming from Cyprus: in spite of a stubborn defence, in which the owner, Giovanni Zen, risked his life, she too was eventually robbed of all goods of any value as well as her weapons and guns.[35] From the report read in the Senate by Giust' Antonio Belegno at the beginning of 1609 there seems to be no doubt that in the preceding years the Knights of Malta had on their own account fitted out small *bertoni* and successfully attacked Venetian shipping. These lesser freebooters acted in collaboration with the galleys of the Order: the booty was divided on their return to the island of Gozo, in such a way that everything that remained to the pirates was regarded as their lawful prize.

In the same report the Venetian admiral stressed how differently the Knights of St Stephen and those of St John conducted themselves in Levantine waters. The Florentines scarcely ever departed from the instructions issued to them by the Grand Dukes in the course of the sixteenth century: these ordered them not to inspect the ships of the Venetian Republic even when there was information that they were transporting merchandise belonging to Turks or Jews. Moreover, they forbade them to approach Venetian territory save in circumstances beyond their control. After the death of the Grand Duke Ferdinand I these orders were formally reissued, not only to the commanders of the galleys of St Stephen, but also to captains like Dupuy and the Count of Viredoré who had put themselves at the service of the Tuscan princes.[36] However, the Knights of St Stephen continued to prefer the eastern Mediterranean to the waters of Barbary, and regularly patrolled there — not without damaging Venetian trade, at least indirectly. Thus in 1607 the galleon *Livorno* — a ship which, in the words of its captain, Scipione Cortesi, 'seems very small when its prow appears, and thus deceives everybody' — attacked the *Giustiniana* and an English vessel in Cypriot waters. Only good fortune allowed the *Giustiniana* to escape in the course of the battle; the English ship was captured. During the years that followed, other merchantmen were to be the object of Florentine attacks — though it is hard to establish which flag was flying from the two *bertoni* that attacked the *Zena* and the *Andrizza* on their way to Constantinople.[37]

On 19 March 1607, in the waters of Cerigo, these two ships 'were attacked by a pirate *bertone*, with which they fought bitterly for many hours. When the pirates realized that they could no longer resist, they ceased defending the *bertone* and took it away, leaving the two merchantmen, and went off to find another *bertone*, which was heavily armed and was also a pirate. These *bertoni* then joined together and went back to find the ships, attacking them with savage fury, and fought with them afresh for nine days. These ships, being unable to resist the savage and inhuman fighting of the pirates, were captured by them with great slaughter and loss of life in a place described as above Sciro, 500 miles from Zante; and those who survived kept nothing but their bare lives.'[38] According to Giovanni Battista di Grassi, mate of the *Andrizza*, the battle centred on Strivali and the encounter was a little shorter — lasting from Palm Sunday to the following Wednesday. The pirates must have been Florentines, but the captains were Jacques Germain, a Frenchman, and Agostino Faenzo, a Maltese. Their *bertoni* were accompanied by a *galeotta* and two *tartane*, with a total of 800 soldiers.[39]

At this time the fleet of the Catholic King or some of his Mediterranean squadrons continued to carry out raids in the Levant, including those organized by the Admiral Anthony Sherley, an adventurer of English birth. Nevertheless, partly because of the measures taken by the Senate, the number of Venetian ships which fell into Spanish hands was much lower than in the terrible decade 1596–1605. However, there were many attacks on the numerous Dutch, English and even French ships which frequented the port of Venice. As for the Maltese, their treachery did not cease, and 'although they outwardly profess to be good friends', writes Belegno in his report, 'and to respect Your Serenity's shipping, nonetheless they have always in fact done precisely the opposite'.[40] It was they who, in spring 1605, fought for many hours with the *Rizzarda* from Syria; who plundered the *marciliana Carminati* in 1607; and who snatched the galleon *Mondo* from the Barbary pirates and bore it to Malta in 1614. The galleon which in 1608 was bombarded by Venetian galleasses for refusing to make any sign of recognition belonged to the Grand Master.[41] But if all the Westerners seemed less dangerous after 1608 — except for Ossuna's adventure in the Adriatic — this was doubtless partly because the strength of the Venetian merchant marine had been terribly reduced. Entangled for decades in the deadly network stretched out on one side by Turkish and Barbary corsairs, and by Westerners and Englishmen on the other, the

Venetians had not only lost a considerable part of their commercial fleet: they had almost entirely ceased to fill the gaps by the work of their dockyards. After their progressive withdrawal both from the Adriatic trade routes and from the western Mediterranean, by about 1615, as we shall see, they were very frequently forced to rely on foreign ships, even for Levantine trade.

Chapter 4

The English

The final blow to Venetian seapower was undoubtedly dealt by the northern fleets and especially by the English. This process began about 1580, gradually became more menacing, and by the end of the century was distinctly alarming. The threat showed no signs of diminishing, and by 1606–09 it was apparent that irreparable harm had been inflicted. The Northerners had gained the upper hand in the Levant, where Venice had stubbornly persisted in directing, or rather concentrating her own strength.

We have already said that Uskok piracy, though it inflicted much heavier losses on Venice after Lepanto, was in a sense a constant hazard of life in the Adriatic. It persisted in much the same way for several decades, and would continue after the period now under review. The same is undoubtedly true of the Barbary corsairs and the Turks, even if their pirate warfare became more persistent and systematic from the last years of the sixteenth century onwards. Moreover, there was a limit to the power and menace of the Uskoks, despite their extraordinary skill as pirates and the strategic advantages of their base. However many miracles of brigandage they accomplished, their small craft could never ruin the trade of a port like Venice. The Turks of Albania and the Morea, as we have seen, much preferred to attack the Adriatic coasts of the Viceroyalty of Naples and of the Papal States. The damage they inflicted was very serious, but they were striking at Venetian trade in a less important sector. The great shipping lines and the vessels entrusted with the most precious products followed the very quiet Dalmatian route: only occasionally were they ambushed by *fuste* in the Ionian sea. The *galeotte* of Barbary were certainly very dangerous, but their bases were far away and their voyages to and fro between Algiers and Constantinople took place only at intervals. The relative infrequency of their attacks partly compensated for their greater range of action. Concerning western piracy, these remarks about the Barbary corsairs also apply to the Knights of Malta and St Stephen. They, too, undertook voyages, but in the other season — between autumn and spring. And one must remember that, though only the Florentines generally respected the ships of Venice, these galleys chiefly attacked Turkish shipping, a very prominent target in itself and one sufficient to satisfy the appetites of these crusading freebooters.

Compared with the years prior to 1580, the real novelty had been the wave of Spanish-Italian piracy which we have just described. But it is at least doubtful whether this could have caused more than a momentary weakening on the part of the Venetian fleet. On the one hand, diplomatic protests and a recourse to arms by the Venetian navy did produce some effect. On the other, the Spaniards were not merchants, much less commercial competitors with the Venetians. There is no doubt that, even without the intervention of northern ships in the Mediterranean, the pirate warfare with Uskoks, Turks, Barbary corsairs and Westerners, on the scale on which it was waged during these years, would have put the navy and merchant fleet of the Venetian Republic to a very severe test. But we now intend to show that the collapse was caused by the latest arrivals: the Dutch, and especially the English.

The return of English ships and the arrival of northern vessels in general in the Mediterranean undoubtedly stemmed from the struggle which set the Spain of Philip II against Elizabethan England and the rebellious provinces of the Low Countries. The fleets of the Protestant countries at a certain moment felt themselves strong enough to force the Straits of Gibraltar, and through this narrow aperture the great Atlantic rivalry was extended into Mediterranean waters. But the events which had occurred in the Mediterranean itself favoured this penetration. The Turkish Empire, faced with the eclipse of French power, could only be delighted to find new allies against Spain, while, for complementary reasons, the expanding seapower of the Northerners could not spurn a market like the Levant. In fact, there existed all the preconditions for the remarkable changes which soon unfolded. There were, however, other causes of particular importance. The policy of the Grand Dukes, which had opened Leghorn to Jewish merchants, likewise made it one of the principal bases for Protestant trade. From the start, the people of Barbary did not hesitate to make a profit out of the need of the northern ships to call frequently at their harbours. Finally, Venetian resentment against Spain combined with the desire to renew old trading relationships. The Republic took no account of the altered situation or of her own weakness, and she too sought to profit from the new circumstances.

Summing up this problem, Contarini writes: 'The Queen had, by imposts insupportable to foreigners, virtually shut the Venetians out of England, and the English had become most expert and powerful on the seas from here to the Atlantic and, indeed, in every place, and to a large extent they were depriving the Venetians of trade in western merchandise. And, a thing still more hateful, they had entered these seas in the guise of brigands, although they brought merchandise too; and they treated every ship they met as an enemy, without distinguishing whether it belonged to friend or foe. This evil was accentuated

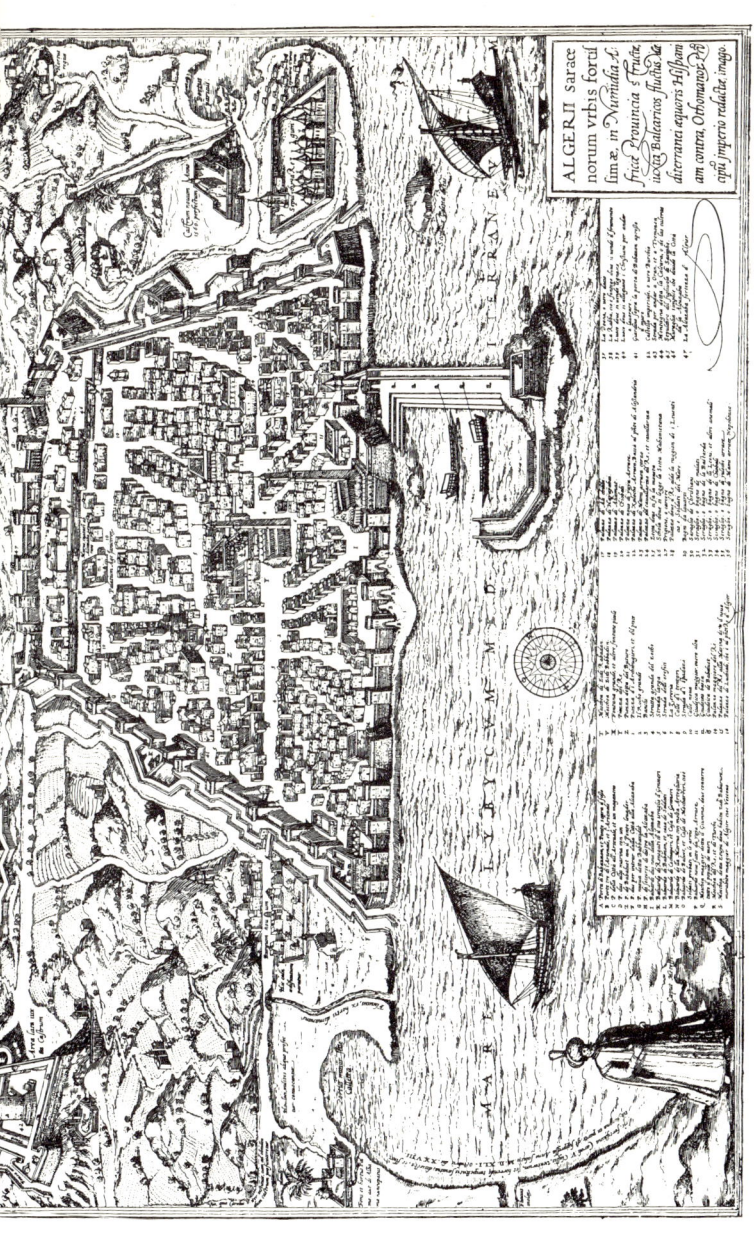

Algiers (from G. Braun, *De praecipius totius universi urbibus liber secundus*, Colonia, 1575)

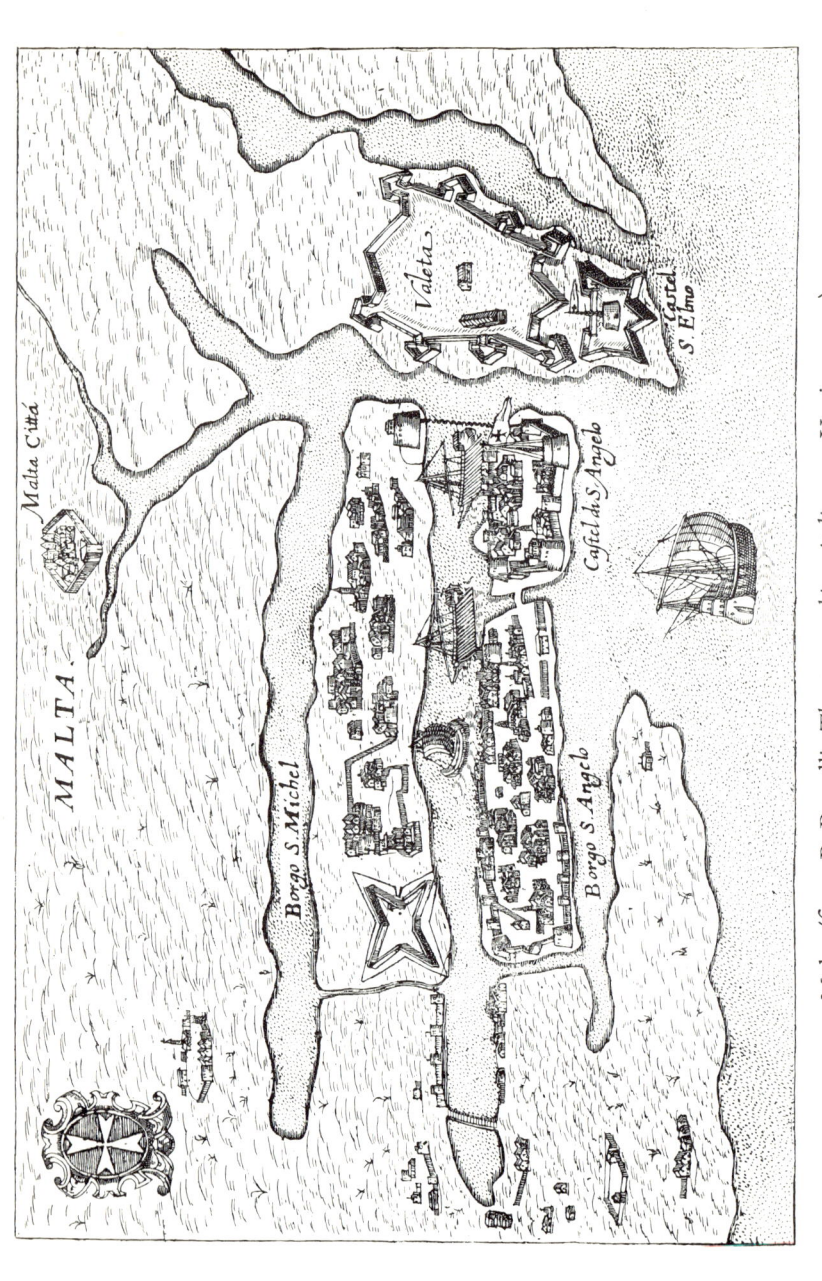

Malta (from P. Bertelli, *Theatrum urbium italicarum*, Venice, 1599)

by the Dutch acting in the same way: they were now bringing up their ships, had penetrated within the Straits of Gibraltar, were even coming to Venice, and had learnt how to sail the Adriatic as well as any native of the country. They were favoured in every place and especially at Venice. Since nobody foresaw how far this new navigation would be taken and since it was then bringing some benefit to the city, they were not only favoured generally, as all foreigners are in Venice, but even wooed with bounties by the government so that they would diligently attend to business. But the Dutch, instead of responding with gratitude, attacked every ship that they met on their voyages, no matter whose it was: and, that their misdeeds might not become known, they sewed up the crews in sailcloth and sank them amid the waves.'[1]

With good reason Contarini recorded the stern measures taken by Elizabeth at the expense of foreign shipping, including Venetian. Venetian ships had long continued to carry cargoes for the north, especially currants and wine from Cefalonia, Zante and Crete, and to return from England with wool, cloth, kerseys and tin. Five or six large vessels made this voyage every year. But the Queen had no doubt decided that it was no longer worth using intermediaries. Towards 1580 English merchants were coming straight to the Venetian islands with their products, and, despite prohibitions, were able to lade wine and currants, 'having agreements and understandings with some of the islanders'. On 26 January 1581 the Senate therefore decided upon counter-tariffs, and ordered all their subjects to withdraw from commercial intercourse with Westerners.[2] But the following year a new agreement was signed between Elizabeth and the Venetians, who returned to frequent the English route, at least till the end of the century. In the registers of the notary Giovan Andrea Catti, for example, these voyages are very frequently mentioned: the very names of the galleons *Bon* and *Lombardo*, of the ships *Balancera*, *Lippomana*, *Stella e Vidala* and *Selvagna*, and of the galleon

Tizzon, tell us that between 1583 and 1590 Venetian merchants were still present in the North Sea.

The risks, however, were increasing. War raged between Philip II and Elizabeth: and whilst Philip did not fail to requisition even Venetian ships, like the *Ragazzona*, Elizabeth's vessels considered themselves authorized to lay hands on Venetian merchantmen. Meanwhile negotiations were concluded between the Porte and the English envoy at Constantinople: the first official contacts took place in 1575. These were renewed in 1578 and culminated in the Capitulations of 1580, which were ratified three years later. There were immediate repercussions. Indeed, an observer from the Grand Duke wrote from Venice on 17 June 1583: 'Here they are feeling very seriously the effects of the trade concessions obtained by the English in Constantinople and throughout all the lands of the Sultan, both because of the duties which used to be paid by the English cloth which originally came to Venice and was subsequently sent to the Levant, and because of the effect on the wool gild and the merchant clothiers. As there are large quantities of cloth arriving directly from England, and as these are sold at much lower prices than the Venetian, scarcely any more cloth will be sent from Venice to the Levant, except for a few very fine scarlet cloths. And we have already heard', the report concludes, 'that when the English galleon and the Ambassador arrived in Constantinople with such a large consignment of cloth, there was nobody who wanted to buy Venetian cloth save at a much lower price than before.'[3]

English vessels gradually reached even the port of Venice itself—some, for instance, arrived at the beginning of December 1583, after only forty-five days' sailing, with lead, wool, tin and kerseys. Two ships belonging to an English merchant described as 'Tommaso Ciolo' set up an almost incredible record in 1586: they arrived, well-laden, from England in twenty-nine days, between April and May.[4] After 1590 there were already many more northern than Venetian ships on the route between Venice and London or Southampton. In addition to the goods mentioned above, they carried grain, — which Venice urgently needed, — sugar, salt fish and tallow. For the return journey, they laded mainly wine and currants. But if the English and Dutch did not spurn the good business which was offered them in Venice, they undoubtedly did better in the islands of the Venetian Dominion. Evidently the Senate did not succeed in enforcing the decree of 1581 any better than its predecessors. Girolamo Contarini, captain of the great merchant galleys employed on the Ionian route, recognized, for example, that the greater part of the 308 *migliara* of currants laded in Cefalonia, Zante and Corfù in 1589 belonged to Englishmen. Much more serious was the admission of Maffio Michiel, *Provveditore* at Zante: in a letter to the Doge, he asserted that the English ships regularly came to take the raisins with the complicity of the inhabitants, and did not fail to make use of their cannon. Thus, at the beginning of March 1604, although Michiel succeeded in expelling from the harbour the two ships *Little Phoenix* and *Greyhound*, nevertheless they stayed for six days in a provoking attitude in front of the city, without the Venetian magistracy being able to reply to their insults.[5]

There is no doubt that the English and Dutch, as soon as they entered the Mediterranean, immediately combined piracy with trade. Their originality lay in their merchantmen being as fully equipped for war as for trade. They showed themselves to be pirates more ruthless and dangerous than any others, and it is certain that only by such methods did they succeed in gaining the upper hand as merchants. The Mediterranean, as we have seen, was not exactly sailed by ships exchanging cheerful greetings at every encounter: to use a contemporary simile, it much more resembled a forest teeming with bandits. Since one had to travel the whole length of it in order to reach Leghorn, Alexandria, Beirut, Constantinople and Venice, it was necessary to be well armed. Moreover, until 1604 England was still at war with Spain, and Barbary corsairs did not let slip good opportunities for attacking her ships, in spite of the Capitulations of 1580. Whilst Turks and Catholics maintained that religious differences were reason enough for fighting one another, the heretics from the north had analogous reasons for attacking Turks as infidels and Catholics as papists. We have seen, however, that pirate warfare was only nominally a crusade: the point of it was not to inflict strategic defeats on one's adversary so much as to plunder, sack and get rich at his expense. The Northerners reached the Mediterranean knowing full well that they would find no friends there. In the sphere of commerce, as in every other, they appeared as direct competitors with the other sea powers. It is not surprising, therefore, that they should have entered as warriors. Nor is it surprising that, when they realized they were the strongest, they should have seized the opportunity to consolidate their growing supremacy.

Even before the English forced the Straits of Gibraltar in great numbers, the Venetians experienced some of their attacks. Towards the end of the sixteenth century Venice had tense relations with Portugal and Spain as well as with England herself, as we have already pointed out. Elizabeth's ships, engaged in full-scale war with Philip II, showed no scruple in attacking every ship which visited the Iberian ports. Thus, at the beginning of 1586, the galleon *Lombardo*, master Francesco Fighetto, with a cargo of wine, was captured off Cape St Vincent. The *Uggiera e Selvagna*, master Dimo Popogianopuli, suffered a similar fate in the same waters at the end of 1590. In these years incidents multiplied. The *Stella* and the *Barozza*, for example, were blockaded in the harbour of Cadiz; a few months later, the *Stella*, together with the *Vidala*, had to withstand a tough battle with two English pirates near Cape St Vincent. Worse befell the galleon *Tizzone*, master Zuane Plaidemo. She was attacked below Cascais by a vessel belonging to the Earl of Cumberland, and wrecked while being taken to

England. The *Manicella* was completely sacked and reached Cadiz in a lamentable condition.[6]

In the Mediterranean, the Venetians were not the first or the only people to pay for the support of northern pirate warfare. Only towards the end of the sixteenth century did they become its principal and most rewarding victims. In the spring of 1581, shortly after the conclusion of the Anglo-Ottoman negotiations, two *bertoni* captured three Turkish caramousals in the Archipelago and sank others which were carrying victuals to Constantinople. In 1587 news arrived from Crete that a large English galleon was now at Algiers: it had square sails, 'but oars also; it goes plundering wherever it can, and hence no ships are being sent out unarmed from these ports'. Another pirate ship sacked the Ragusan vessel *San Rocco*, master Pietro Vadoppia, between the Balearic Islands and Barcelona as it was coming from Leghorn.[7]

By about 1590, nonetheless, the English were quite at their ease in Venetian waters also. In October 1589 a ship from Trapani and the vessel commanded by William Nottingham were both calling at the port of Corfù. Nottingham, anticipating a good catch, sent some of his men on board the *Annunziata* to inspect it, and fell out with the captain, Dimo Magrudi. Magrudi abused him, calling him an insolent cur, and challenged him to a duel, but obtained no reply. However, on the night of 7–8 October, when he was leaving the port with the *Sumaca* and a galleon from Perasto, the pirate slipped behind the convoy; after about two miles, the first shots were fired in the direction of the *Annunziata*. 'I guessed at once', said Magrudi, 'that it was the English ship that had been in the the harbour, as indeed it was — I had anticipated that they wanted to annoy me. The ship came round me, firing many guns at us, and so I swung round to return to port. But this English ship, just as I was turning, fired off other cannonades, and then, coming somewhat nearer, discharged three or four more guns and came alongside to board. Seeing that we were resisting them with our weapons, they withdrew some distance and fired off some further shots, and their boat came up to challenge our ship with a falconet and a number of arquebusiers. We then resolved to abandon ship, seeing that we could no longer resist, and so we lowered our own boat from the stern, and when twenty or twenty-two persons had entered it we set out to flee towards the pier; and for a space that English boat followed us.'[8]

Very similar was the behaviour of James Lile, master of the ship *Gift of God*, which a number of Venetian merchants had chartered to carry spices to Alexandria. On his return, the English captain met a Turkish caramousal in the waters of Crete and took possession of it. On 3 September 1590, the two ships reached the port of Cerigo. From the proceedings initiated by the *Provveditore* of that island against the pirates, it emerged that they as a mark of contempt for Catholic superstitions, had laid waste the furnishings of the church of San Nicolò, flinging a crucifix into the sea and foully defiling the altar.[9]

The type of ship mainly used by the English and Dutch for this two-sided activity of piracy and trading was the *bertone*. This was a vessel of medium tonnage with square sails, broad and rounded in appearance, a three-master. Its distinguishing marks were the peculiar solidarity of the hull and the depth of the keel, which enabled it to ride the sea extremely well. The largest *bertoni* probably had a capacity of no more than 800 butts — normally it was about 500, and quite often even less. The crew numbered about sixty men. The possibility of arming these vessels with a large number of guns rendered them very formidable, especially in the Mediterranean, where galleons, warships of a similar type, were rare. Not all the *bertoni* were equally well armed: but pirate *bertoni* carried some twenty cannon, and occasionally more than thirty, in addition to arquebuses and various other firearms. Westerners who gained possession of one of these ships would not hesitate to exploit its capacity to the full, as we have already seen the Grand Master and the Viceroy of Sicily doing. Of the *Elia d'Oro*, which was equipped in Naples in 1604, probably for Vinciguerra, we read that it was 'an English *bertone* and carried thirty-five metal guns and 340 men, including sailors, gunners and soldiers'.[10]

The northern adventurers turned against Venetian shipping only towards the close of the sixteenth century. In April 1593 Captain Bower met the *marciliana Costantina* on the coast of the Morea: he captured it easily, took it to Modone, and there sold the grain and timber which it had been carrying. He would have liked to sell the ship also, but the Turkish *Cadì* removed it from him and put it in custody. Two years later, in the waters of Crete, James Parent's *bertone* seized the *Girarda e Correra*, returning from Cyprus with a cargo of cotton. This pirate had previously been in Venice 'as a merchantman', but once he had left the port he had devoted himself to plundering every ship which came within range. The very terms in which the Senate circulated the news to the fleet and to the governors of the islands suggest that such incidents had not yet become frequent.[11] But in the summer of 1597 a French *bertone* (also described as 'a Provençal vessel'), commanded by 'Giordano Jonet', joined the ship of Hugh Whitbrook, and they went off together, 'inflicting various kinds of damage in the seas of Crete and forcing the masters of ships which they had pillaged to swear nonetheless that they had taken nothing. And moreover we anticipate', concluded the Senate in its letter to the *Provveditore dell'Armata*, 'that the same will be done by other similar vessels from the west.' The warning was fully justified. During these months the *bertone* from Provence plundered the galleon *Martinengo*, master Gasparo di Giacomo, coming from Smyrna, whilst the Englishman, in league with another *bertone* commanded by John Wart, attacked the galleon *Emo*, pursued the *marciliana Cattanea*, and caused very severe damage to various other craft.[12]

The Venetians undoubtedly believed that they were facing a rather larger number of Westerners than this, and once more issued the order to disarm these vessels. Then, observing that the waters of Crete were the zone most frequently attacked, they determined to reinforce the squadron guarding that island. The Northerners, however, proved more than capable of escaping from the galleys and plundering heavily from that year onwards. Thus, on 7 September 1597, near Cape St John on the island of Crete, the English *bertone David* ambushed the *San Giovanni Battista* of Chios, commanded by Giovanni Castello, on its way from Ancona and Zante. Although this vessel carried several guns, the crew at once realized that the strength of their opponent was greater, and surrendered after a vain attempt at flight. In the course of the pillaging, the English discovered that part of the cargo belonged to Diego Lopez de Padilla and to the Ximenes: these, in fact, were Portuguese domiciled at Leghorn, but they refused to believe it, and forced all the crew to declare in writing that this merchandise belonged to Spaniards, in which case it officially became legitimate booty. The proceeds were considerable — over 36,000 crowns'-worth of silken cloth and hard cash: 'and after removing the goods', wrote Nicolò Allegretti later, 'they took hatchets and broke open the sailors' and passengers' chests and removed everything in them: they left them not so much as a single good shirt.' The unfortunate victims, however, were delighted to come out of this adventure alive. Confined below decks for two days and a night, they heard several times that there was talk of killing them: 'We were expecting death', later wrote the pilot Antonio da Sciò, 'like lambs at the slaughterhouse.'[13]

The sea route worst threatened by the *bertoni* was among the most lucrative and possibly the most important for Venetian trade in this period — the one between Zante and Constantinople along the coasts of the Morea and across the Archipelago. Venice's numerous bases, and especially those of Cerigo and

Crete, seemed particularly suitable for breaking up or at least for impeding this pirate activity. But the brilliant expeditions of Filippo Pasqualigo against the Maltese were not repeated by those who succeeded him in command of the Cretan squadron. Nor, for long years, did the other admirals effectually resist the northern pirates. Thanks to their manœuvrability and the skill of their crews the *bertoni* rode rough seas well, and their captains preferred the winter season for their pirate war. Galleys, on the contrary, were often forced to remain in port during the winter, and some of them regularly went to be laid up in Venice at the end of the autumn. One must remember, also, that at the end of the sixteenth and the beginning of the seventeenth century, when Spaniards and Englishmen joined the usual Turkish and Christian pirates and flung themselves upon the merchant shipping of the Venetian Republic, Venice was engaged in war with the Uskoks and persisted in maintaining a substantial part of her own fleet in Dalmatian waters.[14] Finally, it is quite possible that the Venetian commanders were becoming aware of the inadequacy of the light galleys in the struggle against northern shipping. This is apparently confirmed by the fact that eventually, in order to offer them effectual resistance, the Venetians again sent out their glorious galleasses and one galleon.

Venice, in fact, allowed herself to be caught unprepared, and was at first unable to distinguish properly between the type of piracy practised by the *bertoni* and the traditional western type. The Senate did not apparently instruct the fleet commander to treat the newcomers as pirates before the summer of 1600. Nevertheless, despite the promise of its name, the *Friendship* from London had on 18 August 1598 attacked and sunk the *Pigna*, belonging to Antonio della Pigna, in the region of Cape St Vincent when on its way to Lisbon. In the same year, not far off Messina, several *bertoni* plundered the *saettia* whose master was Francesco Ammirabile. Towards the end of 1599, when the English had taken the *orca Santa Maria*, on its way from Portugal, Dutch pirates plundered the *Ponte*, master Antonio Coluri, with a cargo of Venetian goods worth about 100,000 *reali*.[15]

The situation deteriorated at the beginning of the seventeenth century when the regular fleets of the Viceroys of Sicily and Naples, together with other pirate ships armed under Spanish auspices, also turned against Venetian shipping. In the summer of 1600 the Ambassador at Constantinople announced that, in addition to two French *saettie* returning from Syria, the English must also have captured the *Vidala*. His successor Agostino Nani reported that in the following winter, after capturing a Venetian ship and taking it to Algiers, two *bertoni* had burnt it so as not to have to leave it.[16] In 1602, in the west, three vessels chartered at Lisbon for Venice — the galleon *San Marco*, the *orca Speranza* and the ship *Santa Maria di Loreto* — were captured and taken to England: whilst in the Levant William Pierce of Plymouth attacked the *Veniera* in the waters of Cape Malio, on its way back from Alexandria. The booty was in the region of 100,000 ducats.[17] Piero Bondumier, *Provveditore* at Zante, attempted to organize a pursuit, but there were no galleys ready. He then applied, unavailingly, to three English ships: their commanders answered that their merchantmen were utterly unsuited to his needs. As for the great galleys finally armed at Venice, they were at Corfù; but, as their commander Girolamo Contarini later told the Senate, they were 'offering prayers for the health of their crews, who were infected with repulsive diseases.'[18] Thus Pierce, having rented a whole house at Modone to store the booty, was able to depart in peace for Barbary with the *Veniera*.

In 1603 the great galleys went to sea: they travelled through the Ionian and the Aegean seas and patrolled in the region of Crete; the results were unimpressive. Only once, while they were in port at Cerigo, did they succeed in sighting two *bertoni* (the English *Golden Dove*, commanded by Roderick Scut, and a Dutch vessel under Jan Flores) and in capturing them. However, the Governor of the Galleys of the Condemned appeared to equal advantage, and with his four light galleys reduced several *bertoni* to submission, including one especially powerful vessel, the *Angel*, commanded by Thomas Garner (or Gardiner). On returning to Venice, Girolamo Contarini sought to explain the failure of his expedition. The ships which had been committed to him were, in his opinion, capable, not only of fighting, but also of manœuvring to advantage against the *bertoni*. But, he added, 'they cannot adequately withstand the waves and the storms of sea and sky in the winter season: it is not that they cannot keep them out, for they are very strong against them — but, since they are open ships, it is impossible for the crews to resist the violence of sea and sky'. Their stout bulwarks were more than capable, as they had proved at Lepanto, of routing any hostile fleet: but it was not worth spending so much on arming them merely to hunt pirates. 'When necessity compels us to defend the sea against such invasions by *bertoni*', the admiral concluded, 'it will be much better to entrust the task to six or eight light galleys under a good commander, for they, if they take up first one position and then another, will be well able to keep these robbers at bay and force them into obedience by means of their cannon when they want to inspect them: the *bertoni* will not be able to reply with their guns, since for the most part they have only a moderate number of iron guns.'[19]

A rapid glance at the losses suffered by the Venetians in 1603 creates a forceful impression of the inefficiency and especially of the untimeliness of the watch they kept. The northern pirates managed to plunder at least twelve vessels — always important ones. This was the time when the *bertoni* seemed most to regard piracy as a lucrative industry: two merchantmen were plundered twice in succession during these months, as if the pirates were more interested in finding them again with cargoes than in sinking or capturing them. Piero Albertini, captain and joint owner of the *bertone Jesus*, which had just reached Zante from Syracuse, reported that, after being plundered by an English warship, he had then been ambushed and sacked by a *bertone*. More typical was the case of the *bertone Santa Maria di Grazia*, belonging to Vincenzo Marubin. On the same sea route from Venice to Alexandria, she was first captured at Crete in the spring, and then, in the autumn, pillaged in the waters of Venetico. The second attack took place at night, by moonlight: the assailants, having removed even the guns, detained their victim for four days and nights in order to plunder her at leisure.[20]

As we have already stressed, the Northerners operated especially during the winter months. Thus, in February, two Dutch vessels — the *Caldera* and the *orca Salvatore* — were attacked in the Archipelago, where they had gone to lade grain for Genoa, probably by the same pirates who surprised the *marciliana Bersatona*, coming from Crete, in the harbour of Milo. These, again, were Pierce and a larger *bertone*, the *Dragon*, of over 600 butts' capacity, equipped with thirty-four guns, captained by Thomas Sherley. This English freebooter had first visited Leghorn and had made an offer to Ferdinand I to go to war with the Infidels in his name. He had performed this and other robberies with 200 men, Greeks, Venetians and Florentines, under the Grand Duke's flag. It seems that he then tried to excuse himself, writing to the Grand Duke that his crew had mutinied, and promising that he would serve him better the following year. It was from these encounters, indeed, that a new pirate was born: the English vessel *Fox* was in the neighbourhood, and, having managed to instal four cannon from the *Caldera* on board, she determined to suspend her own activity as a merchantman in order to devote herself to piracy.[21]

It is worth completing our account of this dreadful year 1603. In March and April the Englishmen Christopher 'd'Oloard' (or 'Olororen') and Nicholas 'Alvel', in the waters of Zante, plundered the *Buonaventura Giopanditi*, on its way from

Smyrna with a cargo of cotton: the proceeds reached 100,000 ducats. Soon afterwards, these same pirates attacked at Strivali the *marciliana Memma e Constantina*, returning from Crete, and took it to Modone. Fortunately the Turkish authorities prevented the worst from happening, and even put some of those responsible in chains. Almost simultaneously, Thomas Tomkins, with a *bertone* from La Rochelle and a crew of French, Dutch and English adventurers, carried out perhaps the most profitable operation of that year: the capture of the *Balbiana*, headed for Syria with a vast consignment of valuable textiles. Again in April, John Pierce succeeded in sacking, outside Modone, the *San Giovanni Battista*, returning from Athens. Then, in the autumn, a *bertone* above Cape Gallo stripped Stefano Wro's ship of all its property: in addition to the cargo the guns, anchors, hawsers and even the water supply were removed. With great difficulty the crew succeeded in taking it to the harbour of Zante at the beginning of November.[22] That was not all. We also have the information that in the course of this year three large Dutch ships were captured by English pirates: the *St Peter*, which came from Amsterdam, and two others, the *Jonas* and the *Samson*, which probably came from Portugal. Finally, let us mention that when summer turned to autumn the *San Paolo*, headed for London with the baggage of the ambassador Nicolò da Molin, was also sacked by *bertoni*.

So many pirate expeditions and incidents could not fail to have repercussions. Venetian diplomacy, and the embassy in Constantinople in particular, devoted all its energies to procuring the outlawry of the northern pirates. Venice further sought to avail itself of French support, for French trade with the Levant and even with Barbary was also threatened by the newcomers. 'The French Ambassador', wrote Girolamo Cappello from Constantinople with a certain satisfaction, 'is continually making forceful complaints, which, as we hear from all quarters, will eventually be shared by all nations, because these accursed people have become so bold that they will without hesitation enter every place and with barbarous cruelty sink every kind of vessel and carry off the plunder to Patras and other places, where they find others coming their way.'[23] In the belief that his representations were not producing adequate results, at the beginning of 1603 Henry IV's energetic Ambassador at the Porte actually purchased a *bertone* and equipped it with 100 French soldiers. He committed it to two of his sons. All English *bertoni* were to be treated as enemies. On 13 June 1603 this vessel met the *Salamander* in the Gulf of Milo, and, after a deadly struggle lasting four hours, captured it. Again, the Venetians finally managed to overcome the obstinate reluctance which was depriving them of any direct contact with Elizabeth. After long refusing to entertain diplomatic relations with her because she was a heretic, they sent the Secretary Giovan Carlo Scaramelli to England, and he was soon followed by fully-fledged Ambassadors. The work of these diplomats was not wholly unsuccessful. They often succeeded in procuring the confiscation of goods that reached England after being stolen from Venetian ships, and even in getting them restored. Then, on the accession of James I, various measures against the pirates were adopted by the English government: some were arrested, others condemned to the gallows. The King seemed even to be agreeing to the proposal to demand a security from ships which would have visited Venetian ports. For its part, the Venetian Republic reduced the reprisals which it had ordered against northern merchants and their ships, and also agreed to the release of those that had been detained. In 1605 James I agreed that in Venetian waters every English merchantman must prove to any galleys it encountered that it was not a pirate.

Although it was easy to restore normal diplomatic relations, this did not in itself make going to sea peaceful. Men who had devoted themselves to such profitable ventures were not disposed to abandon them. No doubt the English ships which ranged the Mediterranean to engage in ordinary commercial activity less frequently overstepped the mark and took to piracy: but the others found little difficulty in continuing it. In other words, there was a turning-point about the year 1604. Not only did England re-establish good relations with Venice and collaborate with her in improving maritime affairs, she even concluded peace with the hated Kingdom of Spain. But the English pirates then offered their services to the United Provinces, which were still at war with this Catholic power, and they entrenched themselves still more securely in the bases which they had previously found useful in the Mediterranean. These were, first the Barbary ports, and then numerous others in Turkish territory, as well as the Granducal port of Leghorn.

The attitude of the authorities on the outskirts of the Ottoman Empire towards the northern pirates had from the beginning oscillated between obedience to the strict orders of the Porte, and the most barefaced complicity with the pirates. Constantinople almost continually fought against the connivance which the English were able to find in North Africa and the Morea, but there were very few Turkish magistrates who conscientiously carried out the Sultan's instructions. It may be said that a calculating neutrality, which frequently turned into some degree of support for the Northerners, was the usual policy, if not the absolute rule, from Algiers to Tunis and from Modone to Patras: every so long some contrary gesture was made. The Venetian Ambassadors at the Porte and the *Provveditori* at Zante remorselessly insisted on pointing out that the activity of the *bertoni* ultimately depended on the use of Turkish bases. Maffio Michiel, who spent all his energies in trying to halt the invasion of trade and the piracy of the English around Zante, was distinguished for the watch he kept on the behaviour of the Ottoman magistrates in these years.[24] In addition to describing the weaknesses of the authorities of Corone, Modone and Patras, he also pointed out the illicit favours which the *bertoni* enjoyed at Milo and especially their progress in installing themselves in North Africa. Using the testimony of Thomas Gardiner, captain of the *Angel*, he gave warning that at the beginning of 1603 there were some twenty English pirate vessels at Tunis, whose crews had to a large extent been outlawed by Elizabeth herself. Other later reports likewise deal with Tunis, especially one which concerns the extraordinary profits made by its Beilerbey as a result of northern piracy. In September 1603 Giovan Carlo Scaramelli confirmed from London that English pirates had their bases at Tunis, Biserta and other Barbary ports where they subsequently resold their booty at less than half its real value.

But the *bertoni* were not really forced to establish themselves only in North Africa. Another possible solution lay in putting themselves at the service of the Grand Duke of Tuscany. We have already seen how Sherley did so, and one can also refer to the example of the three *bertoni* which burnt seven *galeotte* in the port of Bugia in the spring of 1604. Banished from England two years earlier, these three ships had devoted themselves to piracy off the Barbary coasts until the Porte had ordered their seizure. However, the Beilerbey of Algiers had almost immediately agreed to their resuming their activity on condition that they shared the loot with him. However, when they suggested to Ferdinand I that they should enter his service, he did not hesitate to welcome them and even to grant them a generous subsidy. Moreover, the Grand Duke, as well as replenishing his stocks of gunpowder from England, also acquired there a number of large ships for his pirate fleet, exploiting the fact that with the conclusion of peace with Spain many people wished to rid themselves of warships with a large tonnage. There were, for example, reports from Zante of two *bertoni* of his at the beginning of 1607. A little later, Zorzi Giustinian wrote from London that the Medici Prince was continuing to employ English crews, and had brought from England a large ship laden with guns.[25]

However, England and Tuscany collaborated only occasionally. After 1604, English piracy was organized especially in North Africa, thus entering a new phase. On 6 June, Maffio Michiel wrote from Zante that the *marciliana Vidala* had been attacked by a pirate vessel which was small but excellently armed and whose crew consisted of Englishmen, Turks, Moors and even a Maltese – the pilot. On his way from Crete to Corfù, Giacomo Giustinian, *Provveditore dell'Armata*, had sighted the *bertone* and its victim: both, however, had escaped him and succeeded in taking refuge at Modone. The admiral then attempted to blockade them, meanwhile earnestly demanding that the Turkish authorities should hand them over. After waiting twenty-two days without result, he had to write to Corfù: 'seeing that the conclusion of this affair would still take me several days, and as I have no bread either for myself or for the fleet, save for six days only, I have sent to Venice the galleys *Donata* and *Trona*, so that Your Illustrious Lordships may order them to be laded with as large a consignment of bread as they can carry and to be returned to me immediately.'[26] Like the *Vidala*, the *Girarda* was ambushed on its way from Crete early in September the same year by a *bertone* of 400 butts with forty guns. The crew of about ninety men consisted half of Englishmen and half of Turks from Tunis. This time there was no looting: the assailants simply removed the ship. Now that England and Barbary were so closely in league, there was no reason merely to empty her and let her go: she could now become another unit in the pirates' war.

The change from the first to the second phase of English piracy was anything but clear-cut. Operations of the type just examined continued throughout this and the following years: however, the incidents known to us clearly indicate that from 1604 onwards the English came to appear almost everywhere, but that now they were seldom alone. On 11 October, at Strivali, a *bertone* of 200 butts, with over a hundred men on board, sacked the galleon *Spelegati* which had left Crete shortly before with a cargo of wine and cheese. A week later, in the same place, it plundered the *marciliana Grassa*, which was coming from Venice. This pirate ship was undoubtedly English, but it was flying the standard of Savoy and there were several Knights of St John aboard. The *bertone Morosini*, which had left Cyprus on 14 September, encountered a similar vessel at the latitude of Malta. This ship fired a salute and made reassuring signals, but the Venetians did not trust them, replied with gunfire and went on their way. Something similar happened to the *Pirona* in the Archipelago: after exchanging fire for about an hour with an English *bertone*, the English ship went on towards Constantinople, leaving the *Pirona* only lightly damaged. However, on leaving Zante again on 19 November 1604, the *bertone Morosini* failed to escape from a second attack at the mouth of the Adriatic. Again there were many Englishmen on board the attacking ship, but they were not alone.[27]

The two years which followed marked a relative pause. The Venetian Ambassador in England wrote in the spring to his government that the London merchants who had devoted themselves to business in the Levant were facing a crisis: their annual turnover, which had until recently been at least 250,000 crowns a year, had probably shrunk to 30–40,000. It is probable that a genuinely smaller number of English ships reached the eastern Mediterranean at this time. However, the *bertoni* found an excellent prize, of about 150,000 crowns, in the ship *Vidala*, which at the beginning of 1605 was returning from Alexandria with a cargo of spices. Two of these ships — the first, apparently, commanded by Anthony Sherley — were likewise reported at Sapienza and Corone towards the end of the following year. But this was literally the calm that goes before the storm: indeed, the star of John Ward, the great pirate of England and Barbary, was soon to rise. He was an Englishman, banished from his own country, who had established himself at Tunis and in other parts of North Africa with some 300 men. His plans were to build up a real pirate fleet.

His first stroke of good fortune was probably at the expense of the *Reniera e Soderina*, on its way from Syria and Cyprus, on 26 April 1607. The year had begun ominously for the Venetians, and it is possible that Ward had been responsible for this too. On 28 January, forty miles from the coasts of the Morea, an English *bertone*, having sacked the *Rubi*, coming from Alexandria with a cargo of spices, had ambushed, captured and taken to Barbary the *bertone Carminati*, returning from Nauplia and Athens. The aggressor was flying a Dutch flag, but the 110 men of its crew were for the most part Englishmen, the remainder Turks.[28]

The capture of the *Reniera e Soderina* created a sensation at Venice, and was regarded by some people as proof of the grave risks involved in arming merchant vessels with men unsuited to combat. 'The captain', we read in a report written some months later, 'after deciding on the advice of everybody to fight, divided up all his crew and passengers, and stationed some on the quarterdeck, others on the maindeck and poop, and thus they all seemed to be very gallant soldiers with weapons in their hands. The two ships that came to attack, even though two or three shots were fired at them, strove without further ado to lay themselves alongside, and on coming within range fired off twelve shots, six each, always aiming at the crew and the sails, without firing once into the water. Their plans, designed to terrify, succeeded excellently, because two of those who were defending the quarterdeck were hit by one of their shots, and when they were wounded, indeed torn to pieces, all the rest fled, leaving all their weapons lying on the quarterdeck and all of them running to their own property, even while the two vessels were coming alongside. For all his efforts, the captain was not only quite unable to force the crew to return to the quarterdeck, he could not even make them emerge from below decks or from the forecastle.

Indeed, the ship's carpenter and some others confronted him with weapons in their hands and told him that he should no longer command the ship.'[29]

The Venetian vessel must have been a magnificent one, because the pirate decided to make it his own flagship. Having sold its cargo at Tunis for 70,000 crowns, Ward converted it by re-equipping it in the form of a *bertone* and placing forty bronze guns on the lower deck and twenty on the upper. Meanwhile the great galleys, which had put to sea after the usual delay, were patrolling the waters where these misfortunes had occurred. On the coasts of the Morea, Lorenzo Venier's three warships encountered an English ship of 600 butts. Since its captain, Richard Harris, refused to take in his sails, it was necessary to seize it by means of gunfire in order to get control of it and lead it to Crete. In the summer the squadron thrust its way into the Gulf of Settelia, where it met another *bertone* and compelled it, again by using force, to lower its sails. These were poor results indeed: not only were the two ships soon released, but, as Zorzi Giustinian wrote from London on 25 July 1607, Ward for his part had brought to Tunis booty worth some 400,000 crowns.[30]

By the end of 1607 the fame of the new pirate fleet had spread throughout the Mediterranean. On 9 November the Senate gave special instructions to Girolamo Memmo and Cristoforo da Canal, appointed commanders of the convoys for Syria and Egypt, to prepare themselves to withstand this threat. But on 22 December, when the news that Ward had put to sea had reached Venice, the Senate issued orders to halt the convoys at Corfù or to bring them back if they were already at Zante. What had happened was that 'anticipating that the most excellent general Bembo would have disarmed his reserve galleys and hence there would be fewer obstacles in Ward's path', the pirate had 'recklessly come with four heavily armed *bertoni* to within sight of the harbour of Zante'. After an exchange of fire, Ward, 'seeing that there was no plunder for him there, left for Modone and Corone, where other ships of his were awaiting him, equipped to stay there observing Venetian ships and other vessels'.[31]

This was further evidence of the inadequacy of the Venetian navy and of the Venetians' persistent mistiming. It is not surprising that, in addition to blocking the passage of the Republic's principal trade, Ward was also able to capture with impunity the two ships which he encountered. On 13 January 1608 it was the turn of the galleon *Balbi*, which was taken to Navarino and fitted out to join forces with the other pirate ships. However, this vessel was wrecked as soon as it left port. Shortly afterwards, the galleon *Spelegato*, belonging to Giulio Venier was captured in the waters of Modone. However, the pirate realized that he had created a vacuum around himself, and therefore preferred not to loiter in the Ionian sea, but to leave for the Levant. However, Jan Casten, who had been his accomplice in the deeds of the previous year, chose to remain behind with his own *bertone* and another, smaller one. By the middle of March, he had already seized the ship *Angeli*. But shortly after this, the great galleys had the good fortune to surprise Casten off Modone on 21 March 1608. The Venetian admiral acted with great cunning: he knew that his own guns had a longer range than those of his opponent, and pretended to flee. Having thus placed himself out of range of the enemy, he began to fire on the two *bertoni*. Fifty pirates were killed and forty-four taken alive, whilst the others escaped to the Turkish coast. The *Angeli* was set free, and Venier, by Senatorial decree, received 2,000 ducats as the sum due to him for its recovery.[32]

In 1607 the Venetian Republic, having accepted without question the criticisms of the employment of great galleys against the pirates, had made a last effort, and likewise fitted out one powerful galleon. But in the reports read in the Senate by the captain of this ship and by the *Provveditore dell'Armata*, in quick succession, they both showed themselves opposed to the new warship. On 13 December 1608, Filippo Pasqualigo asserted that 'those who really understand naval affairs do not hold that this galleon is capable of pursuing *bertoni* and other similar pirate ships. There are many reasons for this conclusion — especially the great disadvantage from which the galleon will always suffer, in that it can be seen by enemies eight to ten miles farther off than it can see the *bertoni*. This greatly helps them to get well out of its sight and to escape by taking another route. But even when the galleon does find a *bertone*', continued the *Provveditore Generale*, 'it is obvious that a small, lighter vessel will soon be under sail and can get under way at the smallest puff of wind — whereas, on the other hand, the galleon, being such a large, heavy contraption, can only move with a vigorous wind.' Though not disputing that the galleon could be considered fast compared with large vessels of similar tonnage — 500 butts or more — he repeated that the *bertoni*, which were much easier to handle, could always manœuvre more freely. With a certain irony, Pasqualigo concluded that it would never be successful unless 'some pirate is unlucky enough to be overtaken by the galleon when anchored in a harbour'. For his part, Giust' Antonio Belegno acknowledged that the new warship had earned the astonished admiration of everyone who had seen it and that 'with its excellence, equipment and speed it had surpassed every expectation'. But there was no doubt that for the purpose of pursuing *bertoni* the great galleys were better than a ship that could not move without a favourable wind.[33]

Meanwhile, the transformation of the pirate war in the Mediterranean proceeded further. A considerable number of adventures, mainly English with some French and Dutch, followed Ward's example, and piracy enjoyed another excellent season in North Africa. With the vital contribution of English ships and sailors to techniques and manpower, the new 'men of Barbary' became the Mediterranean pirates *par excellence*. The losses suffered by the Venetian Republic in these years were ascribed almost entirely to them. For example, in 1609 there was the *Perla*, captured during the voyage from Venice to England and taken to Tunis, whilst the *Giovane Piccolo* was plundered on the same route.[34] Tunis, even more than Algiers, ceaselessly absorbed new victims. The *bertone Colombo* and a French *saettia*, both coming from Crete, were carried there in 1610 by Anglo-Turkish pirates. From Tunis, too, came the pirates who, in December of the following year, flying a banner with three half-moons and three swords upon it, captured the *Bonoma e Valnegrina* off Sapienza and shortly afterwards took the *Salvetta* after a furious battle.[35] If the assailants were not always wholly successful, the Venetians now seldom managed to defend themselves. The case of the *Foscarina e Mula* seems to have been an exception. This ship encountered four *bertoni* off Cyprus, resisted them for three days, 'and eventually, having the wind behind it, though damaged succeeded in saving itself by flight and in going upon its way — the *bertoni* were also damaged'.[36] The coasts of the Morea and the waters off Zante, a region of vital importance for Venetian shipping, continued to be severely attacked: ships suffered considerable delays. Thus, in January 1612, the *Tizzona* succeeded in forming a convoy with four other vessels destined for Venice and in obtaining permission to leave Zante after an enforced sojourn of thirty-five days. Pirates were patrolling round the island, and the Venetian *Provveditore* could only pray that God would bring the voyage to a happy conclusion.[37]

Apart from the numerous attacks suffered even by the northern ships which crossed the western Mediterranean to link Venice with England, Holland and the Iberian peninsula, let us by way of conclusion mention three significant operations carried out in the Ionian sea and the Levant. The first was the work of a *bertone* which reached Valona from Barbary in November 1611 with 100 men aboard — sixty Turks and forty English and French. A week later it ambushed a ship from Curzola on the Saseno, captured it and took it to Valona. Another *bertone* on 6 October 1614 attacked off Crete the *Monda* from Alexandria with a cargo worth 100–150,000 crowns. Having removed this cargo, the pirates placed it on one of their own vessels to carry it to Barbary — but on the return voyage the *bertone* belonging to the Knights of St John succeeded in depriving them of their booty after a bloody battle. Finally, in March and April 1615, even the galleon *Balbi* — the great ship fitted out by the Republic in 1607 and recently used as a merchantman — was attacked by the Barbary pirates shortly after its departure from the Saline of Cyprus. One of the two *bertoni* that attacked it was sunk, but the great Venetian ship itself caught fire.[38]

The reappearance of the northerners in the Mediterranean had, then, profoundly changed the interplay of forces which had developed there in the course of the sixteenth century. After Lepanto the great naval duel between the Crescent and the Cross, which had seen Spain and the Ottoman Empire fully engaged the one against the other, lost its decisive and, as it were, mortal character. Although for many years the alarums continued to be raised,[39] another form of struggle, pirate warfare, soon came to replace it. In itself, this is the clearest demonstration that religious fanaticism and the spirit of the crusade had unmistakably declined into mere inertia and frequently become mere pretexts for robbery. Thus, in the Mediterranean at the end of the sixteenth century, a real change was taking place, psychological as well as naval and commercial. But events in the world of the Mediterranean, at once vast and confined, were directly influenced — one might almost say ordered — by the struggles taking place in the Atlantic. It is clear that the Spanish navy could no longer confront its Islamic enemy once it found itself faced by the famous English navy and by the no less formidable forces of the United Provinces. But we have also seen that this change involved the closer participation of Mediterranean life in the great Atlantic struggle. The Northerners reappeared in the Mediterranean in a manner which was far from sporadic. Not only did they firmly establish themselves in some of the best centres — Algiers, Leghorn, Constantinople and Venice: not only did they invade the ports of the Levant — from Smyrna to Alessandretta, from Beirut to Alexandria: they even penetrated to Naples and Ragusa, to Patras and Milo. At first, up to about 1604, they acted simultaneously as merchants and as pirates. Subsequently, however, with the change in relations between Spain and Venice, pirate warfare was once more practised by clearly defined groups of freebooters and pirates. This last point remains to be established in detail. The operations and activities of the Wards and the Danzikers, of the Verneys and the Sansons, to mention only some of the most prominent, mark the beginning of a new system which was entirely different from that of the sixteenth century.

These activities took place on a considerable scale. A few figures should be enough to give us at least a rough idea of their extent. There were, for example, the fifty richly-laden vessels which in a brief space of time were plundered by Algerian pirates in the summer of 1608 on the coasts of Valencia; or the 500 pirate ships which, according to James I's reckoning, were at work in the Atlantic in the autumn of the same year. Some of these frequently forced the Straits of Gibraltar without difficulty. The strength of the Northerners established in Barbary seems to have been much slighter: in 1608 Ward had only two ships and Danziker four. Nevertheless, Danziker had captured at least twenty-nine ships — English, French and Dutch — off San Lucar de Barrameda. For the rest, the composition of these pirate fleets was extremely variable. At the beginning of 1609, when Ward was about to leave Tunis with nine *bertoni*, another eight, likewise 'from Barbary', were reported to be in the Archipelago. On 12 November of the same year, Marc' Antonio Corner wrote from England that Ward was about to head for the Irish Sea with fourteen ships, but the *Provveditore* of Zante was to report four days later that six of Ward's *bertoni* had detained an English ship sixty miles off Zante.[40] Some other evidence was sent by Venetian representatives from the Levant. Towards the end of 1610, according to an escaped slave, there were probably at Tunis some forty *bertoni* fitted out by Osman Missi, including that of Ward himself. At least six of them should probably reach the waters of Crete, and nine the Straits of Gibraltar. According to another slave, at the beginning of 1612 there were six galleys, twelve frigates and four galleons between Tunis and Biserta.[41] The captain of a *bertone* which reached Corfù from Barbary in January 1615 further reported that there they were equipping for the Levant eight large *bertoni*, each with some thirty bronze cannon. Another four ships — including the *Mondo Piater*, captured from the Venetians — were being prepared at Susa for piracy in the eastern Mediterranean.[42]

One thing, however, is certain — that, by establishing themselves in Barbary, where there was no lack of fighting-men, northern adventurers could with relative ease form properly-organized squadrons. The lone *bertone*, embarking on a long pirate cruise, became a rarity. Moreover, these Barbary fleets had extended their range of action to cover a wide stretch of the Atlantic. But what must be stressed most heavily is the change in the working of the system of piracy within the Mediterranean itself. With the passage of the years, interchanges between Christian and Barbary ports became more clearly-marked and more normal. There is no doubt that the Grand Duke of Tuscany and the Duke of Savoy were vying with the Ottoman authorities of North Africa in supporting and sheltering the pirates. Similar things also happened at Marseilles, where Danziker, after three years' resistance at Algiers, transferred himself in the autumn of 1609 with four well-armed galleys and a booty of 400,000 crowns, to place himself at the disposal of Henry IV. He declared himself ready to attack even this recent base of his if he were permitted to fly the French flag.[43]

However, Leghorn and Villefranche were the ports where this form of piracy developed most fully. In 1609, at Florence, there were serious discussions of the possibility of giving shelter to Ward, who would also withdraw from Barbary. The Tuscans would have been ready, not only to welcome him, but also to employ him against the Turks. It was especially after the Spanish attack on Mamurra in Morocco in 1611 that the Northerners headed for these two Tyrrhenean ports. English pirates arrived at Leghorn with their plunder and sold it there without the slightest difficulty, undoubtedly to the benefit of that market. Clearing-houses for the sale of such booty soon emerged, at least in 1612; the principal ones were the bay of Goro and the port of Ancona.[44] Goods arrived there in abundance, anything from textiles to sugar. It was only in March and April 1613 that nine most richly laden pirate ships entered the port of Leghorn and were all warmly welcomed by the Tuscan authorities. In October 1614 two English pirate ships presented the Grand Duke with a gift of some twenty slaves — a gift with a purpose, since His Highness was asked for a safe-conduct for nine galleons laden with booty.[45] In despite of the Medici Prince, the Duke of Savoy offered still better hospitality at Villefranche, which a fair number of pirates preferred. Among them was Peter Eston, who in March 1613 lay at Villefranche with four ships. Ten other ships of his squadron — which had numbered up to twenty-five — were patrolling off Gibraltar and would probably return later to resell their plunder. This adventurer, who seemed determined to abandon piracy, nonetheless shortly afterwards offered to equip a pirate fleet for Carlo Emanuele I so long as the Duke permitted him to fly the flag of Savoy. The Senate was forced to give instructions to the Captain of the Great Galleys, to the *Commissario in Armata* and to the Governor-general of Dalmatia to be ready to face this threat.[46]

This was no longer the Mediterranean of the sixteenth century. One could cite innumerable examples characteristic of it about the year 1610: from the Sultan decreeing that the port of Alessandretta be closed because it had literally become the hunting ground of the pirates, to Sully admitting that the French consuls in Syria were in league with them; from the English merchants sending munitions of every sort to Tunis, to the *bertone* finding shelter in the Gulf of Cattaro or the Dutchmen invading the waters of the Levant — all these were signs of a radical change. The new organization of pirate warfare, which had now become systematic plunder transcending religious barriers, and the refashioned machinery of forces and alliances, lead us to declare without hesitation that these years marked the end of the phase which we set out to examine.

PART II

The Organization of the Venetian Navy

Chapter 5

The Merchant Fleet

Here some analysis must be made of the fortunes of the Venetian merchant navy at the end of the sixteenth century and the beginning of the seventeenth. Piracy affected it decisively in these years, though this was not the only cause of the crisis and change within it. If we had to examine the problem of the Venetian merchant fleet, we certainly could not limit ourselves to discussing the effects of pirate warfare upon it, however profound these were. We should have to consider at length other aspects of the problem of a purely economic nature, such as the profits made by the shipowners, the transport of merchandise, the mechanism for insurance and the recruiting of crews. We must now merely attempt to see how far the pirates, and especially the Northerners, changed the commercial structure of Venice and influenced the entire organization of maritime transport.

Thus it is not appropriate to describe here the establishment of a regular trade route between Spalato and Venice, or of the route between Venice and the Ionian islands which soon followed it. But it is important to show that the idea of taking the great galleys out of the Arsenal — where they had lain unused since the battle of Lepanto — was put into practice about 1586 under the stimulus of the Uskok threat. 'Henceforth, to prevent the depredations of the Uskoks', we read in a report from Venice of April 1586, 'the Senate has recently decided to keep four *galere bastarde* in the Adriatic, in addition to the usual number of galleys, and to charge them with carrying freight from Narenta and other Turkish ports to Venice, doubling the freight charge and forbidding all other ships to carry goods to those ports. This means that the galleys will easily recoup their expenses, and all the loss will fall upon private persons and foreigners who have no trade other than such carrying.'[1] The employment of two great merchant galleys for the voyage to Corfù and Zante, 'to collect the merchandise which arrives there from Bastia, Castel Tornese and other nearby parts of Greece, and from Constantinople and other ports in Asia', was likewise justified in the Senate by the need to ensure 'safety from the risk of pirates, Uskoks and other evildoers'.[2] These merchant galleys, as we have already seen, were not in themselves safe enough to brave all the ambushes laid by the tireless brigands of Segna, and the Senate was anxious to get them escorted as much as possible by galleys designed for battle. Later, Venetian captains on the Ionian run drew attention to the inadequacy of the armed escort allotted to these vessels (only twenty-six men), and to the permanently insecure state of communications between Corfù and the Albanian coast, both because of the Cimmerioti and because of the very poor quality of the crews.[3]

This period saw the last stage in a process involving, not only one single trade route, but the whole of the Venetian Republic's maritime commerce. After 1580 Venice's classic role as intermediary between east and west — gravely shaken and increasingly challenged in the course of the sixteenth century — totally changed its meaning without being completely extinguished. From the end of the sixteenth century, the merchant fleet of the Venetian Republic no longer performed its double task of supplying the Turkish east with

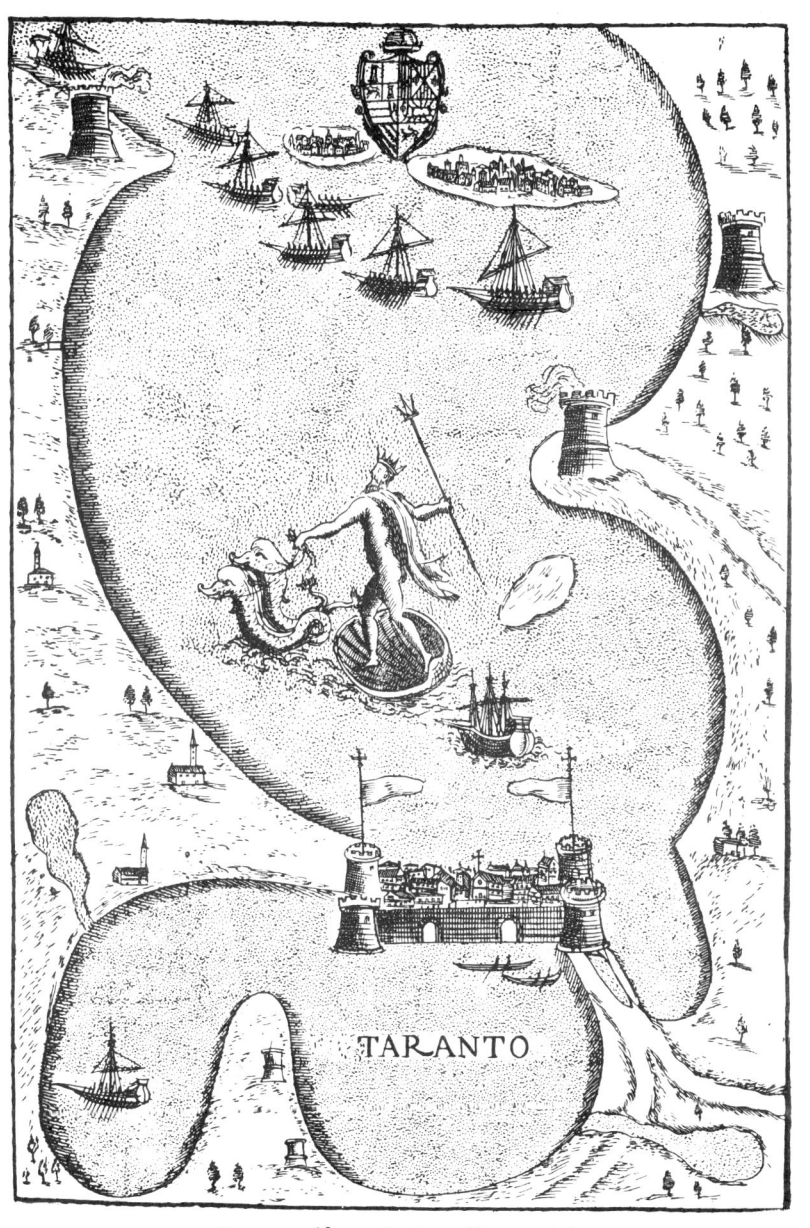

Taranto (from P. Bertelli, *op. cit.*)

The northern ships called *bertoni* by the Venetians, which, especially in English hands, proved themselves to be formidable pirate craft (engraved by H. Cock, from a drawing by F. H. Brueghel, *circa* 1565)

THE MERCHANT FLEET

western manufactures, and of guaranteeing the transport of Levantine foodstuffs and industrial products to the countries of northern Europe. Although between 1580 and 1590 Venetian ships still sailed to England and an attempt was made to establish a shipping line extending to Sweden, the number of their voyages subsequently contracted almost to zero. We have already seen how much the pirate warfare waged by the English during their conflict with Spain had damaged the surviving Venetian trade in the Atlantic. It succeeded in so obstructing it that after 1600 the presence of Venetian shipping in the North Sea was quite exceptional. Trade between Venice and England or Holland was by no means stopped by this — indeed, it increased — but it was from then onwards conducted by northern vessels. The *bertoni* which, originally used as warships, had eliminated Venetian merchantmen by force, acted as complete substitutes for them when peace was concluded between Spain and the Protestant powers.

The Venetian fleet had also to abandon almost completely another zone which was less distant but no less dangerous — Portugal and the Atlantic coasts of Spain. English, Dutch and German ships were now regularly chartered by Venetian merchants for this route, especially for Lisbon. The situation in the western Mediterranean was not much more favourable. By tradition, Venetian shipping was absent from the seas of Liguria and Provence, but towards the end of the sixteenth century it still frequented the Spanish ports of Malaga and Alicante, the harbours of Sicily and also the port of Naples. However, just as the Venetian government was seeking to shorten voyages to the east by means of the galleys of Spalato and Corfù, and to cause goods from the Balkans and even from Asia to flow into the Adriatic and Albanian ports, even so did Venetian merchants adopt a similar remedy to save their trade in the Tyrrhenean sea from the dangers threatening shipping beyond the Straits of Otranto. Instead of assigning their goods to ships which had to cross the dangerous Ionian sea, they laded them more and more frequently on smaller boats or *marciliane*, which followed the Adriatic coastline and ended up in some of the Abruzzo ports. Thence the goods were transported overland towards Naples. Moreover, when the Spanish Viceroys fitted out pirate *bertoni*, others — Apulians and men of Taranto, Calabrians and Sicilians — imitated their example with numerous ships of smaller tonnage which made the southern Italian routes even less navigable.

These brief hints, some of which have already been thoroughly documented,[4] point to a sharp reduction in the scale of Venetian maritime trade. One can, however, try to examine the problem a little more closely in order to convey at least a rough idea of the naval crisis whose severity was constantly being increased by the very frequent attacks of the pirates. Addressing the Doge in July 1607, Cristoforo da Canal asserted that 'Everybody knows that in the last few years this port has suffered irreparable damage, even devastation, through so many ships and so much treasure being plundered by *bertoni*, which — allured by the extent of the gain — come together from many regions to attack Venetian shipping especially without the slightest respect, in order to deprive it of the trade which has for many centuries notably increased the prosperity of this Most Serene Dominion'. Another contemporary document frankly spoke of the 'now abandoned shipyards of Venice, where in former times ships and boats were constantly being built', and of seeing that 'the few vessels which were still in use were being dismantled by thrifty persons, since it was better to make use of the timber and iron than to expose their ships, with other capital of theirs, to manifest danger'.[5]

These documents, which contain very few exaggerations, emphasize the point made elsewhere in describing the activity of the pirates: that is, the striking contrast between the period immediately following the battle of Lepanto (during which the forces capable of bringing about dramatic developments were strengthened, but the naval situation remained outwardly similar to that of the mid-sixteenth century), and the phase which began about 1595. A new situation arose precisely at the turn of the century. For many years the Venetian fleet had seemed capable of withstanding the wear and tear imposed upon it by the assaults of the Barbary pirates, the ambushes laid by the Uskoks and the operations of the Knights of St John and St Stephen. It is true that there existed one fundamental problem — the crisis in the shipbuilding industry — which the various measures taken by the state had not succeeded in solving. We shall now touch on this, and see that in the development of this crisis also the decade 1595–1605 marks a vital turning-point.

The lack of adequate studies of Venetian shipping in the fifteenth century prevents us from critically assessing the legendary figures handed down to us from various sources concerning the hundreds of ships which may have constituted the Venetian merchant navy at that time. It seems, however, that from the beginning of the sixteenth century the number of large ships capable of sailing the longer and more important routes ought to be reckoned in tens rather than hundreds. Moreover, even if reliable estimates were available for the period immediately before the battle of Lepanto, we should still have to take due notice of the decree of 23 August 1579, by which the Senate extended the permit to buy foreign ships, with the right to get them subsequently treated as Venetian, 'because of the present need which we have of ships, since many have been lost in recent years'.[6] The Republic, however, continued the policy which it had initiated some time before of granting subsidies to encourage the construction of ships in Venice itself and in the shipyards of the Venetian Dominion. It always attempted to treat permits to buy ships abroad as exceptional. Most of the loans were made to the shipowners when the ship was still in the yard, and repayment was deferred for several years. Thus, for example, at the beginning of 1559 the government had decided to lend 2,700 ducats to anyone who would build a ship of over 500 butts and 5 ducats per butt to all who built ships of between 300 and 500 butts. In November 1581, acknowledging that prices had risen considerably and that no one was willing to lay down a ship's keel even with state assistance, the Senate raised the subsidy to 3,500 ducats for ships of over 500 butts and to 6 ducats per butt for those of 300–500 butts.[7] The amount of these loans continued to increase during the last twenty years of the sixteenth century. In 1589 Bernardino Sebastiani Rosso was receiving 6,000 ducats for every ship of 600–800 butts, and 7,000 for anything larger. Repayment was to be made over the next ten years, in annual instalments. What might have seemed like an exceptional concession made to a shipbuilder such as Rosso, who had already built a score of ships and was now promising to begin the construction of another ten, soon became the general rule. From 1589, the loan for the larger ships was raised to ten ducats per butt.[8]

This policy was not wholly unsuccessful. There is information about numerous other shipowners and merchants who availed themselves of state aid in order to build ships even at Curzola, Lesina and Cattaro. But at the same time the privilege of treating as Venetian ships which had been bought abroad was increasingly in demand. From the information provided by the notary G. A. Catti, it is pretty clear that by about 1580 they already cost much less than those constructed at Venice. A galleon of 300 butts was sold for 1,700 ducats in 1579, whilst a *saettia* of 400 butts built in the west cost only 1,500 in 1582. In 1584 a Catalan galleon of 300 butts was sold to Raimondo and Girolamo Vitali for 1,400 ducats, and a ship of some 400 butts, built at Lesina on behalf of Vincenzo Barozzi, was valued at 2,955 ducats in 1586. At the beginning of 1590 a *marciliana* with a capacity of 2,000 *staia* cost 2,416 ducats, while a ship from Hamburg of 5,000 *staia* cost no more than 4,200 ducats.[9] Very soon the magistracies most concerned with maritime problems urged the Senate to suspend the prohibition on treating as Venetian ships bought abroad. The *Provveditori e Patroni all' Arsenal* succeeded in this in 1595, and the *Cinque Savi alla Mercanzia*, who had previously supported them, succeeded in 1597 in getting the suspension extended for at least one year in favour of the larger ships. 'By the laws of the most excellent Senate of 10 October 1487, 23 October 1479 and 30 December 1531', they maintained in a special memorandum, 'it appears that the prohibition on treating foreign ships as Venetian was passed solely to ensure that ships and other vessels should be built in Venice in order to support and maintain the master shipwrights and the great number of workmen who were employed and supported by their construction. This was done at that time because the business of marketing and shipping goods for every part of the world was then flourishing in this city. But as the amount of business transacted by your subjects has decreased whilst that of foreign nations has expanded, shipbuilding is at present declining in this city so catastrophically that there are very few persons engaged in it. This, in its turn, results mainly from the heavy expense which is necessary to the construction of a ship in this city. Hence there will be few people in the future who want to undertake this, for they will find it better in every respect to build them abroad, rather than in Venice. However, considering the need this city has of ships and the many benefits which have always accrued from them, and as there are now very few left, it is in our opinion necessary to give your citizens the means of buying them from foreigners and of sending them to sea as Venetian under the laws and ordinances of Your Serenity.'[10]

Among the papers of Leonardo Donà preserved in the Correr Museum in Venice, there is an important statistic which can enable us, at least roughly, to estimate the strength of the merchant fleet at the end of the sixteenth century. This is a list of all the ships which, between 1 September 1598 and

1 September 1599, paid the anchorage tax or berthing fee in the port of Venice.[11] There are some sixty larger ships mentioned there — roundships, *bertoni*, galleons, *galeoncini*, *saettie*. Only one-third of these were foreign ships — foreign because they had been built abroad, or because of the nationality of the owners. Almost all came from the Atlantic and were commanded by English, Flemish or Hanseatic captains. However, it is possible to try to distinguish between the Venetian ships and to pick out those which had been built outside Venice and its Dominion — perhaps fifteen out of forty. The most common type was the *bertone*, owned by nobles like the Balbi family or Francesco Morosini, or by prominent merchants like the families of Stella and Balbiani. It is difficult to claim more than about fifteen large vessels which had undoubtedly been constructed at Venice, because about a number of ships there is no precise information available.[12]

In the last years of the sixteenth century there was thus still a precarious balance between the merchant shipping which was most truly Venetian and the ships of foreign origin. A rapid glance at the naval policy of the following years shows how, in the brief space of five years, the situation became critical and then the balance was tipped. The defence of the privileges enjoyed by Venetian ships seems to become more rigid and stubborn, as though new measures were constantly being devised to alleviate the losses suffered by native shipowners or to encourage their activity. For example, one Vincenzo Bacetich was allowed, after his ship had been wrecked in Sicilian waters, to defer the repayment of a loan of 4,000 ducats. This is not the only example of its kind.[13] Still greater favour was shown to the owner of a galleon of 900 butts built with a state loan at Crete and captured by Barbary pirates. Another vessel was allowed to sail even though the owner was not up to date with the repayments of the subsidy which had been given him.[14] On the other hand, in August 1601 the Senate reasserted that 'all the ships, vessels, galleons, *bertoni* and foreign vessels of every other sort which are sold in this city or outside it to any subject of our Dominion, notwithstanding any privilege which they may have to pay as Venetians on account of the status of the owners or their cargo, must pay dues as foreigners until they receive our gracious permission' to be regarded as Venetian. The following year, with what hope of success no one knows, the government reiterated the old prohibition on exporting raisins to the west from Zante and Cefalonia without first passing through Venice.[15] Again, in August 1602, an attempt was made to discourage the purchase of foreign vessels by forbidding them to call at any port in the Adriatic save at Venice itself; by ordering merchants not to lade on them goods for or from the Levant until Venetian-built ships were fully laden; and by limiting insurance to two-thirds of the value.[16] But on 29 July 1603, although these restrictions were not abandoned, there was a clear majority in the Senate which favoured the renewal of the suspension of the decree forbidding 'making foreign ships Venetian', 'so that when they are recognized to have a capacity of over 500 butts ... they may be made Venetian by decree of this Council and may enjoy all the privileges of Venetian ships just as if they had been constructed in this city'.[17]

At the beginning of 1605, as appears from a memorandum presented to the Doge by the *Cinque Savi alla Mercanzia*, the Venetian merchant fleet now included more ships built abroad than built in Venice: fourteen against twelve. These figures, however, related only to ships of 600 butts or more.[18] Other documents make it possible to state that there was soon a considerable number of *bertoni* among the smaller ships also.[19] 'The ships of Venice', wrote Giust' Antonio Belegno in his report to the Senate on 4 February 1609, 'which used — especially the large ones — to be numerous in this city, are now no more. The main reason is the practice which arose some time ago, with disastrous consequences, of buying *bertoni* and sending them to the Levant with the same foreign officers and sailors as before. These are more skilled than the Venetians and the *bertoni* are swifter than Venetian ships, which leads the merchants to lade their goods upon them and to abandon the great Venetian ships. And so,' concluded the captain of the galleon, 'as there are no ships built in this city and as Venetian sailors are not wanted on foreign ships, the old ones go to serve elsewhere and no new ones are trained, so that the seaman's craft is dying out.'[20]

It has been necessary to draw attention to the crisis in Venetian shipbuilding to make it clear that this had been happening for many years past, and to emphasize that the pirate offensive in the years 1595–1605 marked its culmination. It is clear, as we shall soon see, that great importance was attached to other aspects of this. But it is certain that the inability of the Venetians to fill beyond a certain point the gaps blown by the pirates made their attacks during these years of decisive importance. Every ship captured or sunk meant a loss much less easily repaired than the mere loss of merchandise. Pirate warfare inevitably resulted in a decline of Venetian prestige and testified conclusively to Venice's political decadence. Disasters at sea were to accentuate no less heavily the prevalence of financial and landed investment over the traditional commercial activities.[21] Thus, in the report quoted above, Giust' Antonio Belegno pointed out that, although at the beginning of the seventeenth century cotton from Cyprus was still reaching Venice in large quantities (some 8,000 sacks, all of it on Venetian ships), the Dutch were now removing the greater part of it, and not more than 2,000 sacks were arriving every year. The same thing was happening in Syria, to the advantage of direct trade with the North Sea or with the port of Marseilles, whence Levantine goods were sent on towards Germany.[22]

Moreover, after 1610 there is no sign of a recovery. On the contrary, in October of that year a decree of the Senate 'relating to the deficit caused by the many losses and shipwrecks of recent years' provided that 'all new and sound foreign vessels of over 600 butts that in the course of the next two years are bought by our citizens *de intus* and *de extra* ... shall be regarded as Venetian so long as they are manned by subjects of ours in accordance with the laws'.[23] The number and type of the ships acquired the following year by Venetian owners leaves no room for doubt about the inactivity of the local yards: there was one French *saettia* and as many as seven *bertoni*, some of them being of considerable tonnage.

Other documents confirm that after 1610, as already noted, Venetian sea routes were contracting in scope, and traffic was becoming concentrated in the direction of the Aegean and the Levant.[24] Of the fourteen ships met or escorted by the captain of the galleasses about April 1610, one was headed for Alexandria, three for Constantinople, four for Smyrna and six for Crete. Genuine figures for the movement of shipping in the year 1611 show unmistakably how shipping routes were becoming shorter. As many as fourteen ships left for Crete that year and twelve for Smyrna, but only six for Constantinople. Not more than three ships went to Syria and the same number to Alexandria. There is no need to go on drawing attention to the proportion of foreign to Venetian ships — the Venetian had now become a scanty minority.[25] It is therefore not surprising to find, on perusing the records of the notary Giovan Andrea Catti for the five years 1610–15, many contracts for the hire of northern ships — usually *bertoni* — not only for the western Mediterranean and the Atlantic but also for the Morea, Crete, Zante, Athens and Lepanto. Nor is it surprising to learn that in 1619 many foreign merchants domiciled in Venice, with Francesco Vendramin as their nominal head, 'observing that maritime trade has greatly declined as a result of these disturbances, rather than leave their capital unemployed have chosen to lend it to the government at 5 per cent'.[26]

Apart from the naval escorts which will be discussed later, the Venetian merchant marine could rely on two different systems of defence, by insuring and by arming the ships. The first method should have enabled it to make up its losses rapidly, and the second to reduce deathblows to a minimum.

The system of marine insurance in Venice had worked very efficiently in the sixteenth century. This was emphasized, though in a paradoxical fashion and with some irony, by the secretary Giovan Carlo Scaramelli, who was sent to London to obtain from Elizabeth compensation for losses inflicted by English pirates. 'These disgraceful acts of the English', wrote the Venetian diplomat, 'have multiplied and increased in a way so damaging to Your Serenity's subjects because here it used to be widely believed (as, indeed, it still is) that if any Venetian suffers a loss he will immediately have recourse to his insurer, and so long as he obtains the sum for which he is insured — which is sometimes even more than the capital — he will take no heed of the rest; and that then the insurers, whether acting separately or in unison, each thinking only of his own part in the affair and being preoccupied with more important business of his own, will neglect their own perfectly valid claims and eventually lose what could never justly be denied them. If, as soon as a ship had been plundered, the pirates, the partners in the ship and the guarantors had been promptly confronted by persons with money and skill, there is no doubt that the English, as they themselves admit, would after the first or second time have gone elsewhere to other occupations.'[27]

The remarks previously made about shipbuilding also apply to insurance, at least at one point: up to the end of the sixteenth century it effectively safeguarded merchants and shipowners from the losses frequently caused by shipwrecks and by pirates. It is difficult, if not impossible, to distinguish professional insurers from other merchants. Insurance firms were unusual, though some did exist. There were few people who invested their capital wholly in this activity. Usually the merchants who invested in maritime trade were at the same time insurers

THE MERCHANT FLEET

and did not hesitate to underwrite insurance policies to cover other people's risks. People were almost invariably insured, and the interested party quite often insured himself for more than the real value of his goods, though it is impossible to say how much this happened. It was hard to find anyone willing to underwrite large sums. Sometimes merchants would distribute their goods between several ships to reduce the risks, but even more often they would apply to a large number of insurers in order to secure them. It was roughly true that the number of insurers varied directly with the value of the goods insured. In this way, all persons involved would suffer less from strokes of adverse fortune.

There is no doubt that the insurance business was very prosperous up to the close of the sixteenth century. The profits were very considerable, even apart from their more purely speculative manœuvres.[28] At the turn of the century, the premium — if the route for Syria and Alexandria be taken as a specimen — varied between 2 and 6 per cent according to the condition of the ship, the type of merchandise, and the season. But the alarms which were frequently raised (inevitably and often justifiably, for pirate attacks and shipwrecks were so frequent) caused premiums to increase considerably, even up to 30 or 40 per cent. Dullo Cochini in 1607 admitted that 'When the trade of Venice was not in the low state in which it is at present, underwriters used to gain vast sums of money from insurance premiums'.[29] Indeed, not only did they pay no taxes on their transactions, but they even in a sense enjoyed a monopoly of them, since no merchant could insure himself outside Venice.

But it was inevitable that pirate warfare should not only accentuate the faults of this system, which had on the whole functioned fairly well, but also impair its soundness and efficiency. As the risk grew, the premium had to go up: when the normal risk became very great, the premium tended to become intolerably heavy. In a memorandum dated April

1605 — which, had it been in verse, could easily have been entitled 'The Merchant's Lament' — the heads of the merchants' corporation begged the Doge for a prompt remedy for the misfortunes which had afflicted their trade. 'Sea trade with the Levant', we read, 'on which this market chiefly subsists, is now reduced to such a wretched state, due to the heavy losses and severe depredations hitherto suffered at the hands of English *bertoni* and other pirate ships, and to the obvious and imminent danger of similar or even greater misfortunes, that unless the government in its wisdom and charity adopts some effective remedy it will completely collapse and disappear.' After surveying the very serious consequences to the whole city if maritime trade were interrupted or depleted, the climax of the paper came with these words: 'Your Serene Highness, even now in this city there are ships destined for the Levant ready to sail, but unable to leave, because the merchants cannot and will not expose their capital and wealth to the certainty of loss — both because of the depredations which have recently occurred, and on account of those which the ships of various nations are armed, equipped and on their way to carry out to the loss and ruin of Venetian shipping, as they themselves let it be known, and as we have recently been reliably informed by letters received by the merchants. Hence their ships lie in these docks in lamentable idleness, and this malaise is so great that there is nobody who wants to insure them, even at the highest rates.'[30]

The very high premiums mentioned in this memorandum had become a reality shortly after 1600. Dullo Cochini indirectly confirms this with his proposal to establish a tax on insurance transactions. According to his calculations, had the underwriters made over to the state 'twelve per cent of the value of the goods insured', the Republic would thereby have received a sum sufficient to equip two large ships and ten *fuste*. In return, these ships would have restored peace to the seas and obtained for the underwriters so large a volume of business as to compensate them for the profits they had lost. But now, 'because bad news keeps arriving — though it is frequently not verified — those concerned insure themselves at excessive rates, paying 50–60 per cent or even more'.[31] Such premiums were certainly exceptional; but even the normal ones had doubled. 'All the merchandise at present going to or from Alexandria', reports another document of 1607, 'pays 10–12 per cent on the outward journey and as much again for the return, and sometimes as much as 14 per cent; and at present no one can be found to insure unarmed ships at any premium.'[32] Again in the Senate registers one reads that if the armed great galleys were used for the transport of goods rather than for escort duty not only would 'thousands of ducats be gained on the hire' but 'the merchants will save the 18–20 per cent which they now spend on insurance'.[33]

It is clear that with these liabilities Venetian sea transport was unable to withstand competition. But anyone inquiring how Venetian shipping could work efficiently is bound to agree that the system of insurance still represented its only effective safeguard. It is indeed very difficult to find anything in this period more defective than the armed protection which was in theory compulsory for every medium-sized or large vessel, or a collection of laws less scrupulously observed than those governing shipping movements. A decree of 1569 forbade all Venetian ships to sail during the winter, from the month of November to 20 January. It does not appear, however, that much action was taken against the very frequent infringements of this law. But in 1598 the prohibition was renewed, it being supposed that the endless series of shipwrecks ought to be ascribed to infractions of the law. Only in 1600 did a more enlightened view of the question induce the Senate to remove the veto: they had realized that other seapowers were taking advantage of it to oust the Venetians.[34]

But the real trouble lay, not in disobedience to this rather questionable law, but in the technical and human deficiencies of the merchant navy. One of the chief shipowners at this time admitted, for example, that the *bertoni* 'are continually at sea and are capable of turning even a contrary wind to their advantage and so making much headway, a thing which our ships cannot do, while our sailors know not how'.[35] Nevertheless the Senate — apparently for the sole purpose of keeping an ancient type of vessel unchanged — obstinately opposed the attempt to introduce on the galleons (the only ships resembling *bertoni*) the square sail used by the Northerners instead of the traditional triangular sail 'of the Latin type'. Moreover, the undetected use of a very popular type of smaller ship, the *marciliana*, caused a considerable number of losses at sea. By ancient law, *marciliane* were not to venture beyond Zante: their hulls were little suited to the open seas, and, more important, the scantiness of their crews and the impossibility of installing guns upon them made it unwise to employ such ships in regions infested by pirates or inadequately patrolled by galleys. However, with the progressive disappearance of the larger ships and the difficulty of finding substitutes for them, the Venetians finally yielded to the temptation to permit even *marciliane* to sail as far as Crete. They first partially revoked the law for a period of two years in 1602, extending this further in 1605. Only on 2 May 1606, 'after suffering so many shipwrecks and misfortunes, with the loss of so much capital', were these vessels again forbidden to make the journey to Crete.[36]

But the shipowners, increasingly disinclined to invest their capital in the over-expensive large vessels or 'roundships', skirted the obstacle by causing *marciliane* which had been barely refitted to pass as roundships. In July 1607 Nicolò Balbi wrote frankly in a memorandum that 'I must needs point out to Your Excellencies... that the roundships *Reatta* and *Solda*, which are destined for the voyage to Alexandria, were both *marciliane* only the other day, and very bad ones at that'.[37] In August of the same year, advocates and opponents of this malpractice faced one another in the Senate. The former maintained that 'The *Gottardo, Gottardino* and *Rigolo* have now been under sail for many days in Venice, ready to leave for Crete, but some people have objected that they do not fulfil the requirements for that voyage'. Availing themselves of the support of the *Cinque Savi alla Mercanzia*, those involved proposed to despatch them nonetheless, 'as they are already laden with goods, including some government property, and are insured and everything else that is necessary'. On the other hand, their opponents maintained that the laws which had been repeatedly violated ought at last to be enforced, and proposed that neither on this occasion nor in the future should these three vessels 'which in a fraudulent and deceitful guise and in defiance of the decrees have dared to take freight for Crete, nor any other *marciliana* even if it has been converted like these' be authorized to make journeys to the Levant. The narrow majority (77 votes to 62) by which the proposal of the second group was carried showed how deep this serious and meaningful disagreement had become.[38]

Venetian ships, especially the larger ones, had long been obliged to carry large numbers of guns and several armed men. Thus, at the beginning of the seventeenth century, ships of 600 butts or more had to be equipped with at least eighteen guns: six six-pounder cannon, four twelve-pounders and eight mortars for hurling boulders. These guns were generally made of cast iron, and the *Savi alla Mercanzia* themselves proposed in 1605 to add two bronze culverins. Their suggestion does not seem to have been favourably received, since it had to be revived two years later by the Commissioner for the Navy in a paper addressed to the Doge. From surveys compiled in 1607 it is possible to ascertain that although guns were not altogether missing from Venetian ships they were almost always held to be inadequate. Thus, the galleon of Bernardo Giustinian, which had been at sea for twelve years, was in that year carrying six mortars, two iron guns and as many as ten bronze ones:

THE ORGANIZATION OF THE VENETIAN NAVY

its capacity was 600 butts. A ship of 500 butts like the galleon *Tapino* carried four mortars and twelve iron guns. Vessels of 300 butts also carried many guns: the galleon *Venier* had fourteen iron guns, and Francesco Morosini's galleon carried twelve (six cannon and six mortars, both made of iron). By comparison, a Dutch ship of equal capacity seemed no better armed, with its seven cannon and four mortars.[39]

But at the same time, those concerned with the matter did not conceal from the Venetian authorities their opinion that these armaments were totally insufficient. The *Balbiana*, of 600 butts, was equipped with eleven bronze cannon and ten mortars. Before sending her to the Levant, there were proposals to add another eleven cannon and two mortars. Of the galleon of Giovanni Emo, already equipped with four bronze cannon, ten of iron and two mortars, it was written: 'If we wish to make use of this, it will be necessary to equip it with fully twelve pieces of artillery and two hundred-pounder mortars in addition.' Other figures were given for the larger vessels. It was suggested that in order to send the *Salvetta*, of 800 butts, to Syria, it should be equipped with another fourteen cannon and two mortars in addition to the fourteen cannon and twelve mortars already on board. Another ten cannon should be placed on the *Giustiniana e Zagura*, a ship of equal tonnage with a cargo for the Levant, to add to the twenty-seven guns already installed. Two large new ships of 1,000–1,100 butts ought to be armed as follows: the *Pigna* with thirty-seven guns (twenty-seven cannon and ten mortars), and the *Perastana* with fifty: thirty-eight cannon and culverins and twelve mortars.[40]

The gap between the number of guns demanded and the number actually possessed had naturally to be filled by the government. Guns were a heavy charge on the shipowner. For example, it was calculated in 1607 that the twenty-one bronze guns of the *Balbiana* were worth 5,000 ducats. These consisted of four twelve-pounder guns, seven six-pounders,

Bertoni at sea (engraved by H. Cock from a drawing by F. H. Brueghel, circa 1565)

Typical renegade Christians, who formed the crews of Turkish pirate ships (from N. de Nicolay, *Les quatre premiers livres des navigations et pérégrinations orientales*, Lyon, G. Roville, 1568)

THE MERCHANT FLEET

with two fourteen-pounder mortars and twelve eight-pounders. Their total weight was 21,507 pounds. Moreover, a ship of 600 butts like the *Balbiana*, on the voyage to Alexandria, would need sixty soldiers and forty sailors. Pay and victuals for soldiers for a period of eight months would cost 5,000 ducats, for sailors 2,000. Added to these expenses was another 1,500 ducats for insurance and port dues, whilst the ship could not be expected to yield more than 10,000 ducats, including the freight charge.[41] It was obvious that both private owners and the state itself would attempt to avoid these expenses, or at least some of them. Even in the convoys — started in 1607 and directly supervised by the state — there were ships inadequately armed.[42]

The gravest, the most lamentable defect of the defence system of Venetian merchant shipping lay in the escort crews and especially in the men themselves. On this point a number of admissions were made of so significant and distressing a nature that one cannot fail to report them. They are at the same time so numerous and so much in agreement that they leave no room for doubt. In a paper of 10 April 1605, Nicolò Lion asserted that 'the men that now sail on ships and small craft' were for the most part 'worthless and unscrupulous creatures, so that when attacked by raiders they not only help them but take to plundering themselves'. A memorandum of the *Cinque Savi alla Mercanzia*, dated two years later, provides an authoritative and well-documented confirmation of this. 'On more than one occasion', they admitted, 'we have seen that merchant ships, even though armed in accordance with the regulations of the most excellent Senate, have proved unwilling to fight, whether because they hope that being plundered may afford them the opportunity of making large profits, or because they have discovered that they will get excellent treatment from the pirates if they do not fight — as happened to the *Zena*, the *Silvestra*, the *Zustignana*, the *Perastana* (which refused to sail in convoy according to the government decree) and many others.' Giust'Antonio Belegno, Commissioner for the Navy, added some information, with a touch of the picturesque, which complemented this and covered similar ground. 'Up to the present time', he wrote, 'the shareholders, having in their own fashion profitably insured their ship, spurred on by greed and eager to save expenditure on victuals and pay, have chosen to arm them, not with men with any military training, but with mariners of very little experience, children and striplings, with no training for the sea, let alone for battle should there be any need for it, and not enough of them either. Whenever pirates have attacked, no sooner have they sighted the enemy ship than they have hidden below decks in fear of their lives to avoid fighting and have allowed themselves to be captured in this ignoble fashion. And had they all been brave professional seamen, just the regulation number, no more, they could easily have defended themselves and saved the ships and merchandise.'[43]

This aspect of the naval situation — little known, like everything which hides the sufferings of a society — illustrates the crisis in Venetian shipping and finally assists us to understand it. Describing this to his brother the Doge, Nicolò Donà showed himself unmistakably aware of its gravity. 'My most illustrious lord,' he said, 'this is a serious matter — more serious even than war, because the city is weighed down, oppressed and demoralized by losses. Trade is suspended, you suffer loss of revenue and duties, shipbuilding ceases, we lose our sailors, and victuals are imported with difficulty. The government is dishonoured, the merchants speak ill of it, some talk of emigrating and everyone is scandalized....'[44] But for some years already, especially since Spaniards and Englishmen had taken to pirate warfare, it had been notorious that Venetian merchantmen only seldom or half-heartedly employed against assailants the means of defence at their disposal. This was clearly pointed out by Giovan Carlo Scaramelli in 1603, and confirmed in 1607 by the fleet commanders with the full weight of their authority. Pasqualigo, Canal and Bondumier wrote from Corfù that there must be no more falling into 'the errors made in the last few years in recruiting troops for the security of ships, since the cabin-boys and apprentices of the ships themselves have been enrolled as soldiers, parading in old leather jerkins borrowed from a secondhand shop, when they have never before seen or handled firearms. The result of this (as is well known) has been that whenever they encounter enemy ships they are the first to lay down their arms, surrender, and plunder the cargo of their own ships.'[45] Some years later, Antonio Foscarini, Ambassador in England, repeated that the cause of the collapse of Venetian trade in the Levant was the very fact that they sent there ships 'with bad crews and worse captains, so that, as experience has shown, the sea can easily sink and any petty pirate plunder them because they will not fight'.[46]

It was, then, mainly for technical and human reasons that the Venetian merchant marine emerged so badly from the tests imposed upon it by pirate warfare. Confident of encountering slighter resistance and of gaining equally rich plunder, *bertoni* and *galeotte* more readily attacked the shipping of the Venetian Republic and persistently ambushed the routes it used. It is well known that all the sea powers of the Mediterranean and the Atlantic had to face piracy at this time and that nearly all of them withstood the impact. But for some time Venice had ceased to send the best of her nobles and citizens into the merchant fleet — they were now increasingly attracted by finance or by the profits to be made from the mainland possessions of Venice. This long process of transformation which had been changing the structure of Venetian society since the second half of the fifteenth century had not been much in evidence before Lepanto. The pirates, and especially their activities in the years 1595-1605, brought the organization of Venetian trade and shipping to a crisis which could only accentuate the results of a secular trend.

Chapter 6

Light Galleys

Before embarking on this discussion of the Venetian navy, it should be said that the two chapters into which it has been divided ought to be considered as complementary halves. The problems of victualling and manpower, to mention only the chief ones, were common to all Venetian warships, and there is no justification for describing how they affected every different type of ship over the short period chosen. We shall depart from the scheme adopted in order to analyse at the most convenient moment the individual features of naval organization. We wish to admit and even to emphasize the fact that the light galleys were not abandoned at the beginning of the seventeenth century, but continued their campaign against piracy even when the galleasses and the galleon had entered the field. There are, therefore, good reasons for discussing, first the light galleys, and then the larger craft. The strongest of these is undoubtedly that up to the beginning of the seventeenth century the Venetian fleet still consisted only of light galleys, and that the duty of fighting the pirates therefore fell to them. This task was later entrusted mainly to the great galleys, which, together with the galleon, were rearmed specially for the purpose. Moreover, at the very beginning of

THE LIGHT GALLEYS

the seventeenth century, the fleet was reorganized, or at least some attempt was made to enact a collection of reforms which ought to have produced that result. We believe, therefore, that the problems of the Venetian fleet cannot only be described in separate chapters, but that such a separation may serve to throw clearer emphasis on the two distinct phases in the Venetian struggle against the pirates.

The structure of the Venetian navy in the years after Lepanto differed little from that of the mid-sixteenth century. It consisted almost entirely of a single type of warship, the fighting galley, also called the light galley to distinguish it from a similar one which had hitherto been used mainly for commercial purposes. Armed boats or *fuste*, smaller vessels with some fifteen benches of oarsmen, were rare. The famous government Arsenal enjoyed a monopoly of naval shipbuilding. In the sixteenth century, this enormous industrial complex, almost unique in its time, was capable of fitting out dozens of galleys in the space of a few months.[1] The design of the light galley dated from the Middle Ages. It was nearly fifty metres long and had a mainmast with a triangular sail. But its distinctive feature lay in its being propelled by oars. The oarsmen sat in groups of three on benches, each working his own oar — hence also the name 'trireme' which was given to this vessel. During the sixteenth century experiments were also made with models on which the three rowers together moved a single oar. The great galleys also used one oar per bench, and so, very likely, did those of the squadron commanders. On normal galleys there had to be at least 164 oarsmen on twenty-seven benches, each bench being divided into two by a central gangway, with three men on either side. On both light and great galleys, the crew had no deck to shelter them, but were in the open and therefore exposed to foul weather. In tactics and strategy, the serious disadvantages of this layout were partly cancelled by the fact that some of the pirates (from Barbary, Malta and Florence, but not, as we shall see, from Holland or England) were using very similar ships: *fuste, galeotte* or genuine galleys. Nevertheless, the need to protect the oarsmen became increasingly pressing, and in any case always made it difficult to employ galleys, especially the light ones, in bad weather and when the sea was especially rough. But, by way of compensation, the galley was faster than any other vessel, since it made use of a double motive power: wind and oars.[2]

In the second half of the sixteenth century there was at Venice a radical transformation of the method of recruiting and, as a result, in the composition of galley crews. Before 1545 it was very rare to make use of forced or at any rate unfree oarsmen. In imitation of the methods already introduced in other navies (to say nothing of pirate ships), as a result of the ever-increasing shortage of 'free' oarsmen, Venice too decided to fall back on other sources of labour. Unlike the Pope, the North Africans, and the Knights of Malta and St Stephen, they rejected slaves and began to use convicts. Only persons imprisoned for common offences for which the penalty could be commuted into galley service were eligible for this. Those guilty of serious crimes against the state or the Catholic faith were excluded. Thus, instead of suffering the physical penalties which had been usual, these men began to be sent to Venice and thence, with chains about their feet, to the navy. At first only three or four galleys were manned in this way. The personal ability of their first commander, Cristoforo da Canal, and the progressive decrease in the number of voluntary oarsmen later resulted in a decision to arm further galleys with convicts. After Lepanto, prisoners from Venice and its mainland possessions were no longer sufficient, and the Senate had to apply to neighbouring states in order to obtain others. Neither the Emperor nor the Princes of northern Italy nor, at a later date, the Duke of Bavaria refused to make this contribution to the Venetian Republic. Taking the years 1605-10 as a sample, it is possible to assert that over 500 men a year were taken out of Venetian prisons and embarked on the galleys.[3] The number of ships with convict crews continued to grow after 1580 with the full agreement of the Senate, which declared itself satisfied with the arrangement. In the official language of the Republic they had, significantly, begun to be described as 'the chief basis of our navy' — an expression which was regularly used. It was now perfectly accurate. After repeated decrees of this nature, by 1 December 1592 the Senate was ordering that a twenty-third galley should be manned by convicts, so that almost the entire fleet at sea was now thus equipped.

It would be easy to dwell on the sufferings of this multitude of men for the most part unaccustomed to life at sea and treated little better than slaves. It is certain that the inferior status of the oarsmen opened the way to many abuses and that the result was a very steep decline in the efficiency of the fleet. In 1599 Nicolò Donà wrote that 'An enormous number of the convict oarsmen dies. It costs Your Serenity good money to feed, clothe and physic them, but these poor wretches are ill-clad because of the vile quality of the stuff which is not shaped to cover them, scantily fed because they have only bread and soup, and never looked after when they fall sick.' In his Report the admiral specified that 60 per cent of them died: had there been good hospitals, losses could have been reduced to 10 per cent.[4] A hospital for these crews was eventually erected at Zara by Giovanni Pasqualigo, with good results. However, the most serious troubles persisted throughout much of the period under review. In 1587 many suffered frost-bitten feet and others actually died 'of the ghastly cold one feels in Dalmatia': twenty years later, Filippo Pasqualigo was still asserting that 'every year many of the convicts lose their hands or feet as a result of the cold and at last miserably perish'.[5] Giust' Antonio Belegno ascribed the sufferings of these oarsmen to the constant lack of awnings to shelter them from foul weather, and also to the fact that they possessed only one garment each and could not change even if they were soaked to the skin. All too often, he added, their food consisted only of five ounces of biscuit and one cup of wine a day.[6]

The abuses committed at the expense of the convicts were of no slight importance. When a warship was about to re-enter Venice, the best rowers were often taken from it and distributed among other galleys, thus making the original galley almost useless. As a result, it was quite usual for there to be 180 or more oarsmen on some triremes instead of the regulation 164, whilst on others there were only 100.[7] The enlistment and release of the convicts often took place in a haphazard fashion. Instead of sending them all to the fleet commanders, the magistrates of the mainland territories would send a number of them directly to some captain (or *sopracomito*, to use the Venetian term) with whom they happened to be friendly. He would take them on without registering them, and although time passed there was no reduction of their sentence. But even when they had obviously served their term these hapless men continued to be ill-treated or else kept on the galleys by force. For the rest, there was one almost infallible method of holding them — by making them small loans (in money, clothing or services) and waiting for them to pay their debts. It is not surprising, then, that Giovanni Pasqualigo should describe them as 'deprived of all hope of being able to regain their liberty, no matter how long they serve, and having, on account of their poverty, no means of paying their debts ... for it is impossible for them ever to pay off the debt they have contracted with the government for the costs of their trials, their transport and their fines, and for cloth, canvas and leather, and for the services of barbers, when their pay consists of eight lire every thirty-three days'.[8]

The galley captains were not the only culprits: the fleet commanders themselves often infringed the law or adopted abusive measures. Their galleys were supposed to be manned only by free men, but in order to get a large number of oarsmen

THE LIGHT GALLEYS

they would secretly recruit convicts as well. A clever trick had been devised for this purpose. Many delinquents received sentences twice as long as they deserved, and got by way of compensation half the pay of a free oarsman: the admirals therefore thought themselves entitled to keep them on their ships. For all these reasons, there came a time when even the supply of forced labour gave out. Filippo Pasqualigo showed that by 1605 the ordinary needs of the light galleys were being met only with difficulty. 'The galleys of the condemned', wrote Giust' Antonio Belegno, 'are always in need of men, because some of them die, others take to flight and others are released after having served their sentences — so that, though each of them ought to have 160 convicts, some have only 100, others 120, some more and some less.'[9]

It is only too easy to provide a concrete example of the serious breakdowns in the system which resulted from this. In June 1610, before proceeding to Corfù, the *Capitano del Golfo* decided to inspect at Zara the four new galleys which had just reached him from Venice. His despatch is a precise and objective analysis of the deplorable situation he was witnessing. He ascertained that many convicts were missing from these galleys, but their captains had a reply ready: there was nothing to be done, as there were none to be found. As Francesco Molin immediately pointed out to the Senate, 'this shortage, together with the illnesses which normally attack new crews when they first go out, gravely weakens these galleys, which means that for a long time we cannot hope to receive from them the desired benefits'. Continuing his survey, the *Capitano del Golfo* drew attention to the abuse which made these vessels virtually useless. For some years the galley captains had been receiving a grant for the specific purpose of engaging forty-eight free and experienced oarsmen, so that the convicts — automatically reduced in number to 144 — might under their guidance become accustomed to wielding the oars. As Molin trenchantly remarked: 'When the unfortunate new convicts, who are not accustomed to the hard labour involved in these ships or to the toils of life at sea (which most of them have never even seen before), have to carry the whole burden, which is doubly heavy for them because they are not habituated to galley service, it is inevitable that they should fall sick and die. It is almost impossible for them to hold out, because after all they are creatures of flesh and blood — not men of iron.' This 'slaughter of human beings' took place on every galley where the captain did not care to spend as he ought the money entrusted to him. Molin therefore suggested that the money should not be given to them until they had genuinely enrolled the prescribed number of oarsmen. But he was bound to point out that, with the one deficiency contributing to the other, the entire fleet was in danger of being unable to perform even its normal duties that year.[10]

The *sopracomiti*, as already indicated, were noblemen appointed by the Venetian government to the command of galleys. We have already had reason to describe what they did and failed to do, the gallant deeds which they performed, and the real abuses and injustices of which they were guilty. It is now necessary to describe them more fully, because the entire fleet rested upon their shoulders. They were responsible for every decision on each trireme — disciplinary or political, technical or tactical. Only in questions of navigation could they count on assistance from the mate or the pilot. By their side there was no officer or colleague of noble rank, except for the *vice-sopracomito*. Absolute masters of the galleys, they ruled them single-handed, and their faults were accentuated thereby, no less than their good qualities. Unfortunately, just as there was nobody on board in a position to curb their power or give them authoritative advice, even so did the commanders of the squadrons of which they formed part treat them as colleagues rather than subordinates. They were, moreover, all members of the same exclusive ruling class, sometimes relatives, sometimes friends. There were even men who, however youthful, were conscious of belonging to families or circles of greater power or distinction than those of their superior officers. It can be said that the Venetian admirals, at least at this time, usually preferred to complain of their galley captains to the Senate, and to wait for Venice to send the orders or vetoes which they had not dared to issue themselves. Cases of serious indiscipline or open disobedience were rare, but neglect of duty occurred frequently and the sense of responsibility was feeble. In March 1585, when eleven *fuste* were leaving Valona to plunder in the Adriatic, the *Capitano in Golfo* was forced to report that in spite of his efforts 'both with letters and with written orders' to reassemble his scattered squadron, two galley captains had failed to rejoin him at Lesina. In March 1594 the Senate, in a letter to all the admirals, spoke of 'the daily complaints we receive of the scant obedience of most of the galley captains, who abandon their guard duties and dally round Istria — an appalling example which causes great loss to the state. This leads every day to Uskok and even Turkish raids upon our subjects.'[11]

The dispersal of the Venetian squadrons was frequently due to the unofficial voyages made by the captains just as they saw fit, as far back as Venice or Venetian waters. Even though they were expressly forbidden to re-enter Venice during their term of active duty, the Senate in 1583 was forced to admit that galleys were still coming without authorization not only to Malamocco and Chioggia but even into the Basin of St Mark. These captains did not care that the regions entrusted to them were left undefended: they took themselves elsewhere at their pleasure and justified their absence from the squadrons with numberless requests for things that were for the most part unnecessary. Neither ancient laws nor Senatorial reprimands produced any lasting effect. 'All the day galleys continue to put into Istria, Chioggia, Malamocco and other harbours near to this city', we read in an official document of 1591, 'on the pretext that they need more biscuit, stopping where and when they please, leaving the commanders without their galleys and abandoning the Adriatic and other seas that they ought to guard.'[12] During the winter season the largest possible number of captains drew near to Venice, some of them without authorization and others with illegal permits. The entire Squadron of the Condemned probably did this in 1588, and certainly did so in 1594, in 1600 (four galleys arrived to lade biscuit, when one would have sufficed), and in 1604.[13] At the beginning of the seventeenth century, even the commanders-in-chief were guilty of a very similar type of laxity. In November 1604 the Senate expressly rebuked the *Provveditore dell'Armata* for having abandoned the seas of the Levant and retired straight to Istria. Shortly afterwards Pellegrino Venier was to write that in his opinion the depredations of the pirates had become greatly intensified since the time of the *Provveditore* Pasqualigo, for none of his successors had imitated his bravery and self-denial. 'Anyone leaving the Levant without galleys, as has now been the practice for some time', wrote Venier, 'was bound to suffer new and significant losses all the while.'[14]

Though not apparently the most serious, vanity was not the smallest fault of the Venetian galley commanders. During the period under examination, the command of a galley was a post ardently coveted by Venetian noblemen: it satisfied their innate passion for the sea and their desire to make themselves a reputation. Some, however, could fulfil their ambitions much more easily — by, for example, decorating the poops of their triremes as they thought best and having them painted in their favourite colours. But the most pernicious claim was the demand for new galleys. At the beginning of the seventeenth century a number of very harmful practices had taken root. In order to return to Venice more gloriously, the galley captains would leave the ship they had been using at Crete and take one of the new ones just sent to the Cretan squadron by the Venetian government. But scarcely had the ceremony of returning been completed than the Arsenal took back the galley, which had completed little more than one voyage, stripped it down and disarmed it as though it were an old one. Again, when a captain was no longer satisfied with his trireme, even if it had been at sea for only a few months, he would exchange it for one of the more defective galleys which were ready to be dismantled and get himself sent back to Venice for repairs. After a few vain attempts to put it right, the Arsenal would allow him a new galley of his own choice. It is obvious that this was detrimental to the fleet, but it seems that it could not be remedied either, since in 1613 and 1614 the Senate had to acknowledge that the captains were coming to exchange their galleys very frequently and with little need, but according to their caprices only.[15]

It thus appears that incomplete crews and ill-disciplined commanders were unquestionably typical of the Venetian fleet in these years. This is not the place to dwell on the other abuses which the galley captains did not hesitate to commit, such as engaging men as soldiers but employing them as oarsmen, or depriving crews of soup and wine and giving them only water and biscuit.[16] We can, however, now point out that all this misconduct on the part of the captains was, in its cumulative effect, the chief reason for the inefficiency of the fleet. It was, moreover, the one most difficult to eliminate. Behind the galley captains were their relatives and protectors, in the Senate or even in the government itself. Making his report in 1599, Nicolò Donà had to admit that 'there are also some disorders in that there are noblemen who do not attend or put in an appearance, and everyone shuts his eyes to this, myself more than the rest: for I am not made of stone, and am dependent on offices and recommendations'.[17]

A rather similar impression is conveyed by a despatch prepared by Isidoro Manfredi, an informant of the Grand Duke of Tuscany. In March 1588 the Senate was discussing the powers to be delegated to the Commissioner for auditing the accounts of the fleet. Antonio Cavalli demanded that all the registers should be consigned to him and that he should not return them until he had completed the check. But the squadron commanders and even the *Provveditore dell'Armata* opposed this on the pretext that this was equivalent to giving him the powers of a commander-in-chief. Manfredi commented that 'this may result either in the commission being revoked or in the Commissioner having to proceed so cautiously that he will have to abandon all hope of doing any good. Today', added the agent, 'they are saying that there will be a conflict in the Senate, since the commanders are equipped with many relatives who will oppose these claims to authority, for if they are allowed they would greatly interfere with the plans of the galley captains. For they make such profits out of those who die or are put back and out of passengers that there is nobody who, when his command is finished, does not return home rich, what with his trading and smuggling.'[18]

Certainly this system of abuses — which has been illustrated only in part — would not have been possible without very definite connivance on the part of the authorities. Peace lasted too long and no vital necessity forced the tolerant Senators to turn on the pressure. When the threat from the pirates loomed up at the beginning of the seventeenth century, it was too late — impossible to carry out the reforms which were hastily launched.

During the whole of this period, the Venetian fleet of light galleys consisted of five squadrons in regular service and of a reserve which theoretically consisted of one hundred warships, never to be diminished. In September 1577 it had been decided to keep one hundred hulls for light galleys and a dozen for galleasses ready in the Arsenal. But ten years later, and again in 1604, the Senate itself recognized the fact that the full quota of reserve triremes had never been fitted out. Up to the

THE LIGHT GALLEYS

beginning of the seventeenth century, the policing of Venetian waters and the protection of merchantmen from pirate attacks were committed to a total force of twenty-nine galleys. The *Capitano contro Uscocchi* had to protect the seas off Istria with his five ships (two galleys and three *fuste*). Four galleys were assigned to the Governor of the Condemned for the purpose of patrolling the Northern Adriatic, from Ancona to the Po and from Zara to Fiume. The *Capitano del Golfo*, with his seven galleys, was responsible for all the rest of the Adriatic — two of these, however, were particularly concerned with protecting shipping round the mouth of the Narenta. The largest squadron belonged to the *Provveditore dell'Armata*, whose twelve ships had the most difficult task: the defence of the Ionian sea. Finally, the seas of Crete were to be guarded by the *Capitano della Guardia di Candia*, with four triremes. This was one of the largest regular fleets in the Mediterranean. It was continually being renewed by the senior galley captains returning to Venice to lay down their arms and by others going to replace them the following spring. Their term of service, originally three years, was increased to four in 1587. In addition to this, another four galleys were fitted out at Crete every year and were united to the squadron of the *Provveditore*, but remained there only until the autumn.

Although this was a genuine regular fleet, the ships available during the winter were little more than half as many as in summer. Those who had to return would leave the squadron as early as September, and those coming to join them often did not depart before the summer. The change of commanders had the effect of immobilizing five or six galleys for the greater part of the year. The practice of lending crews, which deprived some to the advantage of others, caused Bernardo Venier to say in 1606: 'Although Your Serenity may think he has twenty-eight sound galleys at his command, at least one-third of these are in fact missing.'[19] But this Venetian admiral knew from personal experience that there were many other reasons for a squadron being all too often deprived of half its forces. The Senate felt no scruples about employing galleys on active duty for the transport of ambassadors, princes or persons of high rank. The galley captains regarded this employment as a pleasing diversion, well calculated to satisfy their desire for ostentation. 'They do things in great style, making a splendid show', reported Nicolò Donà. 'They let no opportunities pass for acquiring honour and spending money. They spend hundreds and thousands of ducats in conveying public personages.'[20] In addition to the practices of disbanding crews and changing captains, the faulty system for renewing supplies of victuals and money frequently made galleys unusable. As we have seen in the first part of this book, it was quite usual for Venetian men-of-war to have to abandon plans for an expedition, or even to break one off because of the lack of provisions. Bernardo Venier, again, was able to do nothing towards the pursuit of the pirates who had captured the *Mazzoca*. The three Barbary *galeotte* which had taken it at the end of July 1605 were on the point of entering the Adriatic together with two *fuste* from Durazzo. The Venetian fleet commander, after heading for Lesina to intercept them, had soon had to retire to Zara because he was almost out of food supplies. None of his ships carried provisions for more than ten or twelve days, and the depots at Lesina and Zara had no supplies. He wrote on 25 August that 'Instead of pursuing these pirates as was my firm intention, I shall be obliged to go and find bread to keep the men alive: for without bread it is impossible to sail'. Only towards mid-September could he get supplies and reinforcements.[21]

Even more serious, in certain respects, was the poor timing of the payments. Biscuit was made at Corfù as well as at Venice, and there were many depots where it could be stored. But money came only from the coffers of the Venetian government. Once the galley captains had consumed the advance payment and subsidy allotted them at their departure, they had to

THE LIGHT GALLEYS

await the arrival of funds from the capital. The geographical situation of Venice could scarcely have been worse from this point of view, since it lay at the extreme end of the elongated area in which the fleet was operating; suffice it to say that even a single galley would take little less than a month to reach Crete. Of the half-million ducats which the Republic spent every year on the squadrons on active service at this time, about half probably had to be transported by sea. The basic pay and food of those who received pay amounted to over 200,000 ducats, while expenditure on biscuit varied between 150,000 and 200,000 ducats. Whether because of the innate slowness of the state in paying its creditors, or because of the difficulty of transporting so much money, it had become a regular habit to distribute pay after a delay of many months. Arrears were dispensed when the ship's company disbanded.

At the end of 1602 a permanent Naval Commissioner was appointed for the purpose of eliminating some of this inconvenience. But, writing to Giust' Antonio Belegno, who had just been elected to this office, the Senate itself admitted on 12 January 1607 that hitherto the payment of galley crews at monthly intervals had not normally been carried out, 'which causes much inconvenience to galley commanders and their crews and likewise interferes with government service, because, as they are not paid, they are often forced to change course and go in search of the Commissioner'.[22] The situation cannot have improved three years later, since the *Capitano del Golfo* thought fit to send in a long despatch concerning the persistent difficulties caused by delays in pay. In addition to those already mentioned, he drew attention to the way in which soldiers and sailors were escaping from the galleys 'and either going to Segna to turn into Uskoks or else to the west ... or else to take to piracy'. Naturally the difficulty of filling these vacancies was increased by the extent to which the fleet lacked the money or credit necessary to engaging new men. 'I should also mention the fact', added Francesco Molin, 'that this delay in payment has frequently given unscrupulous men (and unfortunately there are plenty of them) what I will frankly call a pretext to steal the property of poor people, pleading that they are forced sometimes to connive at the crimes committed by the galley crews because they have nothing with which to feed and support them.'[23] The following year, in his report to the Senate, the *Provveditore dell'Armata* admitted that, in spite of the disorders which we have mentioned, the distribution of pay had become fairly regular immediately after the appointment of the Commissioner, but had later become very slow because of the shortage of money.[24]

Mention has been made elsewhere of another aspect of the problem, which was closely connected with those just described and more than capable of explaining the deterioration in the ranks of the Venetian navy. We have seen that after the battle of Lepanto the process of gradually substituting convict labour for voluntary oarsmen reached its logical conclusion. Though it was only in 1592 that all galleys were manned by convicts, as early as 1580 most of the fleet on active service was relying on manpower plainly inferior to that of thirty years before. The only warships that could stand comparison with those of the previous generation were the galleys of squadron commanders, for they were forbidden to make use of unfree crews. It was natural, therefore, that at the beginning of our period a new problem should have arisen: how to see that each trireme had a number of free and experienced oarsmen sufficient to prevent the vessel from being wholly entrusted to men with chains about their feet, who knew nothing of the trade. About 1580 there were 145 condemned and twenty-eight freemen on each galley — only one freeman for each bench of rowers. At the beginning of 1587 it was decided to reduce the number of benches from 27, 26 or 25 to a fixed quota of 24, at the same time ordaining that each bench should carry four rowers instead of three, 'because this practice has been adopted by all the Princes of the world ... and even by the pirates as well'. On

24 November 1589 the Senate decided that the crew of the light galley should consist of 140 convicts and 53 freemen. In 1593 they finally fixed the numbers at 144 and 48 respectively. Thus, each bench carried one free oarsmen to every three convicts.[25]

The object of this reform was to avoid inequality in the treatment of free oarsmen serving on ships which still had no forced labour, and of those employed on other triremes. It had been noted for some time that the galley captains, in order to induce the increasingly rare volunteers to serve on their galleys, were obliged to entice them with special monetary rewards. At the end of 1581 the subsidy granted to them was raised from 1,500 to 2,500 ducats, whilst the grant to captains of ships using convict labour was fixed at 500 ducats. But from then onwards the situation deteriorated, because the wages paid by the State to the oarsmen and other free members of the crew and of the armed escort remained stationary. By 1 March 1589 Filippo Pasqualigo was complaining in his report of a grave shortage of seamen, officers and petty officers, precisely because the pay was so low that they could not even exist on it. 'Hence', he added, 'they are much readier to try their luck in the service of a foreign Prince and to sail with any sort of ship rather than the galleys of Your Serenity.'[26]

In the course of a few years the problem became so thorny that Nicolò Donà, though not failing to describe it baldly in the Senate, showed that he already regarded it as insoluble. How, he asked, could a galley commander overcome these difficulties in recruiting if he was forced to give double or treble pay to a single person? If he filled one place, two or three others inevitably remained vacant. By this time, oarsmen were daring to demand in advance a retainer fee of thirty or forty gold ducats, making, moreover, 'so many conditions that it is a scandal'. It was inevitable that the crew should thus get into debt to the tune of three, four or even five thousand ducats. The cause lay in the fact that the official rate of pay had remained at the same level for half a century, and the consequences were very serious. 'Men cannot manage on such pay, and hence no more are trained ... and those who remain are wretched, destitute, down and out, failures, men of no account.'[27] The Venetian government displayed a startling inertia and lack of understanding over this matter. The many candid complaints and warnings of the Venetian admirals went unheeded for too long. By finally introducing the convict galleys the state had effected an economy: the subsidy to all the galley captains had descended to 500 ducats, and the gratuity of 1,200 ducats which had been introduced had not proved an adequate compensation. As if satisfied with this result, the government did not intervene until July 1605. It was then decided to 'rouse the spirits of the nobility' with 'some honourable incentive'. The gratuity was raised to 2,000 ducats and the subsidy to 1,365, so that, having received as usual three-and-a-half instalments of pay in advance (some 635 ducats), the galley captains came to dispose of 4,000 ducats in all. Moreover, the Senate, in order to avoid a foreseeable misuse of public funds, at the same time prohibited the gilding of galley poops — work which their captains were still commissioning — and the decoration of any part of the ship with carvings or other expensive adornments.[28]

A rapid glance at the development of this problem in the years which followed justifies the pessimistic prophecies of Donà. Giovanni Pasqualigo, Bernardo Venier and Pietro Bondumier repeated in the Senate that volunteer oarsmen could not live on pay consisting of only 8 lire a month; but in vain. At Venice gangs of braggarts and parasites were formed, of men who pretended to enrol in order to draw the money and to bear arms, but who then, having committed some misdeed, either failed to embark or took themselves off.[29] On the fleet there grew up a custom which was in itself a grave symptom of crisis, whereby the whole crew was considered collectively responsible for the debts of each individual —

especially when somebody deserted. Hence the free oarsmen were reduced to a condition which increasingly resembled that of the convicts, on account of the ever-growing debts which they owed to the captains — a hundred or even two hundred ducats each. 'Which means', remarked Filippo Pasqualigo, 'that these poor wretches, reduced to a much worse state than convicts or slaves, live in despair, full of the wildest thoughts and producing evil results.'[30] To complete the vicious circle: on the one hand, those who wished to free themselves from the obligation to serve as oarsmen by finding substitutes had to disburse sums ruinous to men of their status. On the other, the captains, in view of the incredible rise in their expenses (5,000 ducats for the forty-eight free oarsmen in 1607), asked for, and more and more frequently obtained, permission to demobilize before the end of their term of service. A shortage of soldiers also followed, mainly caused by the extra duties imposed upon them, such as mounting guard over the prisoners at night, answering for any escapes, and sometimes escorting them to distant and mountainous places. The galleys, therefore, were not only left without enough soldiers to defend them from enemy attacks, but had not even enough men to keep order on board ship. The Venetian fleet at the beginning of the seventeenth century was much as Donà had described it at the end of the sixteenth: 'Concerning the navy, the principal force for attack and defence in this state, which to my great astonishment and displeasure I have found and even left in a very different condition from what I saw thirty years ago, I am resolved to say to Your Serenity only that it is suffering from a terrible lack of good sailors, officers, and free and other oarsmen, and in my opinion is ready to collapse in a short time unless it be somehow shored and underpropped.'[31]

The first part of this book showed that, if light galleys were not suitable for pursuing or fighting Uskok boats, they were excellently equipped for hunting *fuste* and Turkish North African *galeotte*. We have mentioned more than one encounter from which the Venetians emerged victorious; and it is certainly generally true that Venetian triremes (unless handicapped by lack of manpower or victuals, or by other misfortunes) never refused battle with pirates, and that whenever they succeeded in engaging them they always emerged either materially or morally the victors. Nonetheless, the deficiencies which have just been described produced serious disadvantages because they prevented the galleys from being in the right place at the right time. Thus the pirates, whose excellent intelligence service was in practice superior to that of the Venetians, could easily avoid the Venetian warships, and all too often succeeded in getting their hands on Venetian merchantmen. Again, we must not forget that the mentality common to all Venetian commanders almost invariably restrained them from joining battle unless they were certain of their superiority to the enemy. They were as prudent and cautious in starting a fight as they were valiant and resolute once it had been launched. But there was another important consideration in the perpetual struggle between the galleys of the Venetian Republic and the Turkish North African pirate ships. Captains and officers, soldiers and crews alike were not only conscious of their own superiority: they also enjoyed very clear prospects of pillaging and dividing the spoils. This was forbidden in theory, but almost never prevented. The booty did not always fulfil the desires of the victors or compensate for the losses sustained in acquiring it. The point was that the prospect existed, and this greatly and perhaps decisively inspired the light galleys to action. On these occasions they interpreted their duty of policing the seas by releasing the Christian slaves, by (as a rule) cutting the Turks to pieces, and by putting all the rest, including the ship itself, up to auction in order to share it out.

But when the light galleys began to find themselves faced

with *bertoni*, whether pirates or mere suspect merchantmen, it was immediately obvious that they were behaving differently, and it is hard to believe that they were not influenced by the motives just discussed. In the struggle against the galleys of Malta and Tuscany, the Venetians — with the exception of Filippo Pasqualigo — had already proved much less aggressive and resolute. The captains knew very well that they could never count on the sale of those ships, and they succeeded in retaining even the least traceable part of the booty only with difficulty and by means of subterfuge. Even the crews were sooner or later repatriated. But the *bertoni* surely provided the most convincing evidence. Most of the admirals were convinced — and there was no lack of proof — that the light galleys were well capable of fighting ships from England and the Netherlands — but, as already pointed out, they hardly ever engaged them. It was no mere coincidence that those who advocated the employment of light galleys against *bertoni* should at the same time have asked for the right to pillage. Pellegrino Venier, having stressed the fact that neither Maltese nor Florentines hesitated to attack the *bertoni* with their galleys (whose artillery was not superior to the Venetian), and that they won marked successes, asserted categorically that 'If they fought on the understanding that whatever a man takes becomes his, the whole sea would soon be swept clean by light galleys alone'.[32] Piero Bondumier, in his capacity of *Provveditore del Collegio della Milizia da Mar*, had already expressed the same opinion, estimating the number of warships needed for the campaign against piracy at precisely five. Giust' Antonio Belegno recalled that in 1603, when ordered to patrol the waters between Sapienza and Cerigo, he had with a few triremes succeeded in stopping five *bertoni*, one after another. Indeed, having encountered one of 800 butts with 120 Turks and 70 Englishmen aboard, he had forced it to surrender after seven hours of fighting, thanks to the cannon on the bows of the galley, whose range was superior to the enemy's. Filippo

Pasqualigo and Agostino da Canal recognized for their part that it was absurd not to risk light galleys in the struggle against the *bertoni* but to let them 'rot away on various pretexts in Istria and in Venice itself'. But all these naval chiefs insisted on the need to grant the triremes rights of ownership in captured pirate ships and also the right to divide the spoils.[33]

It is true that after 1595, when, through the efforts of *bertoni* flying every sort of flag, pirate warfare was becoming really disastrous for the Venetians, the light galleys put up almost no resistance. Certainly we must not forget that these warships were very poorly adapted to taking the sea in winter, the season which such pirates preferred. But the Senate's hesitation to declare them outlaws and therefore fit to be treated like the Barbary Turks notably contributed to the triremes' passive attitude towards them. It also ought to be said that it was difficult for the galley captains to feel in the presence of the *bertoni* that sense of technical superiority which, as far as all other pirate vessels were concerned, was well-founded. The *bertoni*, though of lesser tonnage, had high sides, and it was hard to think of boarding them from the very low-lying hulls of the galleys. And, even when they were only merchantmen and not pirates, it was very difficult to assess the extent of their armaments and the range of their guns. If the *galeotta* (not to mention the *fusta*) was a ship that held few surprises, the *bertone* was almost always an unknown quantity. It was, in fact, extremely hard to discover whether it was a pirate without coming within range of its guns.[34]

We have now attempted to show what were the fundamental problems of the Venetian navy. There is no doubt that after Lepanto the technical and moral strength of the fleet seemed to have been gravely impaired by the inclusion of non-professional seamen in the crews, by the laxity of discipline, and by the negligence of the government in failing to fight energetically its progressive decline. There were unmistakable

THE LIGHT GALLEYS

parallels here to developments in the merchant fleet; on this too the most important influence was the decline in the quality of manpower, though it was linked to more general causes. Venice would scarcely have agreed or found it necessary to recruit convicts for her own galleys in such a wholesale fashion, eventually to the exclusion of all else, if she had not been obliged to withdraw increasingly from the Levant and even from Dalmatia in order to turn to the mainland and involve herself in it: and if she had not resigned herself to so doing. It was inevitable that this general retreat to the mainland on the part of Venetian economy and society should have repercussions on the Venetian navy just as it affected Venetian commerce. As we have seen, there were urgent warnings from those who saw young noblemen increasingly deserting service in the galleys, sailors abandoning their trade or emigrating, and oarsmen taking to flight. It is certain that the various influences we have discussed were beginning to combine with one another in a manner which was dangerous because it was in a certain sense organic and coherent. After various still unrelated symptoms of malaise, there appeared in the last decades of the sixteenth century disorders which were increasingly widespread and interdependent. They were serious enough to reduce the vitality of the entire fleet. Small wonder, then, that the reforms promoted at the beginning of the seventeenth century should produce very limited and disappointing results.[35] On 12 June 1609 the Senate itself admitted the failure of one of the measures which ought to have borne the richest fruits: the appointment of the Commissioner for the Navy. It was generally agreed that there were in the fleet 'many serious abuses no less grave than those that existed before'. Hence this office, which had undoubtedly wounded the feelings of the squadron commanders, was suppressed so that the navy should return 'under the command, protection and control of the naval chiefs and recover its ancient prestige'.[36]

Chapter 7

Galleasses and Galleon

In a report from Venice dated January 1587, we read that 'These gentry wish to arm two great galleys to send them to Crete, the better to ensure a safe passage for their ships'.[1]

Great galleys — or galleasses — were exactly the same shape as light galleys, differing only in their higher sides and greater breadth. This enabled them to carry over a hundred soldiers and an especially large number of guns — about thirty, compared with the trireme's fifteen or so.[2] The entire crew of the galleass consisted of some 500 men. Of the 288 rowers, three-quarters were convicts and the rest freemen. Expenses, too, were very heavy: some 30,000 ducats a year for the flag-ship and at least 25,000 for the others.

The adoption of this type of vessel came slowly. Following the proposals mentioned by the report cited above, the Arsenal set to work. The object was to overcome one disadvantage which would have wholly precluded these ships from taking part in the struggle against the pirates: their excessive slowness. After years of study and experiment, the solution was found: the huge ship no longer needed to be towed, as at Lepanto, and was now capable of keeping pace with a light galley of medium speed. But only in the summer of 1601 was it decided to employ the first two great galleys. A few weeks later, due to 'the many insults and injuries inflicted at this time by various pirate ships', it was ordered that a galleon should be rearmed and immediately placed upon the stocks. This second decree recalled that 'in time of war such ships have proved themselves a stout defence and able to withstand in battle the full force of the Turkish navy', and proclaimed that 'to protect shipping and to enable us to repress the daring insolence of the pirates' it was necessary to fit out a ship 'equal to this task'.[3]

Despite these confident assertions and high-sounding phrases, not all the Senators felt the same enthusiasm for the decisions which had been taken. Before describing the lively debates which ensued, we can at once indicate the chief motive for the Republic's involvement in this new field. From time immemorial, the Venetians had expressed their veneration for large ships and their conviction that these were, in naval operations also, the best means of attack and defence. Suffice it to mention the system of great merchant galleys which they had established in the Mediterranean, and even in the Atlantic, during the fourteenth and fifteenth centuries, or the eager and enthusiastic description of the two *barze* armed against the pirates which Sanudo has left us in his *Diaries*. Sensations of might and wonder, of enthusiastic appreciation of strength and beauty, came over them. More than once, indeed, and at decisive moments, the great ships of the Venetian Republic had distinguished themselves brilliantly on the field of battle. Time had created a tradition and a legend — men who had fought at Lepanto could scarcely fail to become one.

It was in vain that Nicolò Balbi later sought to change the minds of those who, in his opinion, too easily surrendered to these views. 'The loss of a great galley', he wrote, 'would not only entail the loss of a very important ship, of most excellent and valuable artillery, and of the crew with which it was manned: this famous ship would in a sense lose its virginity by rousing the hostile desires of all foreign Princes. What is more, it would serve as a model for the construction of others, a thing which the Princes have all attempted but never understood or completed.'[4] Nicolò Contarini in his *Histories* recalls the vain efforts of the opponents of the scheme and the unshakeable obstinacy of the majority in the Senate in voting for the return of the galleasses — 'they scarcely wished to listen to those who spoke against it'. It would be hard to quote better testimony than this. Though an opponent of their use against pirates, he could still write: 'Truly, when you saw them sailing with their castles towering above the sea, they seemed like moving fortresses: and it was said to be the unique achievement of the Republic to build floating fortresses, for every expert in sea warfare assured us that no ship, no matter how heavily armed, could possibly have compared with them.'[5]

There was perhaps even greater enthusiasm for the galleon. We have already seen this in the decree for rearmament: significantly enough, orders were given for the galleon to be fitted out and constructed on the 1537 pattern. 'Most noble ship', 'most celebrated', 'most excellent': these were but a few of the adjectives habitually used to describe it. Filippo Pasqualigo, then supreme commander of the fleet, could say that 'The armed galleon is the finest and noblest structure that one could ever see'.[6] The Venetians were prepared to say aloud of the galleon what they probably only thought or hoped for of the galleasses: they believed, in fact, that it had only to take the sea for the pirates to disperse. This paradoxical belief can best be illustrated by the words of a very high-ranking naval authority, Girolamo da Molin, *Presidente del Collegio della Milizia da Mar*. He wrote in March 1605 that 'The mere rumour that the galleon has put to sea (for such is the reputation it enjoys in the minds of all men, even while it lies, still unfinished, in the shipyard) will strike such terror into the hearts of the pirates that they will find it in their own best interests to take to other pursuits and leave the sea in peace. This stratagem will serve Your Serenity better than driving them off the sea by force, since the damage which the pirate ships would suffer at the hands of our fleets might well provoke complaints and remonstrances, to the discomfiture of the government.'[7] Shortly afterwards Nicolò Donà, a man endowed with some critical sense, could thus announce the launching of the galleon: 'For the happy future of this great ship, calling upon the name and help of God, on whom the success of every operation depends, be it ordained that at the launching ... the ship shall be blessed at a solemn ceremony of the Church, with musical instruments making the air resound with a mighty chorus of joy, in the presence of the *Serenissima Signoria* and all the most excellent *Collegio* — things which will greatly enhance our fame and reputation in war.'[8]

These remarks have been quoted only for the purpose of emphasizing the irrational and illogical streak in the mentality of the Venetians. At least fourteen years passed between the formulation and the execution of the original proposal to employ the great galleys, and six more years were needed to bring the arming of the galleon to completion. Thus the Republic, in spite of the urgent need for remedies, wasted precious time waiting for its immense ships, which would miraculously put everything right, to take the sea. When they finally did so, there was, as we shall see, a certain diminution of the number of pirate attacks. But this can be interpreted as resulting as much from the sharp reduction in trade and in the number of merchantmen engaged in it as from the activities of the Venetian Republic's new weapons of war. It is certain that the Venetians did not take account of the perilous change in pirate warfare since the *bertoni* had gone into action. Their understanding of piracy had been wholly inadequate even during the sixteenth century, and it would not be unduly rash to suggest that their ideas on the subject dated from the fifteenth. The Senate's decision at the beginning of the seventeenth century to arm galleasses and galleons was, indeed, closely parallel to that of the end of the fifteenth, to launch *barze* for the purpose of pursuing pirates.[9] These new tactics of the Venetians were in reality inspired by an obsolete mentality which invited failure. We shall now see how almost all the faults that reduced the effectiveness of the light galleys imposed similar limitations on the great galleys. As for the galleon, its only campaign spectacularly demonstrated that it was not worthwhile risking it at sea a second time in order to repress pirate warfare.

Going into action in the summer of 1608, this 'great ship' of 800 butts had, by 19 December 1609, already come to be laid up. Before it emerged from the Arsenal, even the agent of the Grand Duke of Tuscany was describing it as 'a ship of wondrous size, soundness and beauty'.[10] The cost, at first estimated at about 20,000 ducats a year, in fact exceeded 43,000. It failed to fulfil many other expectations – concerning, for example, its speed and its ability to pursue any pirate ship. As its captain, the valiant Giust' Antonio Belegno, subsequently explained in the Senate, 'This most noble ship is extraordinarily fast for its size, but it is not entirely free from the disadvantages from which every roundship must needs suffer'. In other words, if the galleon one morning discovered a ship twenty miles away, a slight calm or a contrary wind would be enough to make it useless for pursuit. In the first case, there was not enough sail to move the huge bulk fast enough; in the second, the fugitive found itself to windward, and thus still more favourably placed for flight. Indeed, if a pirate were to be overtaken before nightfall (which, nine times out of ten, would give him the opportunity to escape), the wind had to blow briskly behind the galleon throughout the whole day. Belegno could only propose that it should be accompanied by smaller and faster craft capable of engaging the enemy and delaying his flight.[11] During the seventeen months of its mission, this great engine of war, armed with as many as seventy-six guns, had been kept at sea almost continuously to escort merchant shipping in the waters of the Levant, Cyprus and Crete. However, its captain realized that it was dangerous to keep it in winter near the great trouble-spot for pirate ambushes — which lay between Cerigo, Sapienza and Crete — because that region was open to powerful winds capable of blowing it a long distance away.[12]

All these difficulties had been clearly foreseen by Tommaso Morosini, and he had set them out in a memorandum addressed to the Signoria in July 1605. The one consolation, which Belegno did not fail to offer to the Senate, lay in the confident belief that in a genuine naval battle, 'placing itself in the fore-front of the other ships', the galleon might act 'like a formidable floating fortress'. But pirate warfare was now almost entirely precluding the classic encounters between powerful squadrons, and it was necessary to think of some other way of employing the mighty ship. Moreover, a technical problem was arising. The galleon should have had its keel overhauled every year, but this would have increasingly weakened its hull, and the expense of such an operation would have exceeded that of covering it with lead, which could last for about ten years. The Senate was convinced that this second procedure, used by western ships for voyages to the Indies, and also by Ragusans, was preferable: but the matter was allowed to drag on indefinitely. The galleon stayed in dry dock for two years before it was decided to cover it with lead, and only in April 1611 did the Arsenal acquire the materials necessary for making the metal sheets with which it had to be covered. After further delays, the ship was finally hired by the shipowner Balbi for the purpose of transporting merchandise. But on 24 March 1615, after two hours of conflict with a *bertone* from Tunis, when it was about to get the upper hand, the galleon's powder magazine caught fire and it went to the bottom in the waters of Cyprus.[13]

The Venetians had already suffered a similar disappointment on the return of the great galleys from their first campaign against the pirates. This had lasted some twenty-two months, in 1602–03, and much of this time had been spent at Corfù, waiting for sick crews to get well again. When the men had recovered, in spite of numerous appeals for aid against the *bertoni*, the galleasses had been unable to put to sea because of the foul weather. When they finally left for the Levant, they entered the Archipelago and circled the island of Crete without once catching sight of a pirate. In the whole of their voyage they succeeded in subjugating only two *bertoni*. In his report, the squadron commander, Girolamo Contarini, could only declare that if he had been able to accomplish no more it was by the will of God. Moreover, the reservations which the Senate had introduced into their sailing orders for the galleasses had made their activities less energetic and effectual. For the whole of the year 1604 they remained inactive at Venice, and at the beginning of 1605 the discussion about using them against the pirates was reopened on a grand scale.[14]

The only alternative — favoured by many seafaring men — seemed to be to do as the pirates did and to arm *bertoni* against *bertoni*. The use of these ships had in fact been suggested from 1601 onwards by the shipowner Francesco Morosini, who especially praised their capacity for carrying three rows of cannon, one above the other. But in 1605 the champions of the galleasses again received a hearing. Piero Bondumier, a member of the *Collegio della Milizia da Mar*, held that they should not have recourse to *bertoni*, 'so as not to give rise to any belief in the world at large that this Most Serene Republic, which ... has for thousands of years remained mistress of the seas with ships from her highly esteemed and celebrated Arsenal, is now reduced to having to provide herself with foreign ships in order to serve her needs'.[15] Very similar arguments, inspired by the same human considerations and by stubborn nationalism, were advanced by Lorenzo Venier.

Girolamo Molin went even further: 'Even if this measure were certain of success', he wrote, 'I should still not like it: for it would lead the world to believe that our Republic was forced to buy foreign ships in order to supply its needs.'[16] However, there were some rather more substantial reasons for opposing the employment of *bertoni*. It was suspected that those fitted out at Venice would not prove to be of the same calibre as those of the pirates. Bondumier did not hesitate to specify ('and I am sorry that it should be so') that it was impossible to find anywhere in the Venetian dominions seamen equal to the English or the Flemish, especially as the Venetians would have been mere hirelings, whilst all the pirates were personally interested in the activities of their ship and in its booty. The *Cinque Savi alla Mercanzia* claimed that the estimated annual cost of four *bertoni* — 60,000 ducats — was too great: the merchants would not be able to contribute so much, especially as their business 'was diminishing and falling into the hands of foreigners'.[17] On 30 April 1605, therefore, the Senate felt itself entitled to conclude that for the protection of shipping and the extermination of the pirates there was no surer method, and none likely to produce better results, than the employment of galleasses.

Opponents of the great galleys returned to the attack two years later, trying to make the most of the grave defects which they had once more revealed. In August 1607 the Commissioner for the Navy, Giust' Antonio Belegno, declared that the four such warships then on duty were ill-furnished with oarsmen, soldiers and even with gunners and sailors. Moreover, it would have been little use sending them other men, because it was very rare for new recruits to turn out well there. He therefore proposed to reduce the squadron and to substitute two galleys and two *bertoni* for the great galleys. In a memorandum addressed to Giovanni Bembo, the other fleet commanders expressed even more radical views. They maintained that neither light nor great galleys were suited to fighting pirate *bertoni* and that not even the galleon would be capable of overtaking them. The only possible solution was to employ ships of the same type against the *bertoni*.[18] It is not surprising to find among the signatures that of Filippo Pasqualigo, who as early as 1605 had drawn attention to the inability of the galleasses to remain for long periods at sea, and to the fact that it was impossible in winter for the crews, 'being out in the open, to withstand the cold and the accidents and injuries inflicted by the weather, as well as the other innumerable discomforts that used very frequently to bring these poor wretches to their death or at least to very prolonged sickness'.[19] It is interesting, however, to see the name of Pietro Bondumier, who had shortly before expressed such a different opinion: firsthand experience as *Provveditore dell'Armata* had certainly helped to convince him of the soundness of the arguments which he had formerly opposed.

Many others campaigned with no less energy against the great galleys. Tommaso Morosini, then a member of the *Collegio della Milizia da Mar*, had written very prudently in 1605 that although their hulls were very stoutly built they were so low that waves washed over the top of them. If that happened they were unable to keep the protective awnings spread out, because the sea would have torn them to pieces; the crews, therefore, were inevitably drenched, with serious effects upon their health. Nicolò Balbi, who shared the same opinion, repeated these objections in 1607, and added that even the oars would be unable to withstand the ferocity of the waves.[20] Nicolò Donà drew up a formidable indictment against these ships, since it seemed to him that from every point of view they were ill-equipped for the battle against the *bertoni*. To those who objected that at one time the great merchant galleys had been capable of sailing in winter, he replied that those were other times and different men. Then everybody had a stake in the success of the voyage, and also a change of clothing. Now the crews were composed of 'poor, naked wretches, deprived even of their proper rations, drenched by the rain above and the sea below, without even a change of raiment. Often the very bread that they have to eat is soaked. They have little rest, because the sail has at intervals to be raised or lowered, and they are always busy with some task, so that in a little while they fall down and die.' Donà added that a round ship or one with high sides, like the galleon or the *bertone*, could carry victuals for many months and water for a whole year, but the galleass had to replenish its water supply at least every fifteen days. Again, on the galleon and *bertone*, the crew could sleep and rest — but not on the galleass. The great galleys needed calm weather to pursue pirates, and this was rare in the months in which they operated. Again, when it came to a fight, the galleass could triumph only thanks to its guns, but even a slight swell, let alone a rough sea, was sufficient to make their aim inaccurate. The *bertone* would always prove more manœuvrable, for the galleys 'are equipped with lugsails, their sails are inordinately large, the yards very heavy, and their seamen sluggish and perhaps scared out of their wits, and before they can move the sails the *bertone* can slip away from them so far as to reach safety'. Psychologically, too, the Venetians were at a disadvantage. 'It is sheer foolhardiness and tempting Providence', thundered Donà, 'to take soldiers to sea to fight high and low in the open against those who are completely covered by the decks above them. With due respect, this is a venture which should never be undertaken. . . . Nor do I think that any captain should ever think of boarding a roundship like the *bertone*, manned by pirates, from a great galley, even if he has two of them: he would undoubtedly come out of it badly.' In conclusion, Donà expressed a wish that the great galleys should be 'kept locked up, to be used only on great occasions'.[21]

This uncompromising stand was all the more justified in that the galleasses continued to produce such poor results. The three warships that the Senate had decided to send out against the pirates under the command of Lorenzo Venier had indeed left Venice in July 1606, but they had achieved nothing worth while in the whole year. They had, in fact, restricted themselves to sailing to Zara, only to return subsequently to Istria. The opposition of the best qualified naval commanders to the employment of the great galleys eventually succeeded in the summer of 1607, when the Senate finally decided to fit out four *bertoni*. But their triumph did not last. On 14 August the decree was annulled. 'Experience has shown', so runs the preamble, 'that it is impossible to execute this very useful decree adequately on account of the shortage from which this city is suffering of ships capable of the task.'[22] This was the result of an inspection being held in the harbours of Venice to see whether there were any *bertoni* that could be employed in the campaign against piracy. It had been impossible to find even as many as four, among Venetian-owned and foreign-owned ships. Hence it was thought necessary to rescind the decree, which had obtained the support of Cristoforo da Canal and Lorenzo Venier, as well as of the personages mentioned above. There was no attempt to buy other *bertoni* in Holland, which would have been easy. The prejudices described above now proved to be insurmountable: rather than make use of efficient ships of foreign build, they preferred to rely on Venetian vessels, even if these were ill-adapted to repressing the pirate war. The *bertoni* and their supporters took their revenge ten years later — a bitter blow to the Republic. From 1616 onwards ships of this type laden with soldiers began to flow into Venice: this was the aid which Venice had asked of the Protestant powers in order to face the threat from the Habsburgs of Austria and Spain. The naval operations of the following years were dominated by the presence of these northern *bertoni* in the Venetian fleet. In the summer of 1618, there were already eight English and twelve Dutch *bertoni*, and the Venetians were about to ask for at least another ten. Thus at the beginning of 1619 the Venetian navy consisted of fifty galleys and of an equal number of *bertoni* and galleons, with one or two galleasses. After losing the battle against the pirates, they finally resorted to pirate ships in order to defend their state in danger. A new era was beginning — we must stop on its threshold.

We have now only to examine the performance of the squadron of great galleys and the results of their campaigns. Dangers to shipping were so great that it was almost useless to think of providing against them: 'for', according to a report from Venice, 'this port is going to ruin and its business with it'.[23] The first compulsory convoys were formed — hitherto so strongly opposed by the merchants — but the monthly cost of a ship armed for escort duties had risen from about 1,500 ducats in 1601 to over 2,500 in 1607. At the beginning of 1608 the Senate was deciding to employ even galleasses more for the protection of merchant shipping than for the pursuit of *bertoni*. In spite of this, in December 1609 it was necessary to admit that 'the injuries suffered by the government and by private subjects of ours on account of the many losses they have sustained through ships being either wrecked or captured by pirates are so grave, and the decay of trade because of the insecurity of shipping is now so obvious' that on all routes to the Levant convoys must become compulsory.[24] The following year the *Cinque Savi alla Mercanzia* even tried to have two galleasses converted from warships into merchant galleys in order to employ them on the Syrian route. But the Senate persisted in its determination to divide them into two squadrons of two ships each to carry on the campaign against the pirates.[25]

These warships achieved their most brilliant success in March 1608. Lorenzo Venier, who the previous year had succeeded only in arresting the merchant *bertone* of Richard Harris in the waters of Navarino, then had the good fortune to take the two ships under Captain Casten by surprise. The larger of these was of 600 butts and was carrying thirty guns in addition to many soldiers. The famous pirate was killed in the fight. Shortly afterwards, Francesco Morosini succeeded to the command of the great galleys, and they allowed a pirate *bertone* from La Rochelle to escape them, though they did succeed in freeing a Cretan galleon which this *bertone* had captured. Later they were unable to prevent the capture of the *Doria* on its way to Smyrna, even though the *bertoni* attacked it at Cerigo whilst the galleasses lay at Crete. A contrary wind sufficed to stop them from emerging in time from the harbours of that island.[26] In the autumn of 1610 the Venetian squadron ventured as far as Syria in order to escort two ships, the *Mula* and the *Tizzona*; but in his report to the Senate Morosini expressed disapproval of such voyages. Not being openly at war with the pirates of Malta, Tuscany and other Catholic nations, Venetian warships were in danger of being caught in the middle between them and the Turks. Either they attacked the Catholics without justification, or they failed to comply with the clauses of the treaty of friendship with the Turks. The Venetian admiral suggested leaving the field open to the Knights of St John and St Stephen. They would have done their best to drive all other pirates away from that region. At the end of his tour of duty, the commander of the great galleys was unable to refer to the capture of one single pirate vessel. By way of compensation, he drew up a long list of ships he had escorted, claiming that in the course of nearly four years only four vessels had been plundered in his area, and two of these had been recovered by Venetian squadrons.[27]

Compared with the last years of the sixteenth century and the first of the seventeenth, the situation at sea therefore appeared to show marked improvement, thanks to the employment of the great galleys. Members of the *Collegio della Milizia da Mar*, in a memorandum of August 1611, maintained that shipping was already showing signs of picking up, that insurance premiums had been reduced, and even that the merchant fleet was being rebuilt. But there was no general agreement. Some, like Nicolò Donà, Teodoro Balbi, Antonio Bragadin and Tommaso Morosini, retorted that the cost of the galleasses had proved to be enormous. They had already swallowed up 800,000 ducats, 'a loss far greater than any profit one might have hoped to obtain, let alone actually received, from their services'.[28] The argument of these men and of Alessandro Contarini and Iseppo Michiel finally won the day, and the number of galleasses was reduced to two. The Senate, having approved the advice of Francesco Morosini not to send the great galleys any more into Syrian waters, no doubt held that, if it was necessary to abandon attempts to repress pirate warfare, two great galleys would be sufficient to patrol the stretch of sea between Cerigo and Sapienza. However, controversy over the value of employing them had not died down, but the Venetian Republic had now recognized that these 'most noble vessels', though they might be supremely useful in a naval battle, were really not adapted to suppressing the daring insolence of the pirates.[29]

This conclusion was reached in Venice after many years of stubborn attempts to make use of great galleys to withstand piracy. As already indicated, the operation of these warships could not escape being affected by the deficiencies of the entire Venetian naval system. It is, however, necessary to examine more closely the difficulties they encountered, against which all the efforts of the Venetian government eventually proved in vain.

Unlike the light galleys, and even after a number of severe trials, the great galleys did not suffer chiefly from a weakness in their crews. In 1607 and 1608 their commanders were still speaking of the 'great lassitude and poor quality' of the oarsmen, and of their inadequate numbers. On his arrival at Corfù, Francesco Morosini described them as 'tattered, mangy and diseased, so that they look like lost creatures'.[30] But complaints of this sort afterwards ceased and were heard no more. The Senate decided to issue the crews with clothing for winter and summer. After a considerable delay, they were provided with awnings as well. Complaints of an opposite sort began to be uttered instead, with the commanders protesting against the other hindrances which immobilized their ships even after so much had been spent on providing them with rowers 'of the highest calibre'.[31] Likewise, the troubles connected with the irregular and slow distribution of pay appeared to be serious only at the beginning, and subsequently disappeared almost completely. Thus in April 1607 Lorenzo Venier and Antonio Ciuran left Venice without funds and lay up for a long time in Istria because the Senate did not wish to hand the money over directly but to send it with the Commissioner for the Navy, and the two commanders did not know when to meet him. A year later Venier protested against the order to escort the convoy for Syria, which had reached him whilst he lay at Zante with no money: eight months' pay was already owing to his squadron. At the end of 1609, when the new commander was ordered to leave Corfù for the Levant, he answered that he had not the means of doing so. The pay had not yet arrived, 'and without it is impossible to set sail, because everyone knows that no private person (to say nothing of myself) has enough to maintain so large a number of men, since it is necessary to spend at least 2,000 ducats a month'.[32]

This argument of Morosini's throws light on another aspect of his conduct also: the particular way in which he considered himself obliged to carry out his orders. Certainly, these incidents were more widespread, since Pellegrin Venier could say in 1607 that 'for some time now there has been a certain kind of mild disobedience, with men saying: "I will not obey unless I receive further orders, since the most excellent decrees can on account of the delay in reaching us cease to be of value to the service of the state" '.[33] It is quite usual to find in the despatches of Morosini replies in which the Senate's instructions are treated as conditional imperatives. 'If', wrote Morosini from Corfù to the Doge, 'if you wish me too to fit out my galley to escort the ship, may it please you to send me the provisions I have listed, and I will at once set my men to work, for I certainly cannot put to sea like this without very obvious danger'.[34] It was not surprising that on his return to Venice Morosini had to defend himself against charges of insubordination. This he did with some spirit, recalling all the orders and counter-orders with which he had had to deal during his tenure of command.

Things were not always as simple as they looked from Venice. When Paolo Tiepolo was ordered to proceed to the Levant, no matter what repairs the galleasses needed, he, though promptly replying that he had left Corfù, specified that the other great galley in his squadron was leaking to such an extent that it could scarcely put to sea. In the autumn of 1609, at Corfù, certain parts of the great galley *Valiera* were discovered to be rotten, and in June 1611 Antonio Pisani wrote from his ship that 'she can scarcely stand up to the slightest roughness on the sea, and the whole ship shudders and shakes at the buffets and blows of the sea, thus clearly revealing her age and weakness, and I am especially worried that she may give me dangerous trouble when there is occasion to use the guns'.[35] After eight years of service Tiepolo's great galley was in such a state that the nails were no longer holding; and on that of Giustiniano Morosini, which had been at sea for five years without a proper overhaul, it was necessary to work continually at the pumps. But the Senate attached little importance to the fact that it was absolutely necessary for these ships to be caulked every year. This could be done only at Corfù, since the harbours of Crete were too unprotected and that of Candia was not deep enough. The squadron commanders preferred to carry out this operation in April and May, at the time when the *bertoni* were returning from their raids in the Levant. Repairs to each galley consumed many days, and it was impossible to get two of them caulked at the same time because of the shortage of labour. The workmen, having little experience of such ships, worked slowly and inefficiently. Delicate situations arose in this way, like the one mentioned by Paolo Tiepolo in November 1616. 'Here I am constantly on the alert', he wrote from Sapienza, 'in all matters relating to my office, and am always looking out for these galleasses, which for lack of repairs are leaking extensively.'[36]

There was yet another defect of this kind, no less serious and indeed quite astonishing, in the exasperating and incomprehensible slowness of Venice to meet requests for materials and tools. The great galleys were much more dependent than light galleys on the Venetian Arsenal for replacements: everything, from planks to cables, from nails to masts, had to come from Venice. The Arsenals of the Levant had none of these things, for such warships had not been at sea in their area for several decades. And now nothing was done to remedy this anomaly. Although everything cost twice as much in Venice, lack of materials continued to immobilize the squadrons of the great galleys for long spells at a time. In 1605 Filippo Pasqualigo, in his report as Commissioner for the Navy, had vainly informed the Senate of the need to accumulate reserves of materials and spare parts in the Levant. In his report for 1608 the squadron commander Lorenzo Venier was to return vigorously to this point, but always in vain. Ludicrous situations arose as a result for many years afterwards. A great galley, which had left Venice in obedience to the Senate's orders, would then lie up for three months in Istria awaiting the materials necessary for caulking. Another, which had neither cables nor oars, would be obliged to wait for them at Corfù from the middle of March to the end of June. Eventually its commander would discover that they had been sent to Crete. It was little use for the squadron commander to send in his requests a considerable time in advance. Before replacements came, he would receive orders to do things which he was in no condition to undertake. His protests were regularly made every year about the month of September, on the eve of the winter campaign against piracy. He could only declare, with bitter irony, that 'the needs are the same, they have never been fulfilled; on the contrary, they are increasing'. No wonder that, in giving an account of his tenure of command, Francesco Morosini should at a full session of the Senate deliver the following scathing judgment on the past: 'The lack of provisions, mooring-cables, oars and other equipment... has become almost commonplace. In spite of making many respectful representations about this, I have always been kept very short, for I never received supplies less than seven or eight months after urgently demanding them.'[37] But for his successors there was virtually no change. Antonio Pisani and Paolo Tiepolo continued to beg for consignments of oars. Meanwhile the merchantmen lost many precious weeks waiting for the great galleys to be in a position to escort them. In 1608, after waiting in vain for three months at Corfù, the ships left alone for the Levant. In August 1611 the slowness with which the great galleys were being repaired was such that the *Tizzona* decided to proceed to Syria without an escort. Because of the great galleys' lack of victuals or of oars, the pirates were able to ply back and forth all round the Morea, and frequent the harbour of Modone to their own advantage.[38]

Conclusion

Viewing as a whole the picture which has been rapidly sketched, it is possible to claim originality for the period we have examined. Venice has provided the opportunity to examine in detail, in a particular sphere, the mechanism of pirate warfare and the extent of its impact on the maritime organization of the Venetian Republic. It is clear that from 1580 onwards pirate warfare was gradually, but at the same time profoundly, changing its character throughout the Mediterranean. The religious aspect of it undoubtedly took second place, giving way to a system of sea robbery dependent on very specific political and social forces, and obeying equally explicit rules. The long period of official peace, or rather the decline of the classic form of sea warfare, gave the primacy to a type of conflict from which practically no region of the Mediterranean escaped.

To this day, the Barbary corsairs have always been considered the archetypal Mediterranean pirates — almost the only pirates known to history; and so Algiers has been regarded as almost the only base for piracy. It would now be a mistake to consider the operations of the Knights of Malta or of St Stephen or those of innumerable Spanish, French, Dutch and

CONCLUSION

English ships as being essentially different. Previously, it was well-known that the manpower of Barbary was recruited from Christian nations almost as much as from Islamic peoples — not only the crews of the *galeotte*, but also their captains. By stressing the decisive contribution in ships and manpower which was made to them especially by the English, we have attempted to trace more accurately the features of pirate warfare at this time. This is also well revealed by the policy of the Grand Dukes of Tuscany and the Duke of Savoy, who threw themselves without hesitation into this Hobbesian *bellum omnium contra omnes*.

Without doubt, no seapower felt this impact so gravely as the Venetian Republic. Hence our desire to make a first specific examination of its naval forces, of ships and men and their organization. It may appear that their weaknesses, errors and deficiencies have sometimes been overstressed. But it has seemed necessary to do this in order to reveal the elements of a crisis. We cannot, indeed, describe and seek to understand only the origins and growth of new forces, and concern ourselves with a state only when it is rising to power or at the height of its development. One must know likewise how and when the founts of its energies diminish, and how its long-established structures face up to certain moments of crisis, so that the will and intelligence of ruling classes and *élites* fail to prevent these crises or to arrest their dramatic development.

Glossary

NOTE Unless otherwise stated, the descriptions of ships are based on the account given in Pantero Pantera, *L'armata navale* (Rome, 1614), Book I, ch. iv, pp. 40–8; cf. also H. and R. Kahane and A. Tietze, *The lingua franca in the Levant: Turkish nautical terms of Italian and Greek origin* (Urbana, Illinois, 1958). The translators wish to thank Miss Susan Skilliter for her valuable help in compiling this glossary.

Bertone: a tall, very broad ship with high sides, three masts, seven sails and sometimes one small additional sail at the prow, square-rigged, with two decks. Its capacity was estimated by Pantera at 1,500 to 3,000 *salme*. According to Tenenti, the capacity of an average *bertone* was some 500 butts, and that of the largest *bertone* no more than 800 (see p. 64). The name is probably a corruption of Breton or Briton.

Brazzera: a small boat used by the Uskoks, deriving its name from the island of Brazza, see p. 6. A modern dictionary of nautical terms describes the *brazzera* as a small two-masted boat propelled both by sail and oar, with six rowers and a steersman. (*Dizionario di marina medievale e moderna*, Rome, Reale Accademia d'Italia, 1937, p. 101.)

Brigantine or *bergantino:* a small, very fast boat more used by Turks than Christians – a miniature version of the *galeotta*, which it essentially resembled. One deck and a single sail; 8–16 benches, with one oarsman at each.

Butt or *botta:* a measure both of weight and capacity, roughly equivalent to 0.725 freight tons or about 29 English cubic feet. F. C. Lane, *Venetian ships and shipbuilders of the Renaissance* (Baltimore, Maryland, 1934), discusses at pp. 246–9 the problems of estimating the *botta* and translating it into modern terms.

Cadi: a Muslim district judge. A province of the Ottoman Empire, governed by a *Sancak*, was subdivided into a number of judicial districts, in each of which a *Cadi* presided. (H. A. R. Gibb and H. Bowen, *Islamic society and the West*, 2 vols., Oxford, 1950–57, I, pp. 153–4.)

Capitano: commander of a naval squadron. For the duties of the various commanders, see p. 121.

Caramousal: a very light and manœuvrable ship used in the Levant, long and narrow, with a single deck, a tall stern and not more than five sails. The freight capacity was 1,000–1,500 *salme*.

Chiaus: the Çavuses were officials employed in the Ottoman Empire, sometimes as guards and attendants, and sometimes as ushers in the courts of the Grand Vizier. (Gibb and Bowen, *op.cit.*, I, pp. 87, 349–50.)

Cinque Savi alla Mercanzia: the Venetian Board of Trade, a magistracy with five members or 'sages', originally founded as a temporary measure in 1506 and permanently established in 1517. (A. Da Mosto, *L'Archivio di Stato di Venezia*, 2 vols., Rome, 1937–40, I, pp. 196–7.)

Collegio della Milizia da Mar: a Board created in the mid-sixteenth century to take charge of the fleet of 100 light galleys which the Senate had resolved to build for the defence of the Adriatic. This body dealt with recruiting and with the equipment of galleys in general. (Da Mosto, *op.cit.*, I, p. 199.)

Crown: between 1609 and 1629 the crown or *scudo* was valued by decrees of the Venetian Senate at 8–9 silver lire. (N. Papadopoli-Aldobrandini, *Le monete venete descritte ed illustrate*, vols. II and III, Venice, 1907–19, III, pp. 1003, 97, 98; G. Mandich, 'Formule monetarie veneziane del periodo 1619–1650', *Studi in onore di*

GLOSSARY

Armando Sapori, II, Milan, 1957, pp. 656–7 — also in *Il Risparmio*, V, 1957.)

Ducat: the Venetian ducat of account was equivalent to 6 lire and 4 *soldi*: each lira consisted of 20 *soldi*, so that 124 *soldi* were equivalent to one ducat of account. The silver equivalent of the gold ducat or *zecchino* changed in the course of the sixteenth and early seventeenth century: it rose in 1584 from 8 lire 12 *soldi* to 9 lire 12 *soldi*, and in 1619 stood at 12 lire 8 *soldi*. (Papadopoli-Aldobrandini, *op.cit.*, II, pp. 356, 750–1; III, pp. 97, 1004.)

Feluca: a small Islamic craft, sometimes described as 'a boat of European model'. (Kahane and Tietze, *The lingua franca*, etc., cit., pp. 211–13.) A light, very swift vessel with a single sail and 6–10 oars.

Frigate or *fregata:* rather similar to the brigantine, but with a lower stern. A single sail; 6–12 oars.

Fusta: a smaller version of the galley and *galeotta*. According to instructions left by a Venetian galley-builder of the mid-sixteenth century, a Venetian *fusta* was then $88\frac{1}{2}$ feet long from stem to sternpost, 13 feet wide and $4\frac{1}{2}$ feet deep from freeboard to keel. The corresponding measurements for a light galley were 131 feet, $16\frac{1}{2}$ feet and $5\frac{1}{2}$ feet (B. Landström, *The ship*, London, 1961, pp. 132–3.) According to Tenenti, Barbary *fuste* had on average about fifteen ranks of rowers, with two galleots to an oar, see p. 19.

Galeotta: a small galley with 17–23 or 24 benches. In North Africa, many genuine galleys were superficially disguised as *galeotte* in order to escape the duty of serving the Sultan. See also p. 19.

Galleass or *great galley:* an enlarged version of the light galley. Pantera describes this as being almost a third as long again as the light galleys and proportionately broader. In the mid-sixteenth century, measurements of a great galley were: length, 151 feet, breadth $24\frac{1}{2}$ feet and depth 10 feet. The corresponding measurements of a light galley were then 131 feet, $16\frac{1}{2}$ feet and $5\frac{1}{2}$ feet. Landström, *op.cit.*, see pp. 130–5 for reconstructions of the sixteenth-century galley and galleasses.

Galleon: a three-masted, square-rigged vessel, longer and faster than the roundship, with two and occasionally three decks. The

GLOSSARY

freight capacity was normally 2–5,000 *salme*, but occasionally as much as 12,000.

Galley: a long, narrow single-decked craft powered by sail and oar, normally with 26–30 benches of oarsmen. See Part II, chapter 6 of this book.

Germa: a Levantine freighter, with four enormous sails, one deck and a capacity of 1,000–1,500 *salme*.

Governatore delle Forzate: commander of the convict galleys. For his duties, see p. 121.

Lira: see ducat.

Marciliana: smaller than the roundship or galleon, with a more massive and a rounder prow, six square sails and one lateen sail, two decks, and a freight capacity of 2,500–3,000 *salme*.

Migliaio: a thousandweight, equivalent to 1050 English pounds. (Lane, *Venetian ships*, p. 248.)

Nave: most of the merchant ships not otherwise described in the pages of this book were roundships or *navi*. The prow and sides were rounded, flattening out at the poop, with high castles. There were two or three decks, and the cargo was kept on the lowest deck. These were the largest merchantmen, with a capacity of 3–10,000 *salme*.

Orca: very similar to a *marciliana*.

Provveditore: a general-purpose term for a Venetian magistrate or high-ranking officer on land or sea. This was applied to magistrates who held office in Venice itself, like the *Provveditori e Patroni all' Arsenale:* a magistracy of medieval origin, consisting of three *Patroni* and two or three *Provveditori*, responsible for the custody of the Arsenal and for reporting to the *Collegio* or Cabinet on its activities. From 1565, they formed part of the Arsenal's governing body, the *Collegio sopra l'Arsenale*. (Da Mosto, *L'Archivio di Stato*, I, p. 160.) Governors of certain Venetian possessions, e.g. Zante, were also known as *Provveditori*. Among naval officers, the *Provveditore generale in Golfo* was the admiral appointed in 1592 to fight the Uskoks, and the *Provveditore dell'Armata* was the squadron-commander responsible for the defence of the Ionian sea, see p. 121.

GLOSSARY

Rais or *Reis:* the captain of a Turkish galley.

Saettia: a lateen-rigged ship with three sails. The larger ones apparently used square sails.

Salma: a measure of weight and capacity originating from Sicily, Naples and Apulia. The *salma* seems to have been equivalent to $3-3\frac{1}{2}$ Venetian bushels or *staia*, and ten *staia* made one *botta* or butt, so that about three *salme* were equivalent to a Venetian *botta*. This is suggested indirectly by F. Edler, *Glossary of mediaeval terms of business: Italian series, 1200-1600* (Cambridge, Massachusetts, 1934), pp. 256, 318; by Lane, *Venetian ships*, etc., *cit.*, pp. 245-6; and by J. Delumeau, *Vie économique et sociale de Rome dans la seconde moitié du XVIe siècle*, 2 vols., Paris, 1957-59, II, p. 536. Miss Edler describes the *salma* as equivalent to 10-11 Florentine bushels: one Florentine bushel is about a third of a Venetian *staio*, therefore the *salma* = approximately $3\frac{1}{2}$ Venetian *staia*. 10 Venetian *staia* make one *botta*, so about 3 *salme* are also equivalent to a *botta*. M. Delumeau estimates the *staio* at 76 litres approximately (to Professor Lane's 83 litres) and the *salma* at 240 litres.

Senate: the Council mainly responsible for directing Venetian policy on such matters as finance, the coinage, commerce, the armed forces, the declaration of war and the making of peace. For a time the secret Council of Ten had competed with the Senate for control of financial and foreign policy, but at the constitutional crisis of 1582-83 its powers were curtailed. The Senate consisted of sixty Senators proper and sixty members of an additional body or *Zonta:* its numbers were then swelled by magistrates who enjoyed an *ex officio* right of entry, so that the total number of persons entitled to attend its sessions was in the region of 300. In practice, not many more than 150 persons usually attended any given session of the Senate. (E. Besta, *Il Senato veneziano*, Venice, 1899.)

Soldo: see ducat.

Staio or *staro:* a Venetian bushel, equivalent to 2.3 imperial bushels. 10 *staia* were equivalent to one *botta*.

Tartana: a boat with three or more small sails and a single deck, popular in Provence, with a capacity of 150-600 *salme*.

Notes

ABBREVIATIONS

The following abbreviations have been used:
A.S.F. Archivio di Stato, Florence
A.S.V. Archivio di Stato, Venice
B.M.V. Biblioteca Marciana, Venice
M.C.V. Library of the Museo Civico Correr, Venice

PART I

CHAPTER I: THE USKOKS

1. *Relatione dell' illustrissimo signor Nicolò Donato del suo generalato contra Uscocchi l'anno 1599*, f. 7v. (M.C.V., Cicogna MSS 2855, ff. 6–61).
2. Sixtus V also regarded them as excellent suppliers of slaves. 'Concerning the galley crews which the Pope desired', we read in a report from Venice dated 12 March 1588, 'I have been informed from Rome that in the last few days His Holiness gave instructions to the chiefs in Segna and Fiume to make him in those regions some two thousand slaves of persons subject to the Turk — who are called *morlacchi* — so that he can use them as crews for his galleys. When they brought them to Ancona, they should have their money' (A.S.F., *Mediceo del Principato*, busta 3084, f. 598).

3. *Relatione di Almoro Thiepolo, Provveditor generale in Golfo contro Uscocchi*, 31 January 1594 (A.S.V., Senato, Secreta, Relazioni, busta 66, f. 10).

4. A.S.F., *Mediceo del Principato*, busta 3084, f. 37, 48r.–v., 20 September 1586, reports of Isidoro Manfredi from Venice.

5. *Relazione de ser Ferigo Nani, Proveditor general in Dalmatia*, 10 December 1591 (A.S.V., Senato, Secreta, Relazioni, busta 66, f. 2v.).

6. *Ibid.*, and the *Relatione* of Nicolò Donà, cited above, n. 1: at f. 9.

7. *Relatione de ser Filippo Pasqualigo, Proveditor general in Dalmatia et Albania,* – with the authority of commander-in-chief throughout the Adriatic, – 13 February 1614 (A.S.V., Senato, Secreta, Relazioni, busta 66, f. 3). Cf. also the report he delivered in the Senate on 9 November 1602, after holding the office of Provveditore dell'Armata and Provveditore generale da mar in Golfo (*ibid.*, f. 2v.).

8. Cf. A.S.F., *Mediceo del Principato*, busta 3083, f. 11 (6 February 1580); busta 3084, ff. 9, 27 (February–March 1586); busta 3085, f. 44v. (1 March 1586); and A. Tenenti, *Naufrages, corsaires et assurances maritimes à Venise (1592–1609)* (Paris, 1959), pp. 28–9, 190, 200, etc.

9. B.M.V., Italian MSS, class VII, 503. Cf., however, A.S.F., *Mediceo del Principato*, busta 3086, f. 383 and 384v. (2 March 1592).

10. A.S.F., *Mediceo del Principato*, busta 3086, f. 359 (1 February 1592); cf., for example, *ibid.*, busta 3085, f. 54 (15 March 1586).

11. *Relazione* cited above, n. 1: at f. 7.

12. *Relatione di Segna e di Uscocchi all' eccellentissimo signor Filippo Pasqualigo Proveditore generale da mar in Golfo et in Dalmatia*, by Signor Vettor Barbaro, 25 April 1601 (M.C.V., Cicogna MSS 2855, ff. 68v.–69v.).

13. *Relatione de ser Zuanne Bembo, Proveditor general da mar in Golfo*, 12 September 1598, f. 8r.–v. (A.S.V., Senato, Secreta, Relazioni, busta 66). What follows is no less interesting: 'The numbers of the Uskoks are increased for the most part by subjects of Your Serenity: either deserters from service as freemen or soldiers on warships, who take to flight on encountering the slightest inconvenience; or else fugitives from the law. After committing robbery and murder just as they like, if such a life no longer pleases them,

they contrive to get back and return to the service of Your Serenity. It is easy enough for them to do this — most of all for those who have "immortalized" themselves, as they say, with a reputation as murderers. These men get rewarded rather than punished for their criminal activities': *Relatione di Agostino Michiel, Capitano in Golfo*, 22 December 1608, f. 2 (*ibid., busta* 73).

14. Cf. the *Relazione* cited in n. 3, at f. 11.

15. A.S.F., *Mediceo del Principato, busta* 3084, f. 314v., end of May 1587; cf. *ibid.*, f. 345, and — for a different version of the incident — *busta* 3085, f. 455 (23 May 1587).

16. *Relazione* cited in n. 12, at f. 69v.

17. Almorò Tiepolo's most brilliant success was the capture of Scrisa, thirty miles from Segna, where the Uskoks had deposited their booty. Some of it was found still in bales, just as the merchants had despatched it. 'This was in the custody of the imperial commander, with special books recording not only its consignment but also procedure for distributing it' — cf. A.S.F., *Mediceo del Principato, busta* 3086, f. 490, 500 (11 and 25 July 1592).

18. A.S.V., *Senato, Mar*, reg. 67, f. 80 r.-v., letter to the Capitano Generale da Mar.

19. A.S.F., *Mediceo del Principato, busta* 3088, f. 356v. (24 June 1617), 596 (23 February 1619), 621v. (13 April 1619).

20. *Ibid.*, f. 664, 666v. (17 and 24 August 1619).

21. *Ibid.*, f. 32 (28 March 1615), 74 (17 October 1615), 740 (25 April 1620), 868 (13 February 1621) and 878 (1 March 1621).

22. Barbaro's *Relazione*, cited in n. 12, at f. 70; Donà's *Relazione*, cited in n. 1, at ff. 12v.-13.

23. Pasqualigo's *Relazione* (13 February 1614), cited in n. 7, at f. 17.

CHAPTER 2: THE BARBARY CORSAIRS

1. A.S.F., *Mediceo del Principato, busta* 3083, f. 158v. (10 May 1581). No doubt the *fuste* were sighted at dawn, since it was difficult for a galley to travel more than a hundred miles in a day.

2. *Ibid., busta* 3084, ff. 66v. (25 October 1586) and 70 (1 November 1586).

3. Cf. for example, *ibid.*, busta 3083, f. 664 (22 June 1585); busta 3085, f. 306 (18 October 1586); busta 3084, f. 314 (end of May 1587); busta 3086, f. 742v. (3 August 1596); busta 3087, f. 154v. (3 September 1605).

4. *Ibid.*, busta 3084, f. 314 (end of May 1587). In the summer of 1582 a Venetian galley launched an attack with such impetuosity that it not only overtook the *fusta* off Valona, but actually sunk it with all its men and merchandise – cf. *ibid.*, busta 3083, f. 309 v. (11 August 1582).

5. *Ibid.*, busta 3083, f. 59v. (1 September 1580) and 270v. (28 April 1582); busta 3085, f. 452 (May 1587).

6. *Ibid.*, busta 3083, f. 595v. and 615v. (31 August and 15 October 1584).

7. *Ibid.*, f. 417v. (1 April 1583), 457v. (13 May 1583), 557 (9 June 1584), 672 (6 July 1585), and 684 (17 August 1585). Cf. A.S.V., *Senato, Mar*, reg. 45, f. 210 (22 April 1582); reg. 46, f. 183 (23 August 1584) and reg. 47, f. 43v. (12 July 1585).

8. A.S.F., *Mediceo del Principato*, busta 3085, f. 114 (31 May 1586).

9. *Ibid.*, busta 3084, f. 305v. (9 May 1587).

10. L. Firpo, *Lo stato ideale della Controriforma. Ludovico Agostini* (Bari, 1957), pp. 78–9.

11. 'It is understood', so runs a despatch from Venice on 1 October 1605, 'that the pirates who took the *Mazocca* and other Venetian ships went to Durazzo and offered their crews for redemption. The local *cadi* had the slaves turned over to him, promising to pay their ransom, which amounted to a great deal. But then he failed to pay up, asserting that as the slaves were Venetian, and hence friends of the Sultan, they could not be captured, and he did not wish them to be ransomed. Hence the disgusted pirates, having landed on the pretext of parleying with him, proceeded to kill the *cadi*.' A.S.F., *Mediceo del Principato*, busta 3087, f. 182v.

12. *Ibid.*, busta 3083, f. 43 (16 April 1580); busta 3085, f. 121v. (7 June 1586); busta 3084, f. 370 (18 July 1587) and busta 3087, f. 426v. (25 October 1608). It was undoubtedly good fortune as well as her own efforts that enabled the *Gratarola* to save herself when

attacked by seventeen *galeotte* from Algiers off Cape Martin in Spain in the autumn of 1584; cf. *ibid.*, busta 3083, f. 628v. (14 December 1584). In July 1603, two Venetian vessels escaped from three Barbary *fuste* near Gargano, mainly because of nightfall (*Mediceo del Principato*, busta 3087, f. 91v., 26 July 1603).

13. A.S.F., *Mediceo del Principato*, busta 3083, f. 94v. (4 November 1580); busta 3084, f. 37 (2 September 1586); f. 49 (20 September 1586); f. 57 (4 October 1586); busta 3085, f. 165v. (30 August 1586) and 170v. (23 August 1586).

14. *Ibid.*, busta 3084, f. 743v. (August 1588); busta 3086, f. 168v. (6 June 1591), and A.S.V., *Senato, Mar*, reg. 61, f. 153v. (15 February 1602). Cf. Tenenti, *Naufrages*, etc., *cit.*, pp. 324–5, 333–4, etc.

15. *Ibid.*, busta 3087, f. 155v. (3 September 1605), 165 and 171 (17 September 1605); cf. Tenenti, *Naufrages*, etc., *cit.*, pp. 427–50.

16. *Ibid.*, busta 3086, f. 691 bis (May 1594). With Gradenigo, Nicolò Bragadin, Count and Military Governor of Sebenico, his two sons, their Franciscan tutor, and the local chancellor were also taken prisoner. The informant concludes that 'it is feared that all the aforesaid persons, together with the rest of the plunder and the slaves, have been taken directly to Barbary and perhaps hidden, so that by this means the pirates can have some excuse for not obeying any orders for their release which might arrive from the Porte'.

17. *Ibid.*, busta 3083, f. 637 (December 1584); cf. f. 528 (undated). To placate the Turkish government, Venice was forced to commit itself to executing Emo.

18. *Ibid.*, busta 3083, f. 170v. (17 June 1581); busta 3084, f. 370 (18 July 1587); busta 3085, f. 589v. (26 March 1588) and f. 730 (27 May 1589); busta 3086, f. 307 (16 November 1591).

19. *Ibid.*, busta 3086, f. 742v. (3 August 1596); busta 3087, f. 154v. (3 September 1605); cf. busta 3088, f. 912v. (5 June 1621). See A.S.V., *Senato, Mar*, reg. 71, f. 154v. (2 August 1613).

20. A description by Agostini is worth reproducing here, for the concrete information which it contains, although I am not wholly confident of its accuracy: 'From the other side of the city, below Mount Granaro, half a mile off, there appeared a Venetian galley which was coming along the coast from Ancona.... The Infidels

realized they were in danger of being unable to escape. Nevertheless, they roused themselves so fast as to mobilize all their strength immediately, so that, although the Venetian galley made every effort to intercept them, with the sails swelling towards the west which they had chosen, they crossed the galley's path half a mile from it, opposite the harbour mouth. Our men then put themselves to windward and began trying with their guns to frighten them into surrender. Thus, pursuing with all their might a quarry which they believed to be weaker than themselves, they eventually overtook them. But in this belief they were mistaken, for the *galeotta* carried twenty-two benches of oarsmen and the *fusta* twelve, whilst there were one hundred and thirty Turkish warriors on board, nearly all of them desperadoes grown old in wrongdoing.... After many cannonades and numerous encounters, our galley was unable to take in its sail. Hence, being driven to leeward, it was rammed by the *galeotta* and suffered some damage to the stern, and so many arrows were fired at it that it seemed like a boar at bay...'
Cf. Firpo, *Lo stato ideale*, etc., cit., pp. 79–80.

21. A.S.V., *Dispacci al Senato del Capitanio in Golfo, filza* 1266.

22. A.S.V., *Notary G. A. Catti*, reg. 3371, f. 8v. (4 January 1600).

23. A.S.F., *Mediceo del Principato, busta* 3084, f. 655 (23 April 1588).

24. *Ibid., busta* 3084, f. 149v. (16 January 1587) and *busta* 3087, f. 350v. (21 July 1607).

25. *Ibid., busta* 3087, f. 348, 350v. (14 and 21 July 1607); A.S.V., *Senato, Mar*, reg. 62, f. 201v. (8 February 1603); and *Notary G. A. Catti*, reg. 3388, f. 54 (10 February 1610). The affair of the French ship is probably the one described by Nicolò Contarini: 'this ship was under the command of Bortolamio Antiburl [sic] of St Tropez in Provence, and, having laded a cargo of wine and other merchandise, arrived at Taranto. There, having discharged and sold its cargo, it reladed corn for Naples, the property of Michiel Vais. But on the voyage it was attacked by five pirate galleys, three from Biserta and two from Santa Maura, who, after fighting bravely, succeeded in capturing it. Most of the sailors were taken prisoner and transferred to the commander's *galeotta*, and they put a Berber crew on the captured ship, leaving only five of its own sailors in chains aboard it, for they had thought it advisable to divide them

up. Orders were given that they should proceed as quickly as possible, either back to Santa Maura or on to Valona where the wind would be most favourable; from there they would either obtain an escort or go on further. But the wind blew harder than their oars could carry them, whilst the commander's galley was some way in front. On the way they encountered Teodoro Balbi, the Venetian Proveditor dell'Armata, who was sailing with another four galleys in search of the pirates who infested the sea. On the appearance of the Venetian warships, the pirates at once took to flight, but these galleys, which were much faster than the Turkish, were soon upon them. All the pirates, faced with certain death, fought desperately, but were soon conquered and slain after spilling some blood on our side — for the Senate's orders would allow no truce to be extended to these enemies of the human race. The commander's *galeotta*, which carried the French captives and was faster than the others, escaped to Santa Maura.' Cf. his *Historie*, book VIII, ff. 325v.-326 (A.S.V., *Miscellanea Codici*, no. 80).

26. A.S.F., *Mediceo del Principato*, busta 3085, f. 44v. (1 March 1586) and *busta* 3086, f. 620 (22 May 1593).

27. On the movements of the Turkish fleet and problems connected with it, see especially F. Braudel, *La Méditerranée et le monde méditerranéen à l'epoque de Philippe II* (Paris, 1949), Part III.

CHAPTER 3: MALTESE, FLORENTINES AND SPANIARDS

1. A.S.V., *Senato, Secreta, Relazioni*, busta 55, ff. 3-5.

2. 'However', continued the Commissar-General Pandolfo Strozzi in his *Istruzione . . . all'ammiraglio della squadra fiorentina*, 'you must not go too close to Crete or to the western side.' A.S.F., *Mediceo del Principato*, busta 2077, f. 541v., 1 April 1575.

3. 'Telling the ship's crew that they did not want on this occasion to molest the Jews and any goods of theirs on board the ship, for such were their instructions from the Grand Duke'; *ibid.*, *busta* 3083, f. 470 (17 June 1583). However, the Tuscan galleys frequently disregarded the Grand Duke's orders, when they plundered the *Nana* in the Gulf of Settelia — cf. A.S.V., *Senato, Secreta, Relazioni*,

busta 82, *Relazione* of Filippo Pasqualigo, commander of the Cretan fleet, October 1584, f. 4v.

4. On the intervention of the Spanish representative at Venice, Brocchiero was later released from prison. Cf. Pasqualigo's *Relazione*, cited above, n. 3, at f. 3v., and A.S.F., *Mediceo del Principato*, *busta* 3083, ff. 448–9 (22 August 1583) and f. 497v. (19 November 1583). According to the despatch of 22 August: 'There are various opinions about the booty, but it is generally held that there will be some 100,000 gold ducats divided among the five galleys, with a further tenth to be given to the fleet commander.'

5. Cf. Pasqualigo's *Relazione*, already cited, at f. 5, and A.S.F., *Mediceo del Principato*, *busta* 3083, f. 462 (21 May 1583).

6. The sack of the Maltese ships was described as follows: 'At the first impact all our men sprang on board the two galleys which had been rammed. All my authority did not suffice to prevent them from plundering the property of the Maltese, because as soon as the rest of the convoy came up the soldiers and the rest of the crew jumped on board, mixed in with the others, and created the most appalling confusion.' On reaching Crete, Pasqualigo had his men searched one by one in order to recover the Maltese booty. For the whole encounter, cf. the *Relazione* cited above, n. 3, at ff. 5v.–8, and A.S.F., *Mediceo del Principato*, *busta* 3083, f. 489 (14 October 1583).

7. A.S.F., *Mediceo del Principato*, *busta* 3083, f. 575v. (21 July 1584), and Pasqualigo's *Relazione*, cited above, f. 10v.

8. A.S.F., *Mediceo del Principato*, *busta* 3083, f. 597 (1 September 1584), 672 (6 July 1585), 696 (28 September 1585) and 499 (19 November 1583).

9. *Ibid.*, *busta* 3083, f. 685 (31 August 1585); *busta* 3085, f. 310 (25 October 1586) and f. 329 (29 November 1586).

10. *Ibid.*, *busta* 3084, f. 45v. (September 1586) and *busta* 3085, f. 189 (4 October 1586).

11. On the papal decrees, cf. *ibid.*, *busta* 3085, f. 476v. (25 July 1587) and *busta* 3084, f. 423 (August 1587). On the operations of the Maltese, cf. *ibid.*, *busta* 3084, f. 539v. (December 1587); *busta*

3085, f. 519 (17 October 1587) and f. 547 (2 January 1588); see also *busta* 3084, ff. 131r.–v., 148–149v.

12. *Ibid.*, *busta* 3084, f. 644 (6 April 1588); *busta* 3085, f. 427 (18 April 1587) and 605v. (9 April 1588).

13. *Ibid.*, *busta* 3085, f. 660v. (25 June 1588), f. 741 (5 August 1589) and f. 771v. (14 October 1589). For other encounters with the Turks, cf. *ibid.*, *busta* 3086, f. 60, 750, 155, 157.

14. Indeed, at the beginning of May, the *Provveditore dell'Armata* captured three pirate *fuste* which had been plundering the *Silvestra*, master Girolamo Gambilio, bound for Syria, in the waters of Corfù; cf. A.S.V., *Senato, Mar*, reg. 57, f. 50 (30 May 1597) and Tenenti, *Naufrages*, etc., *cit.*, pp. 204–5.

15. Another revolt of Christian slaves had occurred in Cyprus in June 1591: cf. A.S.F., *Mediceo del Principato, busta* 3086, f. 195. In this connexion it is interesting to note that from time to time Christian galley slaves succeeded in rebelling and in seizing control of the Turkish warships. In September 1580, for example, a *galeotta* arrived at Messina, with eighty-three Christians on board who had killed the commander on the voyage (cf. *ibid., busta* 3083, f. 80v., 8 October 1580). Towards the close of 1591, a number of Christian soldiers removed the chains from the slaves of a galley of the Tunisian fleet. At the same time, they killed half the Turks, clapped the others in irons and took the ship to Trapani, where it was to be purchased by the Viceroy of Sicily (*ibid., busta* 3086, f. 338, January 1592). A typical episode was noted in the journal for 23 June 1590: 'The Turkish galley which came to Malta with 264 slaves brought so many gold ducats that the Turks of Tripoli were sending by way of tribute to the government in Constantinople, that in dividing the spoils, the booty came to about 760 gold ducats for each slave. With the aid of a number of freemen, the slaves managed by degrees to unshackle themselves one night whilst they happened to be in a certain Barbary port. They took up arms and cut to pieces all the Turks and Moors on board that galley which was taking the tribute to the Sultan. They had vowed to present the ship to Our Lady of Trapani, but the Grand Master bought it himself and sent the money to be used by that cult...' *Ibid., busta* 3086, f. 56. Again, in the spring of 1615, a Barbary *fusta*, which had been

separated from the rest of its squadron by a storm, was taken to Malta by sixty Christian slaves, including two of the Knights of St John, who had seized this opportunity to free themselves: cf. *ibid.*, busta 3088, f. 41v. (23 May 1615).

16. For this *Breve discorso del viaggio e ritorno fatto dalle galere della Religione in Levante*, see *ibid.*, busta 2077, f. 659–60v.

17. See his *Relazione*, already cited, at f. 90 (M.C.V., Cicogna MSS. 2855).

18. N. Contarini, *Historie*, vol. II, book VIII, f. 220v. and 222 (A.S.V., *Miscellanea Codici* no. 80).

19. Concerning the penetration of the English and Dutch into the Mediterranean, Pellegrin Venier later wrote that 'They have also run across ships belonging to the King of Spain, and have captured them and taken them to the island colonies of Your Serenity, thereby immediately giving the Kingdoms of Naples, Sicily, Sardinia and others the opportunity to fit out galleons on the pretext of self-defence, and to attack Venetian islands. These galleons, sensing their own power and the excellence of their weapons, did those deeds which are now universally notorious': A.S.V., *Provveditori da Terra e da Mar*, no. 1363, f. 92v.

20. A.S.V., *Notary G. A. Catti*, reg. 3356, f. 202v. (19 June 1585); reg. 3358, f. 71 (9 March 1587); reg. 3357, f. 99 (17 March 1586) and f. 250v. (26 July 1586).

21. A.S.F., *Mediceo del Principato*, busta 3084, f. 715v.–716 (25 June 1588) and f. 729v. (August 1588); cf. busta 3085, f. 660 (25 June 1588).

22. A.S.V., *Notary A. Spinelli*, reg. 11914, f. 127v. (10 March 1593); *Notary G. A. Catti*, reg. 3367, f. 258v. (28 May 1596); reg. 3367, f. 414 (9 September 1596), 437r.–v. (20 September 1596) and f. 463v. (8 October 1596). Cf. Tenenti, *Naufrages*, etc., *cit.*, pp. 177 and 184–5.

23. *Notary G. A. Catti*, reg. 3368, f. 170 (24 April 1597); *Notary A. Spinelli*, reg. 11919, f. 161v. (11 April 1598) and f. 478 (15 November 1598). Cf. Tenenti, *Naufrages*, etc., *cit.*, pp. 202–3 and 219.

24. Cf. Tenenti, *Naufrages*, etc., *cit.*, pp. 233, 261, 275, 307, 309–10, 383 and 532–33.

25. *Memoirs du capitan Alonso de Contreras*, French translation by M. Lami and L. Rouanet (Paris, 1911), pp. 16–17.

26. A.S.F., *Mediceo del Principato*, busta 2995, f. 127v.: letter from Venice to the Grand Duke, by Asdrubale Montauto (12 November 1596).

27. A.S.V., *Notary A. Spinelli*, reg. 11917, f. 408 (25 September 1596) and reg. 11918, f. 6v. (7 January 1597).

28. 'At the Prodano, a rock off Morea, they committed another shameful and violent crime. The *Soderina e Memma* had entered the harbour, and the Spaniards had instantly formed designs upon her. But not daring to attack her directly with such a force, they pretended the ship was Genoese and so ran up the Genoese flag, for pirates are in the habit of keeping the flags of all princes by them in order to deceive. Thus they made it appear that they had lost the ship's boat, which is necessary on all voyages, and had suffered damage from storms at sea, and so they begged for aid. The Venetians took pity on them, believing in this disaster, and thinking they were friends, hastily descended into their boats taking the best sailors with them, and so went, careless and unarmed, to help them. Expecting to be thanked and welcomed, they were taken prisoner and threatened with death if they failed to surrender their ship. The Venetians could not resist, and the Spaniards took the ship, the sailors and all the cargo, and carried them in triumph to Palermo. By a similar trick, they plundered extensively the ship of Giovan Antonio Vidali and Cesare Cordes, whilst others were captured by other insidious tricks.' N. Contarini, *Historie*, vol. II, book VI, f. 32v.–33; cf. *ibid.*, book VIII, f. 221v.

29. Cf. Tenenti, *Naufrages*, etc., *cit.*, pp. 261, 295, 303–4; cf. Contarini, *Historie*, book VIII, f. 221v.

30. Contarini, *Historie*, f. 221r.–v.

31. Cf. Tenenti, *Naufrages*, *cit.*, pp. 405–7 and 412.

32. 'The ships were left at Messina, and Orange cheerfully came to Naples bringing six thousand gold ducats to give to the Viceroy's wife. But she, not satisfied with such a sum, wanted the ships to be

brought there so that she could take a share that she deemed more appropriate. The Viceroy's wife took one hundred and sixty-four camlets, valued at thirty thousand ducats, whilst an equal number was deposited in the treasury.' Contarini, *Historie*, f. 221v.: cf. f. 325v.

33. The Capitano in Golfo further specified that 'They often go so far as to commit acts of robbery with barefaced defiance under the very walls of your cities. . . . Moreover, they go plundering in the Archipelago, and freely have dealings with plague-stricken places and people, and take away infected goods and sell them to Your Most Excellent Lordships' subjects in the islands of the Levant, with whom they have continual relations and constantly mingle. There is an obvious danger that one day some unforeseen disaster will result from this, which we shall not be able to remedy as we would like, especially because of the continuous traffic they have had some time now in the Kingdom of Crete with the Sfachioti. They too, fired with the hope of booty, not only buy from them every kind of stolen goods without the slightest regard for health, but even take to piracy themselves. Hence, among other pernicious results, they consider themselves free to rob even their neighbours on the same island, and they have finally taken to open disobedience, not to say rebellion, in which they have already persisted for several months': A.S.V., *Dispacci al Senato del Capitano in Golfo*, 20 June 1609.

34. Nicolò Contarini, too, had occasion to protest against the claims, for once made jointly, of the Spaniards and French after the recovery of a ship from St Tropez laden with Apulian grain. In 1602, the Provveditore dell'Armata, Teodoro Balbi, having snatched it away from five Turkish *galeotte*, sold the ship with its cargo and divided the proceeds among the crews of his galleys, 'being induced to do this all the more because it was proved that all belonged to Michiel Vais, whose ships were openly attacking Venetian vessels and had recently plundered the ship *Pigna*'. Cf. *Historie*, book VIII, f. 326r.-v.

35. A.S.F., *Mediceo del Principato*, busta 3087, f. 183 (1 October 1605) and f. 199 (12 November 1605).

36. *Ibid.*, busta 2077, f. 1316 (24 July 1608) and f. 1322 (1 August

1609); these were two orders issued in the name of Christina of Lorraine.

37. *Ibid.*, ff. 981–82; for other attacks by the *Livorno* on English shipping cf. *ibid.*, f. 1234r.–v. (11 October 1607). For the attacks which followed, see the *Relatione del clarissimo signore Francesco Morosini Capitano delle galere grosse armate* (A.S.V., *Senato, Relazioni, busta* 73) and *Senato, Mar*, reg. 72, f. 179v. (27 February 1615).

38. *Notary A. Spinelli*, reg. 11928, f. 592v. (7 September 1607).

39. A.S.V., *Provveditori da Terra e da Mar*, no. 1364, despatch by Lorenzo Venier, commander of the great galleys, from Corfù, 20 May 1607.

40. A.S.V., *Senato, Relazioni, busta* 73. 'Their own crews', wrote Belegno of the galleys and warships of the Order, 'although they profess to do the opposite, nevertheless when able to board these ships do not let them go scot-free, because, though they never strip it of everything, they always take something from each ship on various pretexts.' *Ibid.*

41. A.S.F., *Mediceo del Principato, busta* 3087, f. 139 (16 July 1605), f. 334v. (7 April 1607); A.S.V., *Senato, Mar*, reg. 70, f. 180 (5 June 1612); *Senato, Relazioni, busta* 73 (*Relazione di Francesco Morosini*, cited above); *Notary G. A. Catti*, reg. 3393, f. 427v. (28 November 1614). It is, moreover, necessary to remember, that numerous pirates went to sea whom it would be difficult to classify as Spanish, Maltese, etc. There is, for example, the concise report *Nota delli bertoni corsari passati per l'Arcipelago* sent by the Venetian consul at Milo to the commander of the great galleys in July 1607. On 12 November 1606 the *bertone Lion d'Oro*, commanded by Antonio Carara and armed with fifty guns, some of iron and some of bronze, was sighted off Milo: 150 persons were on board. On 18 November, the *bertone* of Antonio Rucaforte passed through. It had apparently been fitted out by Genoese and furnished with three hundred musketeers and thirty iron guns. Two French *bertoni* appeared at Milo on 10 December, each with 180 soldiers and twenty guns. They were commanded by a certain Monsieur di Vigia (Vigier?) and by a Knight of Malta, Monsieur de Monturon. A typical case was that of the *orca San Giovanni*, which reached the Archipelago on 24 December 1606; it was probably fitted out in Sardinia, but

placed under the command of one Monsieur de Roville, 'a French knight', with 240 persons and forty guns on board. On 29 February 1607, the Venetian consul noted the arrival of the galleon *San Spirito*, commanded by Simon Galia. This huge warship not only carried fifty bronze cannon and 400 soldiers, but was also accompanied by three *bertoni* and one Ragusan ship under the command of a certain Alfonso, a Portuguese. On 13 April 1607 the galleon *Il Sole*, captain Jacques Germain of Nice, reached Milo with the ship *Zena*, and the following day Count Alfonso di Montecuccoli arrived with at least fourteen Granducal vessels. Shortly afterwards another eighteen *bertoni*, which did not approach the island, were also sighted. Cf. *Provveditori da Terra e da Mar*, no. 1364, commander of the great galleys, despatch of 8 July 1607.

CHAPTER 4: THE ENGLISH

1. Contarini, *Historie*, vol. II, book VI, f. 31v. (A.S.V., *Miscellanea Codici*, no. 80).
2. A.S.V., *Senato, Mar*, reg. 44, f. 271 (26 January 1581).
3. A.S.F., *Mediceo del Principato*, busta 3083, f. 469.
4. *Ibid.*, f. 504 (10 December 1583) and *busta* 3085, f. 99 (10 May 1586). However, there is no room for doubt about the speed of the English ships. Let us mention the example of the ship captured by Sicilian galleys near the straits of Messina: it had left London thirty days earlier. Cf. *ibid., busta* 3085, f. 539v. (5 December 1587).
5. A.S.V., *Senato, Secreta, Relazioni, busta* 73, and *Senato, Dispacci*, from the governors of Zante, *busta* 2 (6 March 1604). 'The English' — so the same Michiel had written the previous year — 'are making themselves the real masters of these seas, because, in addition to the acts of plunder and robbery which they daily commit against every kind of ship, and particularly against Your Serenity's own subjects on the routes travelled by our ships, they are now beginning to destroy your subjects' carrying trade, to reduce your customs revenue and to kill off your sailors, as Your Excellencies may well know. Not content with depriving your subjects of all trade on the western side, they are now contriving to do the same in the Levant, because with their ships they are going in great numbers

to the ports of Alexandria, Alessandretta, Smyrna and other Turkish centres, both in that region and in the Archipelago. Thence they are removing all the merchandise which our ships used to lade, with great benefit both to the state and to the private man. Moreover, they themselves take these goods, with much benefit to themselves, to all these Levantine ports, and there they contract with your subjects without paying any duty other than the ordinary one, which is very small.' *Ibid., busta* 1, 22 February 1603.

6. A.S.F., *Mediceo del Principato, busta* 3085, f. 59 (22 March 1586); *busta* 3086, f. 249 (1 October 1591), f. 263 (12 October 1591) and f. 387 (21 March 1592). Cf. A.S.V., *Senato, Mar*, reg. 52, f. 73v. (5 July 1591) and reg. 53, f. 74v. (17 July 1592) and 114 (3 October 1592).

7. A.S.F., *Mediceo del Principato, busta* 3083, f. 153 (20 May 1581); *busta* 3084, f. 311 (16 May 1587), and *Notary G. A. Catti*, reg. 3362, f. 190v. (28 May 1591).

8. A.S.V., *Quarantia Criminal*, f. 103, *fascicolo* 71, f. 2v–3.

9. *Ibid.*, f. 114, *fascicolo* 134, f. 24 (18 December 1591).

10. A.S.F., *Mediceo del Principato, busta* 2077, f. 906. It is worth pointing out that not all English pirate ships were *bertoni*, nor were all *bertoni* built in England. Flemish and French *bertoni* also existed. Here, for example, is a description of a *bertone* built at Rouen: 'The galleon or *bertone* of the Grand Master was built near Rouen and had a capacity of 1,100 *salme*. When at sea, it carried 28 metal guns and 12 gunners, and, with six knights, and soldiers and mariners and serving men, the rest of the crew numbered 210. It carried victuals sufficient for six months, and kept its armoury on the poop, with fire-trumpets and incendiary bombs, nails and cannon-balls fixed together, "Flemish arrows" to set fire to sails, and *gabbritte piene di savorna* (?). The other weapons were arquebuses, muskets, halberds and other hand-weapons, together with bits of ship's equipment.' *Ibid.*

11. A.S.V., *Senato, Mar*, reg. 55, f. 190 (26 July 1595), and *Senato, Dispacci*, from the governors of Zante, *busta* 2 (26 May 1604).

12. A.S.V., *Senato, Mar*, reg. 57, f. 85 (25 September 1597) and 97–98v. (25 October 1597).

13. A.S.F., *Mediceo del Principato*, busta 2077, f. 665–7 (27 September 1597). The English captain, a certain Giorgio Rijt or Mijr (George Wright or Myers?), had reached Leghorn on other occasions and had also been at Florence. Cf. A.S.V., *Notary A. Spinelli*, reg. 11919, f. 67–71 (9 February 1598).

14. Cf. Vettor Barbaro's *Relazione* of 1601 (M.C.V., Cicogna MSS 2855, f. 90).

15. A.S.V., *Senato, Mar*, reg. 58, f. 114 (9 October 1598); *Notary G. A. Catti*, reg. 3370, f. 284 (9 July 1599); Tenenti, *Naufrages*, etc., *cit.*, pp. 265 and 270–1. Cf. A.S.F., *Mediceo del Principato*, busta 3087, f. 2 (12 February 1600).

16. A.S.V., *Senato, Secreta*, Despatches from Constantinople, busta 51, no. 19 (6 May 1600) and no. 35 (15 July 1600); busta 53, no. 9 (17 April 1601).

17. A.S.V., *Senato, Mar*, reg. 62, f. 47 (6 May 1602); Tenenti, *Naufrages*, etc., *cit.*, pp. 337–8, 349–53, 355–6, 363–4. A large part of the cargo of the *Veniera* belonged to Pietro da Mosto, who was returning home after serving as Consul in Alexandria. For the description of his travels, see *Senato, Secreta*, Despatches from Constantinople, busta 56, no. 20 (23 December 1602), and Despatches of the governors of Zante, busta 1 (23 December 1602 and 14 January 1603).

18. The *Veniera*'s crew attempted to go to Modone to recover their ship. But the vessel they hired at Zante encountered another English pirate, who stole everything that remained. Cf. A.S.V., *Senato, Secreta*, Despatches from Zante, busta 1 (16 January 1603), and *Senato, Relazioni*, busta 73, *Relazione* of Girolamo Contarini, commander of the two great galleys, 19 January 1604.

19. *Relazione* cited above, n. 18; A.S.V., *Senato, Mar*, reg. 63, f. 120 (30 August 1603); reg. 64, f. 24v. and 28 (12 and 23 March 1604).

20. A.S.V., *Senato, Dispacci*, Governors of Zante, busta 1 (17 April 1603 and 11 November 1603); *Senato, Mar*, reg. 63, f. 95 (24 July 1603).

21. A.S.V., *Senato, Dispacci*, Governors of Zante, busta 1: despatches of 19, 22 and 27 February, and 6 and 12 March 1603.

22. *Ibid.*, 18 and 22 April, 17 May, 6 November 1603; Despatches from England, *busta* 2, no. 1, 5 October 1603 (letter of Giovan Carlo Scaramelli to the Doge).

23. *Ibid.*, Despatches from Constantinople, *busta* 51, no. 23, 3 June 1600.

24. This Venetian Provveditore was probably the most active of the high-ranking Venetian officials in the Ionian region. It was he, for example, who obtained the extradition of Christopher 'Oloard', who had been taken prisoner at Modone, and had him hanged in May 1603. The following year he had the same penalty inflicted on two other pirates. The English attempted on other occasions to get their revenge, and in November 1604 they succeeded, at least in part. Hearing that Michiel had laded much of his property on the *bertone Morosini*, bound for Venice, they attacked the ship at the mouth of the straits of Otranto, concentrating their fury almost exclusively on the *Provveditore's* goods and even killing the doves that belonged to the ladies of his household. Cf. Michiel's despatch of 4 December 1604 (A.S.V., *Senato, Dispacci,* Governors of Zante, *busta* 2).

25. Relations between James I and Ferdinand I were often very tense, on account of Tuscan piracy. It was inevitable that the use of *bertoni* by Florentines, Maltese and Spaniards should harm others besides the Venetians, and that the English themselves should occasionally suffer therefrom. In 1604 four such vessels encountered two English pirates and after a tough battle destroyed their ships, with not a single man escaping. Towards the close of the same year, three Neapolitan *bertoni* captured another English pirate who had been infesting the Mediterranean for seven years (cf. *Senato, Dispacci,* Governors of Zante, *busta* 2, 18 May and 28 December 1604). In 1605 a *bertone* flying the Maltese flag, together with a similar vessel flying the ensign of Savoy, seized an English ship with a very valuable cargo of kerseys, weapons and cash (cf. *ibid.*, Despatches from Constantinople, *busta* 63, no. 1, 14 March 1606).

26. A.S.V., *Senato, Dispacci,* Governors of Zante, *busta* 2, 29 May and 6 June 1604; Despatches of the Commissioner for the Navy, letter to Giovanni Pasqualigo of 8 June 1604.

27. A.S.V., *Senato, Dispacci*, Governors of Zante, *busta* 2 (19 October and 4 December 1604).

28. *Ibid.*, *busta* 3, 11 February 1607.

29. A.S.V., *Provveditori da Terra e da Mar*, no. 1363, f. 46r.–v. According to Lorenzo Arrigoni, the *Reniera e Soderina* was overtaken because of a calm spell in the Gulf of Settelia, and fought for three hours. The pirates' cannon had already caused five leaks in the hull when a number of sacks of cotton, which the defenders had been using as protection, caught fire. The Venetian ship carried some 150 men, whilst each of the *bertoni* was equipped with a hundred musketeers and forty guns. Cf. *Provveditori da Terra e da Mar*, no. 1364, despatch from Zante of 10 June 1607.

30. A.S.V., *Senato, Secreta*, Despatches from England, *busta* 6, no. 34.

31. A.S.V., *Senato, Mar*, reg. 67, f. 105 and 125v.; A.S.F., *Mediceo del Principato*, *busta* 3087, f. 374 (22 December 1607).

32. A.S.F., *Mediceo del Principato*, *busta* 3087, f. 391 (26 March 1608), and A.S.V., *Notary G. A. Catti*, reg. 3388, f. 506v. (16 December 1610). The Senate warmly congratulated Venier: 'The news which reached us with your letters of March 28th concerning the capture of two pirate *bertoni*, which occurred between Sapienza and Modone thanks to your valour and that of the commanders Badoer and Ciuran, with the death of Captain Jan Casten the leading Flemish pirate and many of his other men, in addition to the prisoners taken, has given us great joy — as well it may, for we are now free for the most part of our concern at the damage inflicted on Levantine shipping, and this port is free of the dangers therefrom. Our pleasure is all the greater because we have heard that the whole action took place without the slightest damage to our own side, in spite of the formidable supplies of guns, ammunition and arms which the aforesaid pirates had for their own defence, and the resistance offered by the fortress of Modone, beneath whose walls the ships of your squadron pursued the smaller vessel captured by the commander Badoer.' A.S.V., *Senato, Mar*, reg. 68, f. 22 (8 April 1608).

33. A.S.V., *Senato, Secreta, Relazioni*, *busta* 75, *Relazione* of Filippo Pasqualigo, *Provveditore generale da Mar* (13 December 1608); *busta*

73, *Relazione* of Giust' Antonio Belegno, commander of the galleon, 4 February 1609.

34. A.S.V., *Notary A. Spinelli*, reg. 11930, f. 626v. (2 September 1609) and 858v. (26 November 1609).

35. A.S.V., *Senato, Mar*, reg. 69, f. 104v. (15 May 1610); reg. 70, f. 161 (6 April 1611). Despatches of the commander of the Cretan fleet, 20 December 1610, and Despatches of the governors of Zante, *busta* 4 (31 December 1611).

36. A.S.F., *Mediceo del Principato*, *busta* 3087, f. 479 (12 September 1609).

37. A.S.V., *Senato, Dispacci*, Governors of Zante, *busta* 4, 21 January 1612. About a year later, the *Guidotta e Simona*, master Alvise di Girolamo, 'on its way from Alexandria... was attacked outside Zante by *bertoni* from Barbary, wrecked and sent to the bottom of the sea. The ship and all its crew and cargo were lost.' – *Notary G. A. Catti*, reg. 3393, f. 143v. (12 May 1614).

38. A.S.V., *Senato, Dispacci*, Governors of Corfù, *busta* 7, 16 December 1611; *Notary G. A. Catti*, reg. 3394, f. 154 (6 April 1615) and f. 409 (11 December 1615); A.S.F., *Mediceo del Principato*, *busta* 3088, f. 46 (6 June 1615).

39. Cf. Braudel, *La Méditerranée*, etc., *cit.*, Part III, *passim*.

40. A.S.V., *Senato, Secreta*, Despatches from England, *filza* 8, no. 48; Despatches from Zante, *busta* 3, Michiel Priuli to the Doge.

41. *Ibid.*, Despatches of the commander of the Cretan fleet, 20 December 1610, and Despatches from Florence, *busta* 27, no. 9 (11 April 1612).

42. *Ibid.*, Despatches of the governors of Corfù, *busta* 10 (28 January 1615).

43. *Ibid.*, Despatches from Spain, *busta* 42, no. 21 (23 May 1610); letter of Piero Priuli from Marseilles.

44. *Ibid.*, Despatches from England, *filza* 11, no. 27, postscript (24 May 1612) and no. 44 (19 July 1612).

45. *Ibid.*, Despatches from Florence, *filza* 28, no. 1 (2 March 1613), and *filza* 29, no. 55 (25 October 1614).

46. *Ibid.*, Despatches from Turin, *filza* 36, no. 2 (3 March 1613).

NOTES

PART II

CHAPTER 5: THE MERCHANT FLEET

1. A.S.F., *Mediceo del Principato*, busta 3084, f. 33. However, before Nicolò Vidali was granted the two galleys for the voyage to Narenta, many other efforts had been made in this direction. It will be sufficient to mention the decree of 28 October 1574 which 'for the purpose of protecting merchandise' ordered Fausto's galleon to be adapted for lading goods for the Dalmatian ports, from Narenta to Ragusa and Alessio 'by the same methods as are used in despatching the great merchant galleys' (A.S.V., *Cinque Savi alla Mercanzia, Epiloghi*, 9, pp. 35–7) and the proposal of 24 June 1580 to send 'one of the largest light galleys' on the voyage to Spalato (*ibid.*, p. 37).

2. A.S.V., *Senato, Mar*, reg. 48, f. 111 (10 September 1588). This route immediately appeared less fortunate than its predecessor. The first four auctions of the galleys were unsuccessful, and they were eventually, at the beginning of November 1588, 'taken on by my lord Antonio Donà for the sum of one ducat each, he making the Signory a gift of 6,000 ducats to cover the expenses of the crews, and equipping them with all sorts of weapons' (cf. A.S.F., *Mediceo del Principato*, busta 3085, f. 677). On 12 August 1589, an informant wrote to Florence: 'The two great merchant galleys have returned from Corfù and Zante after their maiden voyage, with little profit, or so it is said, and their men are in a poor state, to say nothing of some that are dead.' (*Ibid.*, f. 744.) Cf. in A.S.V., *Senato, Secreta, Relazioni*, busta 73, the *Relazione* of Girolamo Contarini, commander of the great merchant galleys, dated 8 August 1589.

3. Cf. the *Relazione* of Girolamo Contarini, commander of the great galleys, dated 6 January 1590, in A.S.V., *Senato, Secreta, Relazioni*, busta 73. Giovanni Cappello, in his *Relazione* of 16 November 1592, noted the disastrous results of the low wages paid to the oarsmen, 'Germans and similarly rootless people, who, as they say, go a-begging, and have no trade; and some are too young and not suited to the sea, and, God help them, crouch half dead among the benches under the torments they suffer from wind and weather.' (*Ibid.*)

4. Cf. Tenenti, *Naufrages*, etc., *cit.*, pp. 13-27.

5. A.S.V., *Provveditori da Terra e da Mar, filza* 1363, f. 87 (11 July 1607) and f. 3 (25 August 1607).

6. A.S.V., *Senato, Mar*, reg. 44, f. 149.

7. *Ibid.*, reg. 45, f. 85 (4 November 1581). Any galleons which might be built in Crete were not excluded from this new concession. From 5 January 1577 they were granted the right to a loan of 1,000 ducats if the capacity of the ship was over 300 butts, and to a loan of 3 ducats per butt if it was between 200 and 300 butts. On this question, cf. the essential article of G. Luzzatto, 'Per la storia delle costruzioni navali a Venezia nei secoli XV e XVI' (originally published in *Miscellanea di studi storici in onore di Camillo Manfroni*, Padua, 1931, and reprinted in his *Studi di storia economica veneziana*, Padua, 1954, pp. 37–51). The butt was a unit of measurement roughly equivalent to 0.725 freight tons or about 29 English cubic feet — see Glossary.

8. Cf. Tenenti, *Naufrages*, etc., *cit.*, pp. 18-19.

9. A.S.V., *Notary G. A. Catti*, reg. 3350, f. 114 (17 August 1579); reg. 3353, f. 74 (14 March 1582); reg. 3355, f. 81 (14 March 1584); reg. 3357, f. 86v. (5 March 1586); reg. 3361, f. 483 (25 January 1590), and reg. 3362, f. 326 (14 September 1591).

10. A.S.V., *Senato, Mar, filza* 135 (12 September 1597) and reg. 57, f. 64r.-v. (27 September 1597).

11. The full title is as follows: 'Nota delli parcenevoli et patroni di vasselli che hanno pagato l'ancorazo da primo settembrio passado fin hora' (Donà delle Rose MSS, no. 217, f. 278).

12. An appropriate decree of the Senate had authorized Francesco Morosini to 'have built at the present time in the Low Countries a ship with a capacity of some eight hundred to a thousand butts in the normal style of Venetian ships and equipped with iron bolts, to receive a subsidy of ten ducats per butt when the ship has been brought to this city ... with a proviso that the ship shall be made Venetian both in its hull and in its fitments'. The loan was five ducats per butt, to be restored in annual instalments of 1,000 ducats. The ship so constructed was named the *Sant' Agata*. As already mentioned, Francesco Morosini two years later owned at least one

bertone in addition to this. The decree continued as follows: 'As it is greatly conducive to the public welfare to increase the number of large ships, for the sake of the customs revenue and for the sailor's trade . . ., it is appropriate to accept the said offer under suitable conditions. For the other three ships which he has offered to build those terms shall be made that, on the example of this one, shall be judged most beneficial to the service of the state.' Cf. A.S.V., *Senato, Mar*, reg. 57, f. 39 (29 March 1597).

13. A.S.V., *Senato, Mar*, reg. 59, f. 144v. (31 December 1599); reg. 61, f. 146 (26 January 1602).

14. *Ibid.*, reg. 61, f. 43v. and 135v. (26 April and 29 December 1601).

15. *Ibid.*, reg. 61, f. 88 (28 August 1601), and reg. 62, f. 100v.-101 (16 August 1602). The second decree laid down that 'since in the law of 1580 it was expressly prescribed that raisins could not be carried anywhere except to this city and to the west beyond the straits of Gibraltar, it shall now be decreed that in future the raisins which grow in the islands of Cefalonia and Zante may be exported from those islands only in order to send them to Venice in Venetian ships belonging to subjects of our Signory, officered and manned for the most part either by Venetian subjects or by Greeks, as is permitted by our laws'.

16. 'Foreign ships or other vessels bought by Venetians or Venetian subjects may not be insured at this port save for two-thirds of the value of these ships when they have actually set sail.' A.S.V., *Senato, Mar*, reg. 62, f. 111v.-113v. (31 August 1602).

17. *Ibid.*, reg. 63, f. 104v. The motive behind the decree was as follows: 'The acts which forbid making foreign vessels Venetian cause great loss to our Signory's customs revenue, and greatly harm the interests of private persons.' (*Ibid.*)

18. Cf. Tenenti, *Naufrages*, etc., *cit.*, p. 567.

19. Cf., for example, A.S.V., *Provveditori da Terra e da Mar, filza* 1363, f. 111 (July 1607).

20. A.S.V., *Senato, Secreta, Relazioni, busta* 73.

21. See, for example, the following crucial passage from a memorandum addressed to the Doge by the *Cinque Savi alla Mercanzia* on 11 August 1609: 'We are also informed that when the ships of

Sicily and Naples began their piracy, claiming (although they really wanted to do just what they liked) that they were removing from our ships only merchandise belonging to Turks, Jews and similar peoples, the Consul in Syria for the time being, together with the Council of Twelve, decreed for the purpose of avoiding these unfortunate occurrences that merchants of these nations should not be able to lade goods on Venetian vessels. Turkish and Jewish merchants are greatly aggrieved at this prohibition, firmly believing that these orders were made in order to compel them to sell their silk and other merchandise to our Venetian merchants on terms favourable to the Venetians. The result of their objections has been that they are more willing to sell their silk and other goods to foreigners rather than Venetian merchants, bringing not only disadvantages to themselves, but also loss and damage to the customs revenue of Your Serenity.' A.S.V., *Provveditori da Terra e da Mar, filza* 1362.

22. Cf. A.S.V., *Senato, Secreta,* Despatches from England, *filza* 10, no. 30, letter of Antonio Foscarini from London, 14 July 1611. From the Senate registers it appears that, as a result of foreign competition, silk imports from Persia and the Levant had fallen from 1–2,000 bales to between 100–200 a year: cf. *Senato, Mar,* reg. 72, f. 52 (1 May 1614).

23. A.S.V., *Senato, Mar,* reg. 69, f. 148 (14 October 1610).

24. As early as August 1607, Nicolò Donà could write without hesitation that: 'There are now three much-frequented routes, on which all the most important trade of the city is concentrated: on these depend the profits and gains of private citizens, the subsistence of artisans and all other levels of the populace, the glorification of Venice and the maintenance of the public revenues by means of customs duties. These routes lead to Syria, Alexandria and Constantinople, and the Smyrna voyage should be added to these. However', added Donà, 'at present the Alexandrian route is not very much used.' A.S.V., *Provveditori da Terra e da Mar, filza* 1363, f. 27r.–v.

25. *Ibid., filza* 1362 (5 September 1611) and 1364 (April 1610).

26. A.S.F., *Mediceo del Principato, busta* 3088, f. 630v. (30 April 1619).

27. A.S.V., *Senato, Secreta*, Despatches from England, *busta* 2, no. 45 (11 September 1603).

28. Here, for example, are the remarks sent to the Grand Duke of Tuscany by his informant Isidoro Manfredi on October 18th 1586: 'The report that the galleon *Lombardo* had been captured was untrue, because there are official letters announcing its safe arrival in Crete. The rumour was put about by marine insurers, including one or two Venetian noblemen, who by spreading the report cause merchants to take out insurances, and so make a profit themselves. It is held that steps will be taken about this.' A.S.F., *Mediceo del Principato, filza* 3084, f. 58v.

29. A.S.V., *Provveditori da Terra e da Mar, filza* 1363, f. 107v.

30. *Ibid.*, f. 183.

31. *Ibid.*, f. 107v.

32. *Ibid.*, f. 102. The author of the memorandum wished to maintain that had there been well-armed ships it would have been possible 'to insure at 4 per cent and possibly less, since the goods would be very safe'.

33. A.S.V., *Senato, Mar*, reg. 69, f. 147 (12 October 1610).

34. 'The suspension of navigation, which is prohibited only to our own subjects and to our ships, which are at this time reduced to the condition which is well known to everyone, gives the opportunity to the foreigners who are increasingly frequenting our seas, islands and harbours to deprive our subjects of the profits to which they are used, so that many of them, having lost the support which they are accustomed to receive from the carrying-trade, and being unable to maintain themselves and their families, have been forced to apply elsewhere and make use of foreign ships, so that our mariner's trade is extinguished.' A.S.V., *Senato, Mar*, reg. 60, f. 106v. (4 October 1600).

35. A.S.V., *Provveditori da Terra e da Mar, filza* 1363, f. 164v. (7 June 1601).

36. A.S.V., *Senato, Mar*, reg. 62, f. 137v. (3 October 1602) and reg. 66, f. 45 (2 May 1606). Cf. *Senato, Mar, filza* 155, 23 September 1602.

37. A.S.V., *Provveditori da Terra e da Mar, filza* 1363, f. 83v.

38. A.S.V., *Senato, Mar*, reg. 67, f. 81v.–82v. (6 August 1607).

39. A.S.V., *Provveditori da Terra e da Mar, filza* 1363, f. 121v. and 123.

40. *Ibid.*, f. 121 and 123v. We also have precise information about the way in which the guns were to be arranged on the *Perastana*. Beneath the upperdeck, there were to be sixteen guns: two thirty-pounder culverins at the stern, six fourteen-pounder culverins and six twelve-pounder cannon at the sides, two fourteen-pounder culverins at the prow. The rest, to be placed on the upperdeck, was to be sited as follows: two fourteen-pounder culverins at the stern, two fourteen-pounder culverins and two twelve-pounder cannon on the two sides under the bridge, four fourteen-pounder culverins and two twelve-pounder cannon 'at the sides', two fifty-pounder mortars on either side of the mast, two twelve-pounder cannon at the prow, four fourteen-pounder mortars and four twelve-pounder mortars on the gundeck, four six-pounder guns above the bridge, two fourteen-pounder mortars in the master's cabin, two fourteen-pounder mortars and two six-pounder guns on the deck-cabin. Cf. *ibid.*, f. 129.

41. *Ibid.*, f. 100 and 127.

42. Cristoforo da Canal, for example, in a despatch from Lissa, spoke of 'the *Curzolana*, which is of little more than 400 butts and particularly ill-equipped with guns, most of them being of iron and not in the state that the owners described — so that', he concluded, 'this ship and the *Reatta* cannot be of much service to me'. *Ibid.*, commander of the ships, *filza* 1322 (27 November 1607).

43. *Ibid., filza* 1363; cf., in order, f. 181v., 62v. (8 June 1607) and 16v. (31 August 1607). Belegno, proceeding with his indictment, made the following charges against the shipowners: 'Hence, even though the ships might accidentally or otherwise be captured or wrecked, the owners did not suffer any loss as a result, but rather profited from it, because in insuring the vessel they had falsified its value, and old ships were usually insured as new ones.'

44. *Ibid.*, f. 29v. (2 August 1607).

45. *Ibid.*, f. 4v. (25 August 1607). In his despatch of 11 December 1603, Scaramelli wrote to the Senate that the English 'had been

encouraged and persuaded to take to piracy in the Levant by the rumour and fact of the feebleness of Venetian ships both in fighting and in sailing': cf. A.S.V., *Senato, Secreta*, Despatches from England, *filza* 2, no. 45.

46. A.S.V., *Senato, Secreta*, Despatches from England, *filza* 10, no. 30 (14 July 1611). In his despatch from London Foscarini reported the opinion of the English ex-consul in Syria, Pinder.

CHAPTER 6: LIGHT GALLEYS

1. Cf. here the essential article of R. Romano, 'Aspetti economici degli armamenti navali veneziani nel sec. XVI', *Rivista storica italiana*, LXVI, 1954, pp. 39–67.

2. Cf. the article by E. Fasano, 'Au XVIe siècle: comment naviguent les galères', *Annales: Économies, Sociétés, Civilisations*, 1961, pp. 279–96.

3. A statistic from Donà delle Rose MSS 155, M.C.V., gives us the following figures: 1605, 117 from Venice and 351 from the mainland; 1606, 110 and 406; 1607, 96 and 537; 1608, 91 and 497; 1609, 112 and 372; 1610, 105 and 496.

4. Cf. *Relazione*, already cited, M.C.V., Cicogna MSS 2855.

5. A.S.F., *Mediceo del Principato, filza* 3084, f. 163v. (31 January 1587), and *Provveditori da Terra e da Mar, filza* 1363, f. 188v. (21 April 1605).

6. M.C.V., Donà delle Rose MSS 79, no. IX.

7. Filippo Pasqualigo writes very clearly that 'Since convict galleys were first introduced, no galley has ever come to this city to disband with more than one hundred or very occasionally one hundred and ten convicts – on account of the number of convicts who have died or been released in the course of the voyage'. He specified that when they reached Venice some thirty or forty convicts were normally released, so that only sixty or seventy remained. Cf. *Provveditori da Terra e da Mar, filza* 1363, f. 187v. (21 April 1605).

8. A.S.V., *Senato, Secreta, Relazioni, busta* 55: *Relazione* of Giovanni Pasqualigo, commissioner for the Navy, 19 November 1605. On the problem of the cost of a free oarsman and of a convict, Pasqualigo

added: 'The free oarsman, although he receives the normal pay, turns out to be much less expensive than a convict, for convicts incur very heavy expenditure... and a large part of them pay their debts only by dying, so that without the slightest doubt Your Serenity suffers as much loss as with a free oarsman.' (*Ibid.*)

9. Cf. the *Relazione* cited above, n. 6.

10. *Dispacci al Senato del Capitano in Golfo*, 7 June 1610. Pietro Bondumier in his *Relazione* as Commissioner for the Navy in 1606 reports that in an inspection of five galleys, instead of the prescribed number of forty-eight free oarsmen he had found, respectively, twenty-four, twenty-one, nine, nine and three. The galley commanders who had gone to sea that year had received a grant of 2,000 ducats, with another 2,000 for the crews. Cf. A.S.V., *Senato, Secreta, Relazioni, busta* 55.

11. 'On disobedient persons', continued the letter, 'you shall invariably inflict the harshest penalties prescribed in your instructions, since we are resolved that the galleys must do their duty and obey their superiors.' A.S.V., *Senato, Mar*, reg. 55, f. 48v. (15 March 1594); cf. *ibid.*, reg. 47, f. 30v. (16 March 1585).

12. *Ibid.*, reg. 52, f. 141 (22 November 1591); cf. *ibid.*, reg. 46, f. 32v. (18 March 1583).

13. 'We understand', wrote the Senate to the civil governor of Parenzo, 'that many of our galleys are lying idle in the harbours of Istria, having no wish to go to their guard duties or report to their superior officers': *ibid.*, reg. 55, f. 48 (15 March 1594); cf. *ibid.*, reg. 49, f. 65v. (3 June 1588), and reg. 60, f. 83v. (9 August 1600), and reg. 64, f. 159 (20 November 1604).

14. A.S.V., *Provveditori da Terra e da Mar, filza* 1363, f. 93v. (8 July 1607); cf. *Senato, Mar*, reg. 64, f. 114v. (20 November 1604).

15. A.S.V., *Senato, Mar*, reg. 65, f. 27v.–29 (12 March 1605), reg. 71, f. 90v. (8 February 1613), and reg. 72, f. 37v. (5 April 1614). The admission that a used galley could not generally be repaired, 'after being unavailingly subjected to two or three overhauls', seems to imply that Venetian triremes could not stand up to the sea for more than four years at a stretch, this being the normal tour of duty of each galley commander, after which he returned to

Venice 'to disband'. Cf. *ibid.*, reg. 65, f. 27v. The Senate expressly admitted that squadron commanders found it very easy to obtain new galleys, even after only one year. For example, in March 1605 it was ascertained that there were at least twenty-five used hulls, many of which had been 'used by our naval commanders for one single voyage and then abandoned'. Worst of all was that, on being rejected even by the galley commanders ('because these galleys are normally of greater size ... as they have larger crews'), these warships became definitely included among the old galleys, cluttering up the Arsenal and hindering its activities. Cf. *Senato, Mar*, reg. 65, f. 26v. (12 March 1605).

16. This is asserted by Venier, Capitano in Golfo, in his *Relazione al Senato*, of January 1606 (cf. A.S.V., *Senato, Secreta, Relazioni*, busta 73). He also writes that: 'The galley commanders ... constantly lend one another oarsmen, both convicts and freemen, to the obvious detriment of the service of the state, since the older galley commanders take large numbers of rowers from the new ones, stocking up their galleys with five men or more per bench.' As a result, the oarsmen who remained on the new galleys and had to make greater efforts fell sick and often died.

17. M.C.V., Donà delle Rose MSS 2855, f. 50v.

18. A.S.F., *Mediceo del Principato*, busta 3084, f. 616r.-v. (20 March 1588). In another report from Venice, slightly earlier and probably written also by Manfredi, it was stated that: 'A letter has been sent to the Signory under the pseudonym of Ciriaco d'Ancona ... describing how the *Provveditore dell'Armata* and other naval commanders are only concerned to hire out their galleys and trade with them, and make their convicts work in the castles which they own in Dalmatia and Corfù – and hence he argues that a commission on the navy should be set up.' *Ibid.*, f. 356 (end of June 1587).

19. See his *Relazione di Capitano in Golfo*, A.S.V., *Senato, Secreta, Relazioni*, busta 73. In 1588 Bartolomeo Contarini, *Provveditore dell'Armata*, was already writing to the Doge: 'I am certain that, on account of the galleys that are disbanding and others which have to enter the Adriatic on the service of the state, most of the navy has to repair to that region, and the *Provveditore* will always find it

very difficult to get the galleys which emerge from the city even in their second year: and would to God that he had them yet.' A.S.V., *Quarantia Criminal, filza* 91, *fascicolo* 25 (October 1588).

20. *Relazione*, cited, f. 50.

21. A.S.V., *Dispacci al Senato del Capitano in Golfo*, 3, 25 and 31 August and 12 September. Bernardo Venier, in the *Relazione* of 15 January 1606, already cited several times, asserted that the daily rations of 224 oarsmen consisted of 18 ounces of biscuit per head and 36 pounds of rice, 'which', he remarked, 'is barely enough to keep them alive'. Agostino Michiel gave further information about the irregularities committed at this time: 'There is no doubt that large biscuits of good quality sell better than small bad biscuits: hence the soldiers get the best, and the bad stuff is always left in the depots for the use of the galleys. It appears in fact that all ships, great and small, which sail the Adriatic do not use or eat any bread other than government biscuit, which they draw in the manner described above. . . . The unfortunate oarsmen receive a daily ration consisting only of grist and crumbs, and cannot stand up to their hardships. . . . Hence also the prevalence of disease and death'; cf. *Senato, Secreta, Relazioni, busta* 73, *Relazione di A. Michiel, Capitano in Golfo*, 22 December 1608.

22. A.S.V., *Senato, Mar*, reg. 66, f. 140v.–141v. (12 January 1607).

23. A.S.V., *Dispacci al Senato del Capitanio in Golfo*, 13 February 1610. Sometimes the failure to pay the galley commanders bordered on the absurd, as Molin described it on 8 June 1610. He wrote from Zara that 'When new galleys go out from this city it is customary for the Equipment Office to hand over to the galley commanders in bulk the pay of all the men, both convicts and freemen, who are missing from the total numbers which they are obliged to have, so that they can recruit them outside and their pay can promptly be given to these men by the paymaster. But the last group of galley commanders have not been given this bulk payment, but tell me that it was kept back there in the aforesaid Equipment Office.' *Ibid*.

24. A.S.V., *Senato, Secreta, Relazioni, busta* 55, *Relazione di Agostino Canale*, 20 September 1611.

25. A.S.V., *Senato, Mar*, reg. 47, f. 279v.–280v. (24 February 1587); reg. 50, f. 122 (24 November 1589), and reg. 53, f. 143v. (19 February 1593).

26. A.S.V., *Senato, Secreta, Relazioni*, busta 73, *Relazione di Filippo Pasqualigo, Capitano in Golfo*.

27. *Relazione, cit.*, f. 48–9. A contemporary statement coinciding with this in every way was made by Giovanni Bembo: 'In Dalmatia there are no longer any men willing to venture upon this service, both for the scanty pay which they receive – which is not more than ten lire a month, excluding the food allowance – and on account of the many dangers which arise on guard duty and in watching over the convicts.' A.S.V., *Senato, Secreta, Relazioni*, busta 66, *Relazione di G. Bembo, Provveditore generale da Mar in Golfo*, f. 30v. (12 September 1598).

28. A.S.V., *Senato, Mar*, reg. 65, f. 73v.–75 (28 July 1605). By virtue of the same decree, squadron commanders were assigned a free grant of 3,000 ducats (instead of 2,000) and a subsidy of 4,000 (instead of 3,000).

29. 'There is in this city a band of depraved wretches living by their wits who have conceived the notion of maintaining themselves for most of the year at Your Serenity's expense; and so they go and strike bargains on various terms with the galleys that are recruiting men, in order to obtain the pay which is given to them monthly by the recruiting office and also the right to bear arms (with which they subsequently commit innumerable crimes). Thus for the space of eight, ten or twelve months they fraudulently receive the benefit of the pay and abuse the right to bear arms either by committing crimes or by following some lord as his retainer, so that when the time comes for the departure of the galley they are released and remain behind in Venice.' A.S.V., *Senato, Secreta, Relazioni*, busta 55, *Relazione di Giovanni Pasqualigo, Commissario d'Armata* (19 November 1605).

30. *Ibid.*, busta 75, *Relazione di Filippo Pasqualigo, Provveditore generale da Mar*, 13 December 1608.

31. *Relazione* cited above, f. 48 (M.C.V., Cicogna MSS 2855).

32. A.S.V., *Provveditori da Terra e da Mar*, f. 1363, f. 94r.–v. (8

July 1607). The same year proposals were made to grant a right to plunder the galleon also, according to the traditional apportionment. Having first deducted the 10 per cent due to the State, and set aside 5 per cent for those responsible for the division of the spoils and for any expenses incurred in this, the remainder was to be divided into three parts, one to go to the *Provveditore* and the others to all members of the crew, omitting no one. Cf. *ibid.*, f. 48.

33. *Ibid.*, f. 151v. (5 March 1605), 18v. (31 August 1607), 5-6 (25 August 1607). Nicolò Donà and Antonio Pisani, on the other hand, held that light galleys could not effectively fight against *bertoni*: *ibid.*, f. 28 (2 August 1607) and 12 (3 September 1607).

34. The commander of the Cretan fleet insisted on this point: if light galleys had sometimes taken *bertoni*, they had not, he maintained, captured any of those 'That are fitted out and sent to engage in piracy with two or three hundred or more musketeers, with a hundred sailors, with forty or more guns, twenty-five gunners and twice as many mates, like those of Malta, Naples, Sardinia and Savoy' — *ibid.*, f. 12 (3 September 1607).

35. To read the despatches of Francesco Molin, *Capitano in Golfo*, would in itself be enough to establish that the light galleys were working inefficiently about 1609. Here is a quotation from a letter written from Zara on 30 March 1609. After pointing out that he had not a single sound galley in his squadron, Molin continued: 'Of the galleys now out on active service, the best are employed by express decree of the most worshipful Senate on special missions, so that I cannot and must not lay hands on them — like those of Signor Domenico Mocenigo (sent to serve the most worshipful *Provveditore generale* Zane) and Signor Iseppo Michiel (summoned to Venice to pick up the most worshipful Venier), or the *Quirina* (sent there to collect money by the illustrious Lord Commissioner, being reserved to his most illustrious lordship). Or else they are such shaky and battered hulks — like that of Signor Giovan Francesco Loredan — that if I had to take one with me I should go continually in terror, at every puff of wind, of seeing it swallowed by the waves before my very eyes, or else forced to run aground, suffering grave damage, and greater indignity among ourselves and our rivals alike. The *Balba* is new, and its crew not yet fully

recovered from their first illness, nor sufficiently established in health. The *Donata* and *Basadonna*, which have come out most recently, have their crews in the hospitals, which usually happens to all galleys at the beginning of their voyages. Finally, Signor Francesco Pisani, son of the excellent Signor Benetto, is still in Istria, where he has for over three months been awaiting the new ship to be sent him in exchange for his old one.' Cf. A.S.V., *Dispacci al Senato del Capitano in Golfo*.

36. A.S.V., *Senato, Mar*, reg. 69, f. 150v.–152v.

CHAPTER 7: GALLEASSES AND GALLEON

1. A.S.F., *Mediceo del Principato, filza* 3084, f. 131v.
2. In 1595 a Venetian light galley carried a cannon weighing between 4,400 and 6,000 pounds, capable of firing fifty-pound cannonballs, a falcon (of 1,200 pounds, firing six-pound balls), a falconet (250–400 pounds, three-pound balls) and ten mortars (two of 250–400 pounds firing six-pound balls, and eight of 150 pounds firing three-pound balls). Some galleys carried two extra falconets and two less three-pound mortars. Others carried a thirty-pounder culverin weighing 5,800 pounds, or else a twenty-pounder weighing 4,400, instead of a fifty-pounder cannon. The specifications of 1609 were confined to adding a six-pounder falcon and two three-pounder mortars (cf. M.C.V., Donà delle Rose MSS 155). The great galley carried: on the central gangway, two forty-pounder culverins; at the prow, two twenty-pounder culverins; on the gundeck, two fourteen-pounder culverins and four twelve-pounder mortars; opposite the fifth and sixth bench from the prow, two twenty-pounder cannon and two twelve-pounder culverins; amidships, two thirty-pounder cannon; at the fourth bench from the stern, two twenty-pounder cannon; at the sixth and tenth bench from the stern, two twelve-pounder mortars; and at the stern (between the corridors, the castle and the lower part) two twenty-pounder cannon, two fourteen-pounder culverins and two six-pounder falcons; cf. A.S.V., *Provveditori da Terra e da Mar, filza* 1362, f. 23.
3. A.S.V., *Senato, Mar*, reg. 61, f. 63 (14 July 1601) and f. 79 (9 August 1601).

4. A.S.V., *Provveditori da Terra e da Mar, filza* 1363, f. 82 (17 June 1607).

5. Contarini, *Historie*, etc., *cit.*, book VIII, f. 224v. (A.S.V., *Miscellanea Codici*, no. 80).

6. A.S.V., *Senato, Secreta, Relazioni*, busta 75: *Relazione di Filippo Pasqualigo, Provveditore generale da Mar* (13 December 1608).

7. A.S.V., *Provveditori da Terra e da Mar, filza* 1363, f. 154v.

8. *Ibid.*, f. 32v. (1607).

9. Cf. A. Tenenti, 'I corsari in Mediterraneo all' inizio del Cinquecento', *Rivista storica italiana*, LXXII (1960), p. 243.

10. A.S.F., *Mediceo del Principato, filza* 3087, f. 353v. (28 July 1607).

11. A.S.V., *Senato, Secreta, Relazioni*, busta 73, *Relazione di Giust' Antonio Belegno* (4 February 1609).

12. If the galleon lay in wait, ready to give chase to pirates, at the Gozi off Crete, at least forty miles from the island, it ran the risk of being driven to the Barbary coasts, because south-westerly winds blew there which were capable of lasting for as much as eight to ten days. If it stationed itself at Sapienza, storms might drive it as far as Sicily or Malta: 'and if the wind comes out of the sea it is necessary to enter Greek waters and pass beneath Turkish fortresses'. Finally, if it stayed between Cerigo and Crete, it risked being driven either towards North Africa or to the Archipelago. Belegno chose Vatica as base, although it was windy. Cf. *ibid.*

13. A.S.V., *Provveditori da Terra e da Mar, filza* 1365, despatch of Paolo Tiepolo from Corfù, 28 June 1615.

14. The commander of the great galleys thus concluded his *Relazione* of 19 January 1604: 'The use of these vessels to suppress piracy and for the purpose of merely pursuing robbers is, in my opinion, a thing to be avoided, especially because of the expense.' Cf. M.C.V., Donà delle Rose MSS, 43, f. 99v.

15. A.S.V., *Provveditori da Terra e da Mar, filza* 1363, f. 150 (5 March 1605).

16. *Ibid.*, f. 154v. (7 March 1605).

17. *Ibid.*, f. 160 (7 March 1605).

18. *Ibid.*, f. 3-4 (25 August 1607).

19. *Ibid.*, f. 187v. (21 April 1605).

20. *Ibid.*, f. 137 (July 1605) and f. 82 (17 June 1607).

21. *Ibid.*, f. 28v.–29 (2 August 1607). From the same period comes a memorandum in the Donà collection, which states that 'In the past, no-one ever thought of employing ponderous open vessels which needed such numerous crews, such vast quantities of equipment, so many guns and so much victuals, and had to renew their water-supplies on the voyage. Such vessels have to be exposed continuously, like the hardest rocks, to the waves of the sea, especially in the cruellest season of the year, when it is dangerous to fly from misfortune into port, and not easy to emerge from all harbours in the face of contrary winds.' Cf. M.C.V., Donà delle Rose MSS 43, f. 46.

22. However, the following significant passage may be cited from the *Relazione* of Lorenzo Venier: 'Moreover, it would have been desirable to provide a greater counterpoise to the Dutch and English armies, for although they have always shown great skill and finesse it has never been good tactics or reason of state to allow any nation total preponderance in the strength of its armies: especially as the Northerners with us were on ships with sailors of their own country, which made them stronger and could on account of the shortage of money treat them as heavily in their debt.' Cf. A.S.V., *Senato, Secreta, Relazioni, busta* 75, *Relazione di L. Venier, Capitano generale da Mar* (6 January 1621).

23. A.S.F., *Mediceo del Principato, filza* 3087, f. 341 (16 June 1607).

24. 'All the ships or other vessels which want to sail to the Levant on the routes to Syria, Alexandria or Constantinople must sail in convoy together, starting with the March convoy and with the August convoy, nor may any other vessel, whether it belongs to subjects of ours or is a foreign ship carrying Venetian subjects, leave these harbours on the said voyages at any other time on any pretext whatsoever.' Cf. A.S.V., *Senato, Mar*, reg. 69, f. 53v.–54v. (22 December 1609).

25. *Ibid.*, ff. 123–24 (12 October 1610).

26. A.S.V., *Provveditori da Terra e da Mar, filza* 1364, despatches of the commander of the great galleys, 24 December 1608 and 1 April

1610. The Venetian failure was completed by an almost disastrous pursuit of the two *bertoni*. In the course of this operation, as Francesco Morosini described it, 'the look-outs above noticed that the yards above the mainsail were broken, and so they shouted: "Take in the sail, for the yard is broken!" Hence I was forced, by the great danger which threatened me, to reef the sails at once and take in the mainsail.' Observing that the yards of the galleass could no longer hold up the sails, the commander ordered the other warships to stop also. One of them, moreover, was not in too good a state: 'The foresail had come adrift, the sails on the mizzen-mast had been torn to pieces and scattered, and the mainsail could no longer be carried.' 'God knows', concluded Morosini, 'how disappointed I was to see that a scheme so well conceived had not succeeded.' Cf. *ibid.*, despatch from Zante, 5 April 1610.

27. A.S.V., *Senato, Secreta, Relazioni, busta* 73, *Relazione di Francesco Morosini, capitano delle galere grosse armate* (30 January 1612).

28. Cf. A.S.V., *Provveditori da Terra e da Mar, filza* 1362 (11 and 25 August 1611).

29. On this the new commander of the great galleys wrote: 'These are most noble ships, and they will always be most valuable in time of war when many galleys are fitted out, but they are dangerous in these narrow straits, and this guard duty should be carried out by light galleys, as our ancestors have done it for hundreds of years.' *Ibid., filza* 1364, despatch of Bernardo Venier from Zante, 21 February 1613.

30. *Ibid.*, despatch from Corfù, 19 April 1608; cf. the despatch of Lorenzo Venier from Sapienza on 10 June 1607.

31. *Ibid.*, despatch from Corfù, 6 September 1609. On 30 July 1611, Girolamo Morosini, whose galley had been certified 'unfit to sail', wrote as follows from the same place: 'It is a great burden to me that because of the misfortune of the ship I am compelled to stay uselessly in this harbour, and that the vast expenses which I incurred in fitting out my galley turn out to be of no avail — for I had fully equipped it with oarsmen in much greater numbers than Your Serenity prescribes and with soldiers cunning and skilful at every sort of operation.' *Ibid.*

32. *Ibid.*, despatch of 11 December 1609; cf. the despatch of 29 March 1608 and those of 6 and 9 April 1607. In August 1608 Francesco Morosini wrote from Lesina that he had already incurred debts out of his own pocket to the tune of many thousands of ducats. Antonio Pisani, in a letter from Zante on 14 March 1612, was still more precise. He had spent over 30,000 ducats on his crew. *Ibid.*

33. *Ibid.*, *filza* 1362, f. 94 (8 July 1607).

34. *Ibid.*, *filza* 1364, 28 July 1611.

35. *Ibid.*, 3 June 1611, cf. despatch of Francesco Morosini from Corfù, 6 September 1609.

36. *Ibid.*, *filza* 1365, 26 November 1616; cf. *ibid.*, 8 October 1615, and the *Relazione* of Francesco Morosini, cited above.

37. A.S.V., *Senato, Secreta, Relazioni*, busta 73, *Relazione* cited above, of 30 January 1612; cf. *Provveditori da Terra e da Mar, filza* 1363, 28 June 1609.

38. A.S.V., *Provveditori da Terra e da Mar*, *filza* 1365, 15 March 1614 (from Cerigo) and 4 January 1615 (from Zante).

Bibliography

Aspetti e cause della decadenza economica veneziana. Venice, 1961.

BARKER, A. *A true and certain report of the beginning, proceedings, overthrows and now present state of Captain Ward and Dansker, the two late famous pirates.* London, 1609.

BATTISTELLA, A. 'Il dominio del Golfo', *Nuovo archivio veneto, nuova serie*, XVIII, 1918, vol. XXXV, pp. 5–102.

BRAUDEL, F. *La Méditerranée et le monde méditerranéen à l'époque de Philippe II.* Paris, 1949.

Calendar of state papers and manuscripts relating to English affairs in the archives and collections of Venice and in other libraries of Northern Italy, ed. Horatio F. Brown. London, 1894, vol. VII *et seq.*

CANAYE, PH. *Lettres et ambassade.* Paris, 1635–36, 3 vols. in folio.

CHARLE-ROUX, F. *France et Afrique du Nord avant 1830: les précurseurs de la conquête.* Paris, 1932.

CHARRIÈRE, E. *Négociations de la France dans le Levant.* Paris, 1848–60, 4 vols. Collection de documents inédits sur l'histoire de France.

CIALDEA, B. *La formazione dell' ordinamento marittimo nelle relazioni internazionali (secoli XIV-XVIII)*, vol. II. Milan, 1959.

CLARK, G. N. *War and society in the seventeenth century.* Cambridge, 1958.

CORBETT, J. S. *England in the Mediterranean, 1603–1703*, vol. I. London, 1904.

COZZI, G. *Il doge Nicolò Contarini: ricerche sul patriziato veneziano agli inizi del Seicento*. Venice-Rome, 1959.

CRESCENZIO, B. *Nautica mediterranea*. Rome, 1607.

DAL POZZO, B. *Historia della Sacra Religione di S. Giovanni gerosolimitano detta di Malta*. Verona, 1703.

DAN, P. *Histoire de Barbarie et de ses corsaires*. Paris, 1637.

DRACHIO QUINTIO, B. *L'ammiraglio*. B.M.V., Italian MSS, class IV, CLXXVII (5155).

ENGEL, C.-E. *L'Ordre de Malte en Mediterranée, 1530–1708*. Monaco, 1957.

EPSTEIN, M. *The English Levant Company: its foundation and its history to 1640*. London, 1908.

FALCONI, A. *Breve instruzione appartenente al capitano de' vasselli quadri*. Florence, 1612.

FERNANDEZ DURO, C. *Armada española desde la union de los reinos de Castilla y de Aragon*, vol. III. Madrid, 1897.

FERNANDEZ DURO, C. *El duque de Osuna y su marina*. Madrid, 1885.

FISCHER, G. *Barbary legend: war, trade and piracy in North Africa, 1415–1830*. Oxford, 1957.

FURTTENBACH, J. *Architectura navalis, dass ist con dem Schiff, Gebäw auff dem Meer und Seeküsten zugebrauchen*. Ulm, 1629.

GIGANTE, S. *Venezia e gli Uscocchi dal 1570 al 1620*. Fiume, 1904.

GIOMO, G. and VISENTINI, F. *Le galere grosse veneziane nel 1593*. Venice, 1895.

GOSSE, PH. *Histoire de la piraterie*. Paris, 1952.

GRAMMONT, H. D. de. *Études algériennes: la course, l'esclavage et la rédemption à Alger*. Paris, 1885.

GRAMMONT, H. D. de. *Relations entre la France et la Régence d'Alger au XVIIe siècle. Première partie: les deux canons de Simon Dansa, 1606–1628*. Algiers, 1879.

GRAMMONT, H. D. de. *Histoire d'Alger sous la domination turque, 1515–1830.* Paris, 1887.

GUARNIERI, G. G. *Le imprese guerresche dei Cavalieri di Santo Stefano dal 1609 al 1621.* Leghorn, 1914.

GUARNIERI, G. G. *Cavalieri di Santo Stefano.* Pisa, 1928.

HAEDO, D. de. *Histoire des rois d'Alger,* trans. H. D. de Grammont. Paris, 1881.

HORVATH, C. ed. *Monumenta Uscoccorum.* 2 vols. Zagreb, 1910–13.

HUBAC, P. *Les Barbaresques.* Paris, 1949.

JURIEN DE LA GRAVIÈRE. *Les derniers jours de la marine à rames.* Paris, 1885.

KOENIGSBERGER, H. G. 'English Merchants in Naples and Sicily in the seventeenth century', *English Historical Review,* 1947.

KRAVJANSKY, M. 'Il processo degli Uscocchi', *Archivio Veneto, quinta serie,* V, 1929, pp. 234–66.

LANE-POOLE, S. *The Barbary corsairs.* London, 1890.

LANE, F. C. *Venetian ships and shipbuilders of the Renaissance.* Baltimore, 1934.

LA RONCIÈRE, CH. de. *Histoire de la marine française,* vol. IV. Paris, 1910.

LEVI, C. A. *Navi venete da codici, marmi e dipinti.* Venice, 1892.

MANFRONI, C. 'La marina da guerra del granducato mediceo'. *Rivista marittima,* 1896.

MARCHESI, G. V. *La galera dell' onore.* Forli, 1735, 2 vols.

MASSON, P. *Histoire du commerce français dans le Levant au XVIIe siècle.* Paris, 1896.

MERCIER, E. *Histoire de l'Afrique Septentrionale (Berbérie) depuis le temps les plus reculés jusqu'à la conquête française, 1830.* Paris, 1891.

MINUCCI, M. *Historia degli Uscocchi.* Venice, 1602.

NANI MOCENIGO, M. *L'arsenale di Venezia.* Rome, 1938.

NANI MOCENIGO, M. *La marina veneziana da Lepanto alla caduta della Repubblica.* Rome, 1930.

NEGRI, P. 'La politica veneta contro gli Uscocchi in relazione alla congiura del 1618', *Nuovo archivio veneto, nuova serie*, IX, 1908, vol. XVII, parte II, pp. 338–84.

PANTERA, P. *L'armata navale*. Rome, 1614.

PARUTA, P. *La legazione di Roma, 1592–1595*, ed. R. Fulin and G. De Leva. 3 vols. Venice, 1887.

PLANTET, E. *Correspondance des beys de Tunis et des consuls de France avec la cour*, vol. I, *1577–1700*. Paris, 1893.

RAPPENAU, G. *De la piraterie du droit des gens à la piraterie par analogie*. Paris, 1942.

SALVA, J. *La Orden de Malta y las acciones navales españolas contra Turcos y Berberiscos en los siglos XVI y XVII*. Madrid, 1944.

SARPI, P. *Aggiunta all' Historia degli Uscocchi di M. Minucci*. Venice, 1671.

SASSI, F. 'La guerra in corsa e il diritto di preda secondo il diritto marittimo veneziano', *Rivista di storia del diritto italiano*, II, 1929.

SASSI, F. 'La politica navale veneziano dopo Lepanto', *Nuovo archivio veneto, quinta serie*, XXXVIII–XLI, 1946–47, pp. 99–200.

SAVARY DE BRÈVES, FR. *Relation des voyages tant en Grece, Terre-Saincte et Aegypte qu'aux royaumes de Tunis et Arger*. Paris, 1628.

SHERLEY, E. PH. *The Sherley brothers: an historical memoir of the lives of Sir Thomas Sherley, Sir Anthony Sherley and Sir Robert Sherley*. Chiswick, 1848.

STEFANI, G. *L'assicurazione a Venezia dalle origini alla fine della Serenissima*. 2 vols. Trieste, 1956.

TENENTI, A. 'Gli schiavi di Venezia alla fine del Cinquecento', *Rivista storica italiana*, LXVII, 1955, pp. 52–69.

TENENTI, A. 'I corsari in Mediterraneo all' inizio del Cinquecento', *Rivista storica italiana*, LXXII, 1960, pp. 234–87.

TENENTI, A. *Naufrages, corsaires et assurances maritimes à Venise, 1592–1609*. Paris, 1959.

TENENTI, A. 'Schiavi e corsari nel Mediterraneo orientale intorno al 1585', *Miscellanea in onore di Roberto Cessi*, Rome, 1958, vol. II, pp. 173–85.

TENTORI, C. *Saggio sulla storia civile, politica, ecclesiastica e sulla corografia e topografia degli Stati della Repubblica di Venezia*. Venice, 1787–88, vols. VIII–X.

TITONE, V. *La Sicilia dalla dominazione spagnola all' unità d'Italia*. Bologna, 1955.

TUCCI, U. 'Sur la pratique vénitienne de la navigation au XVIe siècle: quelques remarques', *Annales: Économies, Sociétés, Civilisations*, 1958, no. 1, pp. 72–86.

UZIELLI, G. *Cenni storici sulle imprese scientifiche, marittime e coloniali di Ferdinando I, granduca di Toscana, 1587–1609*. Florence, 1901.

VERTOT, DE. *Histoire des Chevaliers hospitaliers de S. Jean de Jerusalem* ..., vol. V. Paris, 1778.

WOOD, A. C. *A history of the Levant Company*. Oxford, 1935.

Index

Abruzzo, 21, 92
Adelantado, the, 45
Adriatic, the, 32, 54, 90; piracy and, xvii, 8, 14, 17, 21, 22, 24, 25, 43, 47, 56; Venetian shipping, 4, 21, 91, 92; informers from, 29; Maltese assault on, 39–40; the Dutch and, 59; patrol force, 121
Aegean, xvii, 25, 99
Africa, North, corsairs from, 16, 19; English pirates and, 73, 74, 75, 77, 80; Ottoman authorities, 84
Agostini, Ludovico, on pirate traders, 23–4; on a Barbary-Venetian encounter, 16 n. 20
Airoldi, the, 25
Albania, hotbed of piracy, 18–20, 24, 31; Turks of, 57; Venetian shipping and, 91
Albertini, Piero, 69
Alessandretta, 83, 86, 170 n. 5
Alessio, 24
Alexandria, 41, 42, 61, 68, 76, 82, 83, 99, 179 n. 24; English shipping and, 170 n. 5
Algiers, and piracy, 19, 25, 38, 57, 68, 74, 150, 160 n. 12; English galleons and, 63; Northern pirate base, 83
Alicante, 91
Allegretti, Nicolò, 66
Alvel, Nicholas, 70–1
Alvise, Pietro d', 48
Ammirabile, Francesco, 67
Amsterdam, 46, 71
Anatolia, 31, 48

Ancona, xii, 8, 12, 22, 66, 121, 157 n. 2; pirate clearing-house, 85
Andrizza, the, 53–4
Angel, the, 69, 74
Angeli, the, 79
Anglo-Turkish pirates, 80–1
Annunziata, the, 63
Antiburl, Bortolamio, 162 n. 25
Antwerp, xii
Apulia, 20, 21, 92, 168 n. 34
Aragona, Ferdinando d', 49
Archipelago, the, xvii, 66, 138; piracy and, 24, 27, 37, 40, 50, 63, 70, 76, 83, 169 n. 41
Argostoli, 44
Arnaut, Memi, Corsair, 25, 26, 27
Arrigoni, Lorenzo, and capture of *Reniera e Soderina*, 174 n. 29
Atlantic, the, extension of rivalry into Mediterranean, 58; and Mediterranean affairs, 82; Northern pirates and, 83, 84; Venetian trade and, 91; use of merchant galleys, 133
Aumale, Prince, 38
Austria, 4

Bacetich, Vincenzo, 96
Badoer, commander, 174 n. 32
Bagosnizza, 26
Baietto, the, 39
Balba, the, 187 n. 35
Balbi, the, 79, 82
Balbi, Nicolò, 104; and great galleys, 133–4, 140
Balbi, Teodoro, 28, 96, 137, 145, 162 n. 25; sells a ship's cargo, 168 n. 38

198

INDEX

Balbiana, the, 7, 39, 71, 106–7
Balbiani family, 96
Bandino, Knight, 36, 38
Barbaro, Vittore, and the Uskoks, 8, 12, 13, 15, 43
Barbary coast, xvii, 17, 24, 30, 57, 58, 165 n. 15; English pirate bases, 73, 74, 77; 'new men' from, 80–1, 83, 84, 175 n. 37; Atlantic fleets, 84
Barbary Corsairs, 56, 96, 151; location of their attacks, xvii, 17, 25; offensive against Christendom, 17; vessels used by, 19–21, 22, 24; feats of daring, 21–2; disposition of prisoners and booty, 23–4, 29, 160 n. 11, raids by, 24–5, 26, 50, 161 n. 16; and slave trade, 26; encounters with Venetian navy, 26–8, 161 n. 20, 162 n. 25; extract tribute, 29; spread eastward, 33; clashes with Maltese pirates, 38; and the Levant, 43; use of *bertoni*, 52; and English shipping, 62; use of the galley, 111
Barella, the, 29
Barozza, the, 62
Barozzi, Vincenzo, 94
Barze, 133, 136
Basadonna, the, 187 n. 35
Basso, Giacomo, 45
Beckmann, Mark, 45
Beirut, 61, 83
Belegno, Giust' Antonio, 14–15, 52; and Maltese pirates, 54, 169 n. 40; on the galleon, 80, 136, 137; on the Venetian *bertoni*, 97–8, 129; on Dutch piracy, 98, on escort crews, 108, 181 n. 43; and sufferings of convict crews, 113–14, 115; appointed Commissioner, 123, 139; and galleasses, 139
Beltrame, the, 30
Bembo, Giovanni, 13, 78–9, 139; and galley crews, 186 n. 27
Berbers, the, 27, 33, 162 n. 20
Bersatona, the, 70
Bertoni, 25, 26, 30, 48; and Mediterranean waters, 52–4, 64, 169 n. 41, 173 n. 25; English use of, 64ff, 72, 73, 75, 171 n. 10; distinguishing features, 63–4, 171 n. 10; armaments, 64, 171 n. 10; route threatened by, 66; Venetian defence against, 67–9, 79–80, 138; used by France, 72, Ward and, 83, 84; replace merchantmen, 91; in Venetian merchant fleet, 96, 97; *vis-à-vis* light galleys, 128–30, 187 nn. 33, 34; Venetian opposition to their employment, 138ff; description of, 152
Biserta, 74, 84, 162 n. 25
Black Lion, the, 45
Bon, the, 59
Bona, the, 26
Bonaventura Giopanditi, the, 70–1
Bondumier, Piero, 68, 109, 126, 129; and use of *Bertoni*, 138, 139, 140
Bonoma e Valnegrina, the, 81
Bower, Captain, 65
Bragadin, Antonio, 145
Brazza island, Uskoks and, 6
Brazzere, used by Uskoks, 6, 13, 152
Brigatine, 152–3
Brindisi, 14
Brocchiero de Anaya, Don Diego, 35, 39, 164 n. 4
Bruzza, Francesco da, 5
Bull, the, 46
Butt, the, 153, 177 n. 7

Cadi, definition of, 153
Cadiz, 45, 62, 63
Calabria, 17, 32, 92
Calamici, 41
Caldera, the, 70
Calvinism, xvi
Canal, Agostino da, 130
Canal, Benedetto da, 15
Canal, Cristoforo da, 78, 92, 109; and convict galleys, 112; on the *Curzolana*, 181 n. 42
Candia, 35–6
Canea, the, 36
Canevala, the, 25
Caorle, 14
Cape Celidonia, 41
Cape Gallo, 71
Cape Lachi, 19
Cape Malio, 32, 68

199

INDEX

Cape Martin, 160 n. 12
Cape Matapan, 25, 34
Cape of Good Hope, xii
Cape of Otranto, 25
Cape St Angelo, 40
Cape St John, 43, 66
Cape St Vincent, 62, 67
Cape Salamon, 36
Cape Sant' Andrea, 48
Capello, Girolamo, 23, 71–2; on poor wages of galley crews, 176 n. 3
Capitulations of 1580, 60, 62
Caramousal, description of, 153
Carara, Antonio, 169 n. 41
Carlo Emanuele I, Duke of Savoy, 75, 84, 85, 151
Carminati, the, 54, 77
Cascais, 62
Castel Rosso, 40
Castello, Giovanni, 66
Castelnuovo, 19, 29
Casten, Captain Jan, 79, 143–4
Cattanea, the, 65
Cattaro, 14, 24, 25, 29, 86; shipbuilding, 94
Catti, Giovan Andrea, notary, 59, 94, 99
Cavalli, Antonio, 120
Cefalonia, 27, 34, 38, 45, 59, 61, 178 n. 15
Cerigo, 34, 35, 40, 53, 64; Venetian base, 66, 68, 129, 137, 144
Cerigo, Manoli da, 45
Cerigotto, 36, 40
Cesenatico, 22
Chiaus, definition of, 153
Chioggia, 14, 22, 23, 117
Chioggia, Francesco da, 19
Chios, 66
Christianity, rivalry with Islam in Mediterranean, xvi, 16, 82; piracy and, 8, 62, 151; victory at Lepanto, 33
Christians, captured by pirate ships, 27, 41, 42, 43
Christina of Lorraine, 168 n. 36
Ciciri river (Crete), 43
Cigala e Mozzocca, the, 26
Cimmerioti, the, 90
Cinque Savi alla Mercanzia, 95, 97, 107, 143, 178 n. 21; definition of, 53

Ciuran, Antonio, commander, 146, 174 n. 32
Classen, Wilhelm, 45
Cochini, Dullo, 101, 102
Coletti, the, 25
Collegio della Milizia da Mar, definition of, 153
Colombo, 81
Coluri, Antonio, 68
Condocolo, Nicolò, 45
Constantina, the, 65
Constantinople, xvi, 14, 24, 37, 41, 49, 50, 57, 61, 66, 99, 179 n. 24; trade concessions to England, 60; Venetian embassy and piracy, 71; and Northern pirates, 73, 83
Contarina, the, 6, 7
Contarini, Alessandro, 145
Contarini, Bartolomeo, 184 n. 19
Contarini, Carlo, 20–1
Contarini, Girolamo, 61, 68, 69, 138; on poor quality of galley crews, 176 n. 3
Contarini, Nicolò, 44, 50, 162 n. 25; on piratical treachery and cruelty, 48–9, 167 n. 28; on losses from piracy, 50, 168 n. 34; on England's sea power, 58–9; on Dutch pirates, 59; and galleasses, 134
Contreras, Alonso de, 47
Convicts, use of in galleys, 26, 112ff, 124; their sufferings, 113–14; hospitals for, 113; abuses of, 114, 115, 182 n. 7; enlistment and release, 114; the commanders and, 114–15; breakdown in the system, 115–16
Convoy system, 107, 143, 145, 146, 190 n. 24
Cordes, Cesare, 167 n. 28
Corfù, Venetian navy and, 19, 21, 28, 30, 34, 37, 40, 68, 84, 122, 138, 147; use of galleys, 44, 90, 176 n. 2; its pesthouse, 48; English ships and, 61
Corner, Marc' Antonio, 83
Corone, 25, 73, 76, 79
Cortesi, Scipione, 53
Council of Ten, 5, 156, 178 n. 21
Crescent Moon, the, 46
Crete, 20, 25, 43, 45, 59, 63, 67, 70,

200

INDEX

Crete (*cont.*)
  78, 82, 99, 168 n. 33; defence of, 34, 66; Turkish grain for, 37; Senate loans for shipbuilding, 96, 177 n. 7; galley captains and, 118–19, 121; its regular fleet, 121
Croatia, 4
Croce, the, seizure of, 39
Crown, the, value of, 153–4
Curzola, island of, 6, 12, 82; shipbuilding at, 94
Curzolana, the, 181 n. 42
Cyprus, 7, 34, 41, 48, 52, 65, 76, 81, 137; Venetian dominion over, xi–xii; Christian fugitives from, 40–1; slaves revolt in, 41, 165 n. 15

Dalmatia, 4, 131; and the Uskoks, 5, 6; pirate refugees from, 10; Venetian naval base, 21, 186 n. 27; Barbary corsairs and, 23, 26; main route of Venetian shipping, 57, 67, 85
Damiata, 41
Dandolo da Milo, 29
Danziger, his pirate fleet, 83; and Henry IV, 84–5
David, the, 66
Diedo, the, 25
Dominicans, at Segna, 9
Donà, Nicolò, 176 n. 2; and the Uskoks, 8–9, 13, 15; on Venetian shipping crisis, 108; on convict labour, 113; on disorders in the fleet, 119, 122; and shortage of crews, 125, 126, 127; and the galleon, 135; condemns galleasses, 140–1, 145; on changed sea routes, 179 n. 24
Donata, the, 75, 187 n. 35
Doria, the, 144
Doria, Andrea, xv
Dragon, the, 70
Ducat, value of, 154
Dulcigno, 24
Dupuy, Captain, 53
Durazzo, and piracy, 19, 24, 29, 122, 160 n. 11
Dutch, the, xi, 50; and decline of Venice, xiii; and Mediterranean affairs, xvii; enter the Mediterranean, 44, 59, 166 n. 19; piracy against their shipping, 46, 54, 70, 71; treatment in Venice, 59; use of *bertoni*, 64, 142; and piracy, 68, 80, 86, 98; ships' armaments, 106

Egypt, 78
Elia d'Oro, the, 65
Elizabeth I, xvi; struggle with Spain, 58, 60, 62; and Venetian trading, 58; measures against foreign shipping, 59; Venetian ambassador to, 72
Emilia, 21
Emo, the, 65
Emo, Gabriele, 26–7
Emo, Giovanni, 106
England, xi; and decline of Venice, xii–xiii, 56, 57; and Mediterranean affairs, xvii; and Barbary corsairs, 17; and pirate warfare, 35, 44, 50, 61, 62, 91; enters the Mediterranean, 44, 58, 166 n. 19; relations with Venice, 44, 59, 72; attacks on her shipping, 53, 62; and trade with Venetian Republic, 58, 59–60, 91; her ships reach Venetian waters, 60–1, 63; speed of her ships, 60, 170 n. 4; at Zante, 61, 170 n. 5; combine piracy and trade, 61–4; use of *bertoni*, 64–71, 142; measures against pirates, 72; collaboration with Tuscany, 74–5, 175 n. 25; organization of her piracy, 75, 80; and the Levant, 76; and pirate manpower, 151
Eston, Peter, 85
Europe, xi, xii, xiii; Venetian importance in, 17–18; Spanish piracy and, 44

Faenzo, Agostino, 54
Famagusta, 41
Fano, 23
Fanzaga, the, 26
Farsi uscocco, 10
Feluche, 46; definition of, 154
Ferdinand I, Grand Duke of Tuscany, 53, 151; Sherley and, 70, 74; employment of English pirates and materials, 74, 84; pirate gifts to, 85

201

INDEX

Ferletich (pirate), 14, 15
Fermo, 22
Ferra, Lorenzo Suarez de Figueroa y Cordoba, Duke of, 50
Ferrara, Duke of, 21
Fighetto, Francesco, 62
Fiume, 3, 121, 157 n. 2
Florence, xi, 23; offensive against piracy, xvii; pirates from, 34, 37, 45, 46, 50; use of *bertoni*, 52, 173 n. 25; and Venetian shipping, 52-3, 57; and Ward, 85; use of the galley, 111
Flores, Jan, 68
Flying Fortune, the, 46
Fortune, the, 46
Foscarina e Mula, the, 81
Foscarini, Antonio, on collapse of Venetian trade, 109
Fox, the, 70
France, use of the Mediterranean, xii, xvii, entente with Turkey, xvi; naval power, xvi; attacks on her shipping, 30, 39, 54, 81, 162 n. 25; and *bertoni*, 65, 171 n. 10; trade with the Levant, 71; campaign against piracy, 71-2; pirate adventurers, 80; in collusion with pirates, 84-5, 86
Franciscans, at Segno, 9; pirate attacks on, 22, 23
Fregate, 7, 14, 19, 34, 38; definition of, 154
Friendship, the, 67
Furegon, Giovan Maria, 47
Fuste, 11, 15, 20-4, 27, 29, 30, 32, 34, 57, 111, 112, 117, 122, 130; the galley and, 128; construction of, 154

Gagliana, the, 49
Galeotta, 19, 32, 46, 57, 151, 160 n. 12; use of, 22, 24, 25, 26, 29, 45, 54, 112, 122, 130, 161 n. 20; its company, 27, 28; capture of, 30; destruction of, 74; the galley and, 128; definition of, 154
Galia, Simon, 169 n. 41
Galleasses (great galleys), 120, 191 n. 29; use against piracy, 110, 132-3, 138ff, 145, 189 n. 14; their oarsmen, 111; crew and armaments, 132, 145-6; use of convicts, 132; vis à vis *bertoni*, 138-42; defects, 139, 140-1, 190 n. 21; miseries of their crew, 140-1; campaigns against their use, 140-2; their performance, 143-5; cost of, 145; reduction in number, 148; irregularities in payment of crews, 146-7, 192 n. 32; lack of repairs to, 147-8; lack of replacements, 148-9; construction of, 154
Galleons, use against piracy, 110, 134-5, 136-7; Venetian admiration of, 134, 135; cost of, 136; disadvantages in action, 136-7, 189 n. 12; armaments, 137; sinking of, 137; construction of, 154-5
Galley, definition of, 155
Galleys, great, *see* Galleasses
Galleys, light, use against piracy, 6-7, 11-12, 19, 20-1, 26-7, 30, 67, 80, 89-90, 103, 110, 127-8, 139-40, 160 n. 4, 169 n. 1, 176 nn. 1, 2; inadequacy of armed escort, 90; poor quality of crews, 90, 130, 131, 176 n. 3, 184 n. 16; fitting out, 111; oarsmen, 111-12, 184 n. 16, 185 n. 21; recruitment of crews, 112, 125; use of convict labour, 112ff, 124-5, 131; responsibilities of the *sopracomiti*, 116-17; behaviour of the captains, 117-18, 183 n. 13, 16; prestige attached to command of, 118, 122; harmful practices concerning, 118-20, 183 n. 15; numbers and duties, 120-1, 184 nn. 16, 18; and Crete station, 121; unauthorized employment, 122; escapers from, 123; payment of crews, 123-4, 125-6, 185 n. 23, 186 nn. 27, 28; reduction in number of benches, 124; proportion of freemen to convicts, 125; pretenders to enrolment, 126, 186 n. 29; collection of crew debts, 126-7; demobilization of captains, 127; shortage of soldiers, 127; prospects of booty, 128, 129-30, 186 n. 32; behaviour towards *bertoni*, 128-30, 187 nn. 33, 35; their inefficiency, 187 n. 35; armaments, 188 n. 2

INDEX

Galleys of the Condemned, 69, 115
Gargano, 21, 160 n. 12
Garner (Gardiner), Thomas, 69, 74
Garzoni, the, 25
Genoa, xi, xii, 38, 169 n. 41
Germain, Jacques, 54, 169 n. 41
Germany, northern, xvii, 45
Giacomo, Gasparo di, 65
Gibraltar, xvii, 85; forcing of the Straits, 45, 58, 59, 83
Gift of God, the, 64
Gilds, the, xiii; and cloth trade, 60
Giovane Piccolo, the, 81
Girarda, the, 75
Girarda e Correra, the, 65
Girolamo, Alvise di, 175 n. 37
Giustiniana e Benvenuta, the, 48, 52, 53
Giustiniana e Zagura, the, 106
Giustinian, Antonio, 13
Giustinian, Bernardo, 105
Giustinian, Giacomo, 75
Giustinian, Zorzi, 74, 78
Golden Dove, the, 68
Gomenizze, the, 28
Goro, Bay of, pirate clearing-house, 85
Gottarda, the, 26
Gottardino, the, 105
Gottardo, the, 105
Governor of the Condemned, 121
Gozo, island of, 38, 52
Grabusce, 36
Gradenigo, Marino, 26, 161 n. 16
Grassa, the, 76
Grassi, Giovanni Battista di, 54
Gratarola, the, 160 n. 12
Greece and the Greeks, 24, 41, 42, 90
Greyhound, the, 61
Grippi, 22
Guidotta e Simona, the, wreck of, 175 n. 37

Habsburgs, xviii; garrison at Segna, 3; and Hungary, 4; and Uskoks, 4–5, 13; threat to Venice, 142
Half Moon, the, 46
Hamburg, 46, 94
Harris, Richard, 78, 143
Hassan Aga, 25, 27, 29, 35
Henry IV, King of France, 72, 84–5

Heres, Flores, 46
Holy Trinity, the, 46
Hungary, 4

Il Sole, the, 169, n. 41
Inquisition, the, 35
Insurance, marine, 97, 100–5, 107, 180 n. 28, 181 n. 43; premiums, 101–3 Ionian islands, 47, 89; and piracy, 24, 28; trading route, 61, 90, 91
Ionian sea, piracy and, xvii, 17, 57, 81; defence force, 121
Islam, rivalry with Christianity in Mediterranean, xvi, 16, 37–8, 82; piracy and, 8, 18–19
Istria, 4, 6, 15, 118; protective force, 121

James I, King of England, 72, 83, 173 n. 25
Jerusalem, Knights of, and papal decrees, 39
Jesus, the, 69–70
Jews, 8, 38, 41, 43, 164 n. 3; intermediaries between Christian and Turk, 24; papal trade with, 38; captured by pirates, 48, 49; and Leghorn, 58; prohibition on, 178 n. 21
Jonas, the, 71
Jonet, Giordano, 65

La Rochelle, 71, 144
Lanciano, 21
Lefteri, Georgio, 50
Leftimo, 28
Leghorn, xvi, 61, 63, 66, 70; geographical advantages, xiii; Order of St Stephen, 17, 30; opened to Jewish merchants, 58; base of Protestant trade, 58; Northern pirate base, 73, 83, 85
Lemos, Count of, Viceroy of Naples, 47, 49, 68, 167 n. 32
Leone, the, 48
Leone d'Argento, the, 47
Leone d'Oro, the, 47, 50, 169 n. 41
Lepanto, Battle of, xvi, xvii, 4, 16, 20, 56, 82, 89, 92; victory for Christianity, 33; use of galleasses, 132

P   203

INDEX

Lesina, island of, 5, 6, 117, 122; shipbuilding, 94
Levant, the, xvii, 17, 137; and Venetian trade, xii, xiii, 18, 43, 60, 102; England and, xiii, 68, 76, 170 n. 5; Venetian territories, 33, 56, 168 n. 33; expeditions to, 34, 35, 43; Spanish squadrons and, 47, 54; Northerners and, 58; Ward and, 79, 84; 'new' Barbary pirates and, 81–2, 83; the Dutch and, 86; Venetian navy and, 91, 118, 131; direct trade from, 98; convoy systems and 143, 190 n. 24; lack of naval repairs, 148
Leyva, Don Pedro de, 47
Liguria, 17
Lile, James, 64
Lion, Nicolò, on escort crews, 107
Lippomana, the, 59
Lisbon, xii, 46, 47
Little Phoenix, the, 61
Livorno, the, 53, 169 n. 37
Livy, on the Uskoks, 3
Lombardo, the, 59, 62, 180 n. 28
Loredan, Giovan Francesco, 187 n. 35
Loredano, Signor, 28
Loreto, pilgrimages to, 21, 22
Low Countries, Calvinism in, xvi; and Mediterranean affairs, xvii; piracy against, 46; relations with Spain, 58
Luber, Hans, 46
Lupo, Nicolò, 13
Lutheranism, 46

Macri, Gulf of, 41
Madrid, 50
Magrudi, Dimo, encounter with Nottingham, 63–4
Malaga, 45, 91
Malamocco, 14, 117
Malta, xvi; offensive against piracy, xvii, 18; pirates from, 34, 35, 37, 38, 45, 46, 50, 54; capture of Hassan Aga's ship, 35; relations with Venice, 37, 39, 51; use of *Bertoni*, 52, 173 n. 25; sack of its ships, 164 n. 6
Malta, Order of St John, 17, 76, 93, 165 n. 15, 169 n. 40; its character, 35; raiding voyages to the Levant, 35–6, 39, 52, 54; encounters with Venetian fleet, 36–7, 54, 57; use of *bertoni*, 52, 82; use of galleys, 111
Mamurra, 85
Mancinella, the, 63
Manfredi, Isidoro, on pirate trading, 23; on navy malpractices, 119–20; and the *Lombardo*, 180 n. 28
Manfredonia, 15
Maqueda, Bernardino de Cardenas, Duke of, Viceroy of Sicily, pirate expeditions, 47, 48, 49, 68; death, 49
Marcello, Donato, 23
Marches, the, 14, 21
Marciliane, 7, 22, 75, use of, 25, 26, 27, 39, 50, 92; restrictions on, 104; passed as roundships, 104–5; description of, 155
Maritime transport, use of the galley for, 89–90; insurance of, 97, 100, 178 n. 16; defence of, 99–100, 105–6; prohibited from winter sailing, 103; use of a galleon, 137
Marmara, Sea of, 47
Marseilles, xii, xiii, 98; shelters Danziger, 84–5
Martinella, the, 49
Martinenga, the, 50
Martinengo, the, 65
Marubin, Vincenzo, 70
Mathcovich, Zuane, 13
Mayner, Pieter, 46
Mazzoca, the, 122, 160 n. 11
Mediterranean, the, xi; rivalled by Cape route, xii; Dutch and English intrusions into, xiii, xvi, 44, 58; Christian and Moslem rivalry in, xvi, 16, 17; scene of pirate battles, xvi–xvii, 8, 16–17, 35, 61, 166 n. 19; theatre of European history, xvii, 17–18; withdrawal of Venetian shipping, 25, 55; Turkish threat in, 33; extension of Atlantic rivalry into, 58, 82; effect of reappearance of Northerners, 82–4; changed character of its piracy, 84–6, 150; use of merchant galleys, 133
Mehemet Remer, 27
Memma e Constantina, the, 48, 71

204

INDEX

Memmo, Girolamo, 78
Merlere, 47
Messina, 35, 46, 47, 50; pirates from, 34, 40, 48,
Michiel, Agostino, 145; on oarsmen's rations, 185 n. 21
Michiel, Iseppo, 187 n. 35
Michiel, Maffio, and English ships at Zante, 61, 73, 75, 170 n. 35; and Ottoman magistrates, 173 n. 34; English attack on, 173 n. 24
Milo, 70, 72; *bertoni* at, 74; Northern pirates and, 83; report from Venetian consul, 169 n. 41
Missi, Osman, 84
Mocenigo, Domenico, 187 n. 35
Modone, 24, 25, 40, 65, 68, 71, 73, 75, 79, 172 n. 18, 174 n. 32
Mola, Angelo da, 19
Molin, Francesco, on a shipwreck, 7-8; on the pursuit of *galeotte*, 28; on Western prisoners, 51; on restoring prisoners, 5, 168 n. 33; and convict galleys, 115-16; on delays in payment of crews, 123-4; on inefficiency of light galleys, 187 n. 35
Molin, Girolamo da, and the galleon, 134-5; opposes use of *bertoni*, 139
Molin, Marino da, 15
Molin, Nicolo da, 71
Monda, the, 82
Mondo, the, 54
Mondo Piater, the, 84
Mongibello, 43
Montecuccoli, Count Alfonso di, 169 n. 41
Monturon, Mons. de, Knight of Malta, 169 n. 41
Moors, 165 n. 15; taken by pirate ships, 38, 41, 42
Morea, xvii, 65, 66; hotbed of piracy, 18-19, 24, 31, 32, 49, 57, 149; English pirates and, 73, 77, 78, 81
Morgante, Giovanni, 47
Morosini, the, 49, 76, 173 n. 24
Morosini, Camillo, 28
Morosini, Francesco, 26, 106, 138; his *bertoni*, 96, 177 n. 12; use of great galleys, 144, 190 n. 26; and the crews, 145, 146, 192 n. 32; his treatment of orders, 146-7; indictment of the navy, 149
Morosini, Giustiniano, 147
Morosini, Tommaso, and the galleon, 137; and the galleasses, 140, 145
Mosta e Moceniga, the, 24-5
Mosto, Pietro da, 172 n. 17
Mount Morlacca, 3
Mula, the, 144
Musli Rais, corsair, 27
Mytilene, Bey of, 29

Naazar, Tirvirch, 46
Nana, the, 25, 163 n. 3
Nani, Agostino, 68
Naples, 32, 57, 65, 162 n. 25; and piracy, 43, 44, 47, 49, 50, 178 n. 21; and Venetian shipping, 47, 91; Northern pirates and, 83
Naples, Viceroy of, *see* Lemos
Narenta, the, its estuary, 4; the Uskoks and, 6, 11, 12, 19; use of galleys and, 90, 176 n. 1; protective force, 121
Nauplia, 77
Navarino, 40, 79, 143
Navy, Dutch, xvi, 18
Navy, English, xvi, 18, 82
Navy, Turkish, 31, 35, 163 n. 27; and Maltese pirates, 37, 39; and Western pirates, 39; Christian slave revolts, 165 n. 15
Navy, Venetian, xiv; and the protection of trade, xvii, 90-1; and the Uskoks, 5, 7, 11, 12, 15; and deserters, 10, 185 n. 13; neutrality in pirate warfare, 16; loss of power, 18; and Barbary corsairs, 19, 22-3, 54; treatment of corsairs, 20-1; protection of ports, 24; fear of pirate ships, 24; encounters with pirates, 24-5, 27-31, 57; reduction of merchant fleet by piracy, 26, 50, 54-5; increased strength, 34; offensive against English pirates, 68; failure against *bertoni*, 69, 79-80, 104; inefficiency of its watch, 69; use of the North Sea, 59-60, 91; changed task of the merchant fleet, 90-1; abandons Atlantic

205

INDEX

Navy, Venetian (*cont.*)
coasts, 91; crisis caused by piracy, 92–3; number of ships, 93; prohibition concerning foreign built ships, 94–5, 96–7, 178 n. 15, 21; strength of merchant fleet, 95–6; balance between foreign and Venetian ships, 96–8; decline in its maritime trade, 99; defence of the merchant marine, 99–100, 103, 180 n. 32; prohibition on winter sailing, 103, 180 n. 34; deficiencies in its merchant fleet, 103ff, 130; its armaments, 105–7; pay and victuals for crews, 107, 110, 122–4, 125–6; defects in escorts crews, 107–9, 181 n. 45; reorganization, 111; strength after Lepanto 111; dispersal of the squadrons, 117; laxity of commanders-in-chief, 118; abuses and malpractices, 118–20, 121–2, 183 n. 15, 184 nn. 18, 19, 185 n. 21; auditing of accounts, 120; protective and patrolling numbers, 120–1; transport of pay, 122–3; appointment of Commissioner, 123, 131; internal disorders, 131; use of the *bertone*, 142–3

Negroes, captured by pirates, 42, 43
Nelson, Nicholas, 46
Nerins, Luke, 46
Nettuna, the, 50, 167 n. 32
New Lily, the, 46
North Sea, 59–60, 98
Northerners, the, and the Levant, 56, 58; incursion into Mediterranean, 58, 62; and Venetian shipping, 65–7, 70; Venetian defence against, 67–8; Turkish attitude to, 73; composition of their fleets, 83; disposal of plunder, 85; and commercial structure of Venice, 89
Nottingham, William, encounter with Magrudi, 63–4
Novigrade, Straits of, 6

Obrovazzo river, 6
Oloard (Olororen), Christopher, 70–1, 173 n. 24
Orange, Pietro d', 50, 167 n. 32

Orange Tree, the, 46
Order of St John, 17, 35, 37; see also under Malta
Order of St Stephen, 17, 30, 35, 37
Ossuna, Duke of, 15, 54
Ottoman Empire, and Venice, xi–xii, 4, 18, 33; relations with England, xiii, 60; united front against, xvi; refugees from, 9–10; Uskoks and, 12, 14; pirate aggression towards Christianity, 16, 18ff, 50, 56, 62, 82; defence of Rhodes, 34; papal trade with, 38; Christian revolts against, 41, 165 n. 15; limits to her power, 56, 57; attacks on her shipping, 57; relations with Spain, 58, 82; attitude to Northern pirates, 73
Otranto, 48; Straits of, 33, 91, 173 n. 24

Padilla, Diego Lopez de, 66
Palermo, 25, 45, 47, 50, 167 n. 28
Papacy, xvi; offensive against piracy, xvii; relations with Venice, 4, 38, 51; and the Uskoks, 4, 5, 8; and Barbary corsairs, 17, 21
Papal States, 57
Paradise, the, 45–6
Parenzo, 13, 22
Pasqualiga, the, 30
Pasqualigo, Filippo, 158 n. 7; and the Uskoks, 6, 8; and Mehemet Remer, 27; Commander of the fleet at Crete, 34, 45, 67, 118, 163 n. 3, 187 n. 34; and Knights of Malta, 35–7, 67; on use of the galleon against *bertoni*, 80, 134; on escort crews, 109; and convict galleys, 113, 115, 182 n. 7; and shortage of men, 125, 126, 127; and light galleys, 130; and galleasses, 140; Commissioner of the Navy, 148
Pasqualigo, Giovanni, and convict labour, 113, 114; on the free oarsmen, 182 n. 8
Patinota, the, 45
Patras, 46–7, 72, 73, 83
Paxu, 28, 34
Penino, Fr., 42
Penzo, Filandro, 7
Perastana, the, 106, 107, 181 n. 40

206

INDEX

Perasto, 24, 63
Perla, the, 81
Pesaro, 22, 23
Philip II, King of Spain, and Elizabeth, 58, 60, 62, 73
Pierce, John, 71
Pierce, William, 68, 70
Pigna, the, 48, 50, 67, 106, 168 n. 34
Pigna, Antonio della, 67
Piracy, and the decline of Venice, xiii; early accounts of, xv; combined with trade, xvi, 61–2, 83; Mediterranean locations, xvii; religious pretexts for, 8, 62, 64, 82, 150; disposition of booty and prisoners, 23–4, 44, 49, 85, 160 n. 11, 167 n. 32; increased activity, 43; private enterprises, 47, 48; tricks practised, 47–8, 167 n. 28; glorification of pirates, 49; effect of release of prisoners, 51–2; proliferation in early seventeenth century, 52; a lucrative industry, 69; replaces naval duels, 82; activity of freebooters, 83, 86; its changed character, 83, 84–6, 150; clearing-houses for, 85; insurance against, 97, 100–5, 107; inadequate defence against, 107–9; dangers to health from, 168 n. 33; difficulties of classification, 169 n. 41
Pirona, the, 67
Pisa, Order of St Stephen, 17, 35
Pisana e Mazza, the, 47
Pisani, Antonio, 147, 149, 192 n. 32
Pisani, Francesco, 187 n. 35
Pizzamano, Giorgio and Bernardino, 36
Plaidemo, Zuane, 62
Plague, the, xiii
Po, the, 21, 23, 121
Pola, 13
Ponte, the, 68
Popogianopuli, Dimo, 62
Portoferro, 27
Portugal, xii, xiii, 62, 91
Prevesa, 28; Battle of, xvi
Primaro, 22
Prodano, 49, 167 n. 28
Protestantism, xvi, 35, 58
Provveditore, duties and offices etc., 156

Provveditore dell'Armata, the, 27, 30
Psoro, Leo, 50

Quarnaro, 4, 6, 13, 24
Quirina, the, 27, 187 n. 35

Ragazzona, the, 34, 60
Ragusa, xii, xvii, 6, 8, 38, 45, 63, 83, 169 n. 41
Ramadan Pasha, 26
Ravenna, 22
Reatta, the, 104, 181 n. 42
Recanati, 21
Red Lion, the, 46
Reniera, the, 50
Reniera e Soderina, capture of, 77–8, 174 n. 29; becomes Ward's flagship, 78
Rhodes, 29, 34, 40
Rigolo, the, 105
Rimini, 22
Risano, 19
Rizzarda, the, 54
Rodosto, 47
Roman Congregation, and trade with Jews, 38–9
Rome, pirate attacks on, xvii, 17; informers from, 29; treatment of heretics, 35
Rossi, the, 49
Rossi, Bernardino Sebastiani, shipbuilding loan, 94
Rota, the, 45
Roundships, 104–5
Roville, Mons. de, 169 n. 41
Rovigno, 13
Rubi, the, 77
Rucaforte, Antonio, 169 n. 41
Rusco, Nicolò, 7

Saettie, 7, 8, 12, 13, 25, 38, 48, 67; definition of, 156
St. Andrew, the, 46
St Mark, Basin of, 23, 117
St Peter, the (two), 46, 71
St Stephen, Knights of, 30, 34, 52, 93; voyages of plunder, 34, 40–3, 53, 57, 163 n. 3
Salamander, the, 72
Salma, equivalent of, 156
Salvatore, the, 70

207

INDEX

Salvetta, the, 81, 106
Samson, the, 71
San Giacomo, the, sack of, 36–7, 164 n. 6
San Giovanni, the, 169 n. 41; sack of, 36–7, 164 n. 6
San Giovanni Battista, 66, 71
San Giovanni di Sciona, island of, 40
San Giuseppe e Bonaventura, the, 48
San Lucar de Burrameda, 83
San Marco, the, 68
San Nicolo della Vlemona (Cerigo), 35
San Paolo, the, 71
San Rocco, the, 63
San Spirito, the, 169 n. 41
Sanson, pirate, 83
Sant' Agata, the, 177 n. 12
Santa Maura, 24, 28–9, 162 n. 25
Sanudo, *Diaries*, 133
Sapienza, 76, 81, 129, 137, 148
Saracens, 38
Sardinia, 166 n. 19, 169 n. 41
Saseno, 27, 40, 82
Savoy, Duke of, *see* Carlo Emanuele I
Scaramelli, Giovan Carlo, 72, 74, 100, 108
Scarpanto, 40
Sciò, Antonio da, 66
Sciro, 54
Scrisa, capture of, 159 n. 17
Scut, Roderick, 68
Sebenico, 6, 26, 161 n. 16
Segna, characteristics, 3; base of the Uskoks, 3, 5, 8, 11; its friaries, 9; reinforced by refugees, 9–10; Venetian offensive against, 12–13, 15; Habsburgs and, 13
Segura, the, 38
Selvagna, the, 59
Senate, the, description of, 156
Setta e Vidala, the, 45
Settelia, Gulf of, 78, 163 n. 3, 174 n. 29
Seven Capes, 41, 42
Sherley, Anthony, 54, 70, 76; and Ferdinand I, 70
Shipbuilding, Venetian crisis in, xiii, 93ff, 108, 109; reduction in, 92, 99; Senate loans for, 94, 96, 177 nn. 7, 12; cost of, 94; rules concerning foreign built ships, 94–5, 96–7; pirate offensive and, 98; the Government Arsenal, 111, 119, 132, 138
Shipwrecks, pirates and, 7–8; losses caused by, 98; insurance against, 100; and winter sailing, 103
Shipyards, 92, 99
Sicily, xvii, 165 n. 15, 178 n. 21; Barbary corsairs and, 17, 25, 38; fits out pirate ships, 43, 44, 45, 92; use of *bertoni*, 52; Venetian shipping and, 91
Sicily, Viceroys of, *see* Maqueda and Ferra
Silvestra, the, 50, 107
Sixtus V, Pope, 157 n. 2
Slave trade, at Brazza island, 6; papacy and, 157 n. 2; pirates and, 26, 41, 42, 43, 160 n. 11
Slaves, Venetian navy and, 20–1; in Christian ships, 33, 36–7; revolt of (Christian), 41, 165 n. 15; presented to Ferdinand I, 85; use of, for galleys, 112
Smyrna, 25, 26, 45, 65, 99; English shipping and, 71, 170 n. 5; Northern pirate base, 83
Soderina e Memma, the, 48, 167 n. 28
Solda, the, 104
Sopracomiti, and convict labour, 114; their position in the galleys, 116–17; neglect of duty, 117–18, 183 n. 11
Spain, xii, xvi, 21, 25, 91, 175 n. 25; and the Low Countries, xvi; rivalry with Protestantism, xvi, 58; offensive against piracy, xvii, 18, 45; relations with Venice, 14, 62, 83; alliance with Uskoks, 15; offensive against Islam, 16, 82; and Maltese pirates, 39; her own piracy, 44, 45ff, and the Westerners, 45; and Levantine waters, 47, 54; limits of her power, 57; at war with England, 62; concludes peace, 73; and English navy, 82
Spalato, 89; use of galleys, 6, 26, 91, 176 n. 1
Spelegati, the, 76, 79
Speranza, 40

208

INDEX

Speranza, the, 68
Spinola (pirate), 52
Squadron of the Condemned, 118
Stella, the, 62
Stella family, 96
Stella e Vidala, the, 59
Strivali, 54, 71, 75
Strozzi, Pandolfo, 163 n. 2
Sully, Duc de, 86
Sumaca, the, 63
Surbi, Domenico, 7
Surian, Nicolò, advice to Venetian squadrons, 32, 34; attitude towards Westerners, 33, 45
Susa, 84
Syracuse, 45, 70
Syria, 7, 25, 34, 48, 50, 54, 68, 78, 179 n. 24; French consulate, 86; use of galleasses, 145; convoy system and, 146; prohibition on Turkish and Jewish merchants, 178 n. 21

Tapino, the, 106
Taranto, 32, 92, 162 n. 25
Tegiachin, the, 7
Textile industry, xii, xiii, 60
Tiepolo, Almorò, and the Uskoks, 5, 11; use of the galley, 11; and Barbary corsairs, 19; capture of Scrisa, 159 n. 17
Tiepolo, Paolo, 147, 148, 149
Tizzona, the, 81, 144, 149
Tizzone, the, 60, 62
Toledo, Dan Pedro de, 47
Tomkins, Thomas, 71
'Tommaso Ciolo', 60
Tosa, the, 26
Trapani, 45, 63
Trau, 6
Tremiti, 23
Tripoli, 19, 25
Trona, the, 75
Tunis, xvi, 37, 165 n. 15; English pirates at, 74, 81, 86; Ward and, 77, 78, 83, 84
Turks, taken by pirate ships, 40, 41, 42, 45, 63, 64, 75; prohibition on merchants, 178 n. 21
Tuscany, 53; Barbary corsairs and, 17, 37, 38; her galleys, 34, 40, 44; piratical cruises, 40-3; collaboration with English pirates, 74-5, 173 n. 25; employment of pirates, 53, 74
Tuscany, Grand Duke of, *see* Ferdinand I
Tyrrhenean Sea, xvii, 85, 91

Uggiera e Selvagna, the, 62
United Provinces, 73, 82
Uskoks, the, their base, 3; an international problem, 3-4; meaning of, 4; their protectors, 4-5, 157 n. 2; their organizations, 5; tactics employed by, 5-6, 11; area threatened by, 6-7; their depredations, 7-8, 13-14; religious pretexts, 8-9, 12; their customs, 9; a community of violence, 9, 14; increased by refugees and deserters, 9-10, 14, 158 n. 13; Venetian offensive against, 12-13, 15, 52, 89-90; renewed attacks by, 14-15; Turkey and, 18-19; and the Adriatic, 43, 53; limits of their power, 56-7; and the Venetian navy, 93

Vadoppia, Pietro, 63
Vais, Michele, 50, 168 n. 34
Valencia, 83
Valiera, the, 147
Valona, and piracy, 19, 22, 24, 27, 81-2, 160 n. 4
Vatica, 189 n. 12
Vendramin, Francesco, 99
Venetian Republic, period of her decline, xii-xiii; effect of piracy on, xiii, 50-1, 54, 56, 151; relations with Turkey, 4, 18, 20, 60; refugees from, 10; relations with Spain, 14, 15; withdrawal of shipping from Mediterranean, 25, 55; attitude to Westerners, 33, 52, 59; relations with Malta, 37, 40; seizure of her shipping, 39, 68; relations with England, 44; Spanish attacks on her shipping, 45, 46, 49-50, 54, 57, 167 n. 28; losses due to piracy, 50, 80-1; and the release of pirate prisoners, 51; treatment of prisoners, 52; Florentine pirates and

INDEX

Venetian Republic (*cont.*)
52–3; withdrawal from Adriatic route, 55; use of foreign ships, 55, 91, 93, 99; and the Levant, 56; main route of her shipping, 57; effect of English sea power on her trade, 58–9; offensive against Northern piracy, 65–7, 71, 78; renewed diplomatic relations with England, 72–3; and the use of galleys on trade routes, 90; and convicts for galleys, 112–13; amount spent on naval pay, 123; and payment of crews, 126; and use of galleons and galleasses against piracy, 133, 135ff, 143, 145; and *bertoni*, 142–3

Venice, expansion onto mainland, xi, xii, 109, 131; and textile industry, xii, 60, 98; effect of piracy on her prosperity, xiii, 89, 92, 98, 109, 143, 178 n. 21; neutrality during pirate warfare, xvii, 17–18, 51; shipping traffic, 4, 18, 30, 59; treatment of pirates, 10; and the Uskoks, 11ff; European importance, 18; attacks on her shipping in port, 54; treatment of the Dutch, 59; entered by English ships, 60–1, 62ff; Northern pirate base, 83; intermediary between east and west, 90; reduction in maritime trade, 92; shipbuilding industry, 94–5; loss of prestige and political decadence, 98, 131; decline in commercial enterprises, 98, 178 n. 21; supply of convicts for galleys, 112–13; the galley captains and, 117, 118; veneration of large ships, 133, 134; lack of understanding of piracy, 135–6

Venetico, 70
Venier, the, 106
Venier, Bernardo, and depleted squadrons, 121–2; lack of provisions, 122; and payment of crews, 126
Venier, Giulio, 79; the Senate and, 79, 174 n. 32
Venier, Lorenzo, 78, 143, 169 n. 39,

190 n. 22; and the galleasses, 138, 142–3, 146, 148
Venier, Pellegrin, 146; on galley commanders, 118; and pillage, 129; on English and Dutch pirates, 166 n. 19
Veniera, the, 25; its cargo, 68, 172 n. 18
Venturini, meaning of, 9–10
Verney (pirate), 83
Vidala, the, 12, 25, 26, 50, 62, 68, 75, 76, 167 n. 32
Vidala e Cordes, the, 48
Vidali, Giovan Antonio, 167 n. 28
Vidali, Nicolò, 176 n. 1
Vigia (Vigier), Mons. di, 169 n. 41
Villefranche, and Northern pirates, 85
Vinciguerra, Giacomo, 49, 50, 65
Viredoré, Count of, 53
Vitali, Raimondo and Girolamo, 94

Ward, John, rise to fame, 76–7; Mediterranean activities, 77–9, 80, 83; number of his ships, 83–4; his employment by Tuscans, 85
Wart, John, 65
Westerners, the, 36, 45; Venetian attitude towards, 33, 37, 52, 59; and the Levant, 43; acts of piracy by, 46, 49–50, 54; and Venetian trade, 48; use of *bertoni*, 64–5
Whitbrook, Hugh, 65
Wilemens, Dirk, 46
Wro, Stefano, 71

Ximenes, the, 66

Zante, 29, 32, 34, 44, 45, 54, 59, 70, 178 n. 15; English ships and, 61, 66, 68, 70, 73, 81, 170 n. 5; Ferdinand I and, 74; Ward and, 84; use of galleys for, 90, 176 n. 2
Zara, 7, 28, 121, 122; convict hospital, 113; convict galleys, 115
Zen, Giovanni, 52
Zena, the, 107, 169 n. 41; attacked by *bertone*, 52, 53–4
Zoistes, Fiche, 46
Zustignana, the, 107